Those who have the good fortune to call Victress a true friend know that she is someone who lives life with an open heart and with courage. *A Tree with My Name on It: Finding a Way Home* invites us to learn about her life—an authentic story of a person living in this world as well as a heroine's journey to self-discovery. It is both inspiring and engaging.

ANAM THUBTEN Buddhist teacher and author of
No Self, No Problem, The Magic of Awareness, and
Into the Haunted Ground: A Guide to Cutting the Root of Suffering

This beautifully rendered memoir tells the story of Victress Hitchcock's two years on a remote ranch in a Rocky Mountain valley, home to harsh winters, and equally tough, big-hearted characters. A skilled storyteller and chronicler of human relationships, she tells us in lyrical prose and unexpected humor, how she boldly pulled back layer after layer of built-up armor around her heart leaving an opening wide enough for tenderness to emerge. A poem of a memoir about what it means to be an American woman, an engaged Buddhist, and a fully alive, open-hearted human being.

BRAD WETZLER Author of *Into the Soul of the World: My Journey to Healing*

A riveting intimate tale of a woman's journey in search of a home, in her body, in her spirit and in the land. *A Tree with My Name on It* is a vividly written, heart wrenching deep dive into life itself in all its beauty and complexity. I couldn't put it down and, in the end, I felt deeply enriched and touched by her honesty and wise heart.

I know the ancient magic of the Wet Mountains where Victress Hitchcock lived at Lookout Valley Ranch, and the warmth and wisdom of the neighbors and friends that we shared. With *A Tree with My Name on It: Finding a Way Home,* she tells her story of that time and place with candor and courage. Her memoir is as compelling and profound as the rugged and spacious landscape that inspired it.

Compelling and beautifully written, this spiritual memoir is the courageous account of a woman's transformation while living on a remote Colorado mountain ranch. Both inspiring and heart rending, Victress brings you along on her extraordinary journey—a powerful story about healing, resilience, and finding inner freedom.

In this vibrantly woven reflection about inner healing, Victress allows us to experience her grief and the wounds caused by childhood tragedy in a vulnerable and open-hearted way. She opens up the reservoir of pain enabling the reader to experience the transformation that unfolds through her newfound relationship with herself and acceptance of life, as it is. Her presence is as solid as the tree that stands amidst the aspen and pines with her name on it.

IRMA VELASQUEZ Author of *Fish Dreams: A Mother's Journey from Curing Her Son's Autism to Loving Him as He Is*

A Tree with My Name on It is a heartrending tale of more than survival in a wilderness. The author takes us along her path of self-discovery in an unknown wild space on a ranch in Colorado. It is an identity crisis of later life, a heroic journey that inspires through tough and beautiful times. She is a friend telling us how it was, a storyteller of the soul, allowing us to also find our inner strength. I thank her.

KAREN ROBERTS Author of *The Blossoming of Women, A Workbook on Growing from Older to Elder*

A heart-wrenching and healing story that embraces pain and joy in equal measures. Victress weaves a powerful tale that draws you in, inviting you to be deeply engaged in her journey of self-discovery. Her story is one of profound wounds that alter her life in an inescapable way. I was moved deeply at the way she learns to embrace her pain, to confront the agony of her trauma and to love both the woman she is and the woman she aspires to become. A truly incredible story.

JESSE RENE GIBBS Author of *Girl Hidden*

A Tree with My Name on It is a raw, courageous, and initiatory memoir for our times, a beautifully written account full of pain, liberation, compassion, and wisdom. This is the story of a woman who stood at the edge of the abyss and didn't blink. In a compelling narrative start to finish, the author insightfully intertwines her journey of loss, healing, and transformation with the adventures and challenges of ranch life in the mountains of Southern Colorado, working with horses and teaching meditation to prisoners in a nearby Federal Prison.

FLEET MAULL Author of *Radical Responsibility* and *Dharma in Hell*, founder of Prison Dharma Network.

Readers are welcomed into the author's world with beautifully rendered details of the struggles and joys and challenges . . . gems of wisdom are sprinkled throughout. The author's inner search for home is very familiar and I benefited greatly from reading this poignant journey. Bravo for all of us to have such a guide.

JUDY VASOS Author of *My Dear Good Rosi: Letters from Nazi Occupied Holland 1940–1943*

This is a book that can't be put down. Hitchcock's commanding storytelling, the weaving of her life, the humans who touch her tender soul, the horses who help to heal her heart and the ever-changing landscape of the valley together create a profound and transformative tale.

JACKIE ASHLEY, LPC, BC-DMT, ACS, ESMHL
Somatic and Equine Facilitated Therapist

A Tree
with
My Name
on It

A Tree with My Name on It

FINDING A WAY HOME

a memoir

VICTRESS HITCHCOCK

BOLD STORY PRESS

CHEVY CHASE, MARYLAND

Bold Story Press, Chevy Chase, MD 20815
www.boldstorypress.com

Acknowledgements for Permission to Reprint
Jack Finley for use of Berna Finley's writings
Laverna Clemens for use of sections from her mother's self-
  published book, *My Life as a Mountain Pioneer.*
Human Kindness Foundation for use of sections from *We're
  All Doing Time* by Bo and Sita Lozoff
Glenna Olmsted, Executive Assistant to Pema Chödrön for use of sections from
  her published writings and from notes taken by the author at her talks.
Frederick Courtright for Shambala Publications for use of a line from *Cutting
  Through Spiritual Materialism* by Chögyam Trungpa Rinpoche.
All Of Me (*Song lyrics on pages 43, 57, 212*)
  Words and Music by Seymour Simons and Gerald Marks
  Copyright © 1931 Sony Music Publishing (US) LLC, Redwood Music,
  Round Hill Songs, Marlong Music Corp. and Bourne Co. (ASCAP)
  Copyright Renewed
  All Rights on behalf of Sony Music Publishing (US) LLC Administered by Sony
  Music Publishing (US) LLC, 424 Church Street, Suite 1200, Nashville, TN 37219
  All Rights on behalf of Redwood Music Administered by Round Hill
  Carlin International Copyright Secured All Rights Reserved
  Reprinted by Permission of Hal Leonard LLC
A Broken Wing (*Song lyrics on pages 170–171*)
  Words and Music by Sam Hogin, Phil Barnhart and James House
  Copyright © 1996 Sony Music Publishing (US) LLC, Sam's
  Jammin' Songs and Suffer In Silence Music
  All Rights Administered by Sony Music Publishing (US) LLC, 424
  Church Street, Suite 1200, Nashville, TN 37219
  International Copyright Secured All Rights Reserved
  Reprinted by permission of Hal Leonard LLC
Desperado (*Song lyrics on pages 250 and 264*)
  Words and Music by Don Henley and Glenn Frey
  Copyright © 1973 CASS COUNTY MUSIC and RED
  CLOUD MUSIC Copyright Renewed
  All Rights Administered by UNIVERSAL MUSIC WORKS
  All Rights Reserved Used by Permission
  Reprinted by permission of Hal Leonard LLC

This book is a memoir and it reflects the author's present recollections of experiences over
time. Some names and identifying characteristics have been changed to protect the privacy of
those depicted, some events have been compressed, and some dialogue has been re-created.

First edition: October 2024

Library of Congress Control Number: 2024919285

ISBN: 978-1-954805-90-3 (paperback)
ISBN: 978-1-954805-64-4 (e-book)

Text and cover design by KP Books
Author photo by David Wright

Printed in the United States of America
10 9 8 7 6 5 4 3 2 1

For Berna Jean,
who loved the ranch as I did.
This book is for you.

CONTENTS

PART 1

Finding the Ranch

The Classifieds

"Listen to this one," I yelled from the living room couch, where I was stretched out drinking coffee on a Sunday morning in September. The year was 1996. My husband, Joe, was in the kitchen of our old Denver bungalow. You had to yell through the hatch in the dining room to get the attention of the person in the kitchen.

"A rare opportunity to own a little slice of heaven in the Wet Mountains. One hundred and sixty acres of lush mountain valley complete with the original 1870s historic homestead." I took a sip of coffee and continued with full sales-pitch verve. "Barns and corrals and a log cabin—Lookout Valley Ranch. Come visit and we guarantee you'll fall in love."

Joe joined me as I finished. He reached for the *Denver Post* folded open on the Classifieds Real Estate for Sale column, and I watched him read the ad slowly to himself. Then he turned to me, perplexed, and asked, "Have you ever heard of the Wet Mountains?"

In my memory this scene plays out in slow motion again and again, like the replay of an improbable game-changing pass.

I can't remember whose idea it was that we should buy a ranch—two middle-aged educational video producers who knew nothing about ranch life. The closest thing to ranch living I can find in either of our ancestral lines was a great-uncle who settled in the plains of Eastern Colorado and raised cattle on a thousand acres of dry land.

Joe grew up in suburban Portland in a 1950s ranch-style tract home. I grew up in London, Paris, and Madrid, the excess baggage to my father's career as a diplomat. They called us "foreign service brats" in those days, which says a lot about child rearing in the 1950s. I was an only child, with a brilliant emotional wreck for a mother and a father who lost touch with who he really was in his ambition to make it in the Ivy League world of diplomacy. I was four years old when we moved to London. Over the next four years, we lived in four different houses—large houses with kitchens in the basement and a separate entrance for the help. Until then, my world had been a two-bedroom apartment in cookie-cutter, postwar housing in suburban Washington, DC, running wild in corduroy overalls with tangled hair. Suddenly I was a proper English schoolgirl dressed in a tweed coat with a velvet collar, living on the top floor of a six-story house. My companion was an unhinged Irish nanny named Madge who, each night, would dress a mannequin in her uniform and carry on long conversations with herself. In a recurring childhood nightmare, Madge lifts me out of a warm bath and hurls me out the window from the sixth story. I land in a vacant, bombed-out lot filled with trash, and no one hears me, no matter how loudly I call for help.

Early on in my life, I vowed that if I made it through the hell of my childhood alive and had children, which I couldn't imagine, I would never subject them to a childhood filled with so much uncertainty, loss, and fear.

I did marry, and Joe and I did have kids—a boy we named Nicholas and, four years later, a girl named Julia. For eighteen years we only moved once, from a small house in Boulder, Colorado, to a larger, rambling place four blocks away. I learned how to make tuna casserole and folded a lot of laundry. But it was the seventies and eighties; we carried the imprint of sex, drugs, and rock and roll into parenthood. And it turned out, I had inadvertently married a man who, a few years in, began hatching escape plans. Wales, Corvallis, Orcas Island, and the most insane of all, Yuma, Arizona. I managed to nip each plan in the bud, but it took its toll on our marriage and my mental health.

Then Julia started high school and struggled to fit in. While Nick sailed through Boulder High, playing on the football team and working on dude ranches in the summer, Julia, who was born an activist with a deep connection with Black culture, had developed a strong aversion to the white privilege of Boulder. By the end of her freshman year, her life had become unbearable. We had to do something.

The thought of leaving the house I loved sent me into a spiral of old grief and fear. My chest hurt from holding the demons of my childhood at bay. But I couldn't say no to Julia's need to find her place in the world, so we moved to Denver.

It felt good to see how much she loved her new life at Manual High School, where white students were a minority, and she was welcomed onto the mostly Black cheerleading squad. Truth be told, it didn't take long for me to settle in and enjoy our new urban reality as well. But, after two years, Joe began to get restless. Maybe it was the fear we were both beginning to feel at the thought of Julia graduating and leaving home. Nick was in his second year of college; once Julia left, it would be just the two of us. For twenty years, we had been the faithful supporting cast in their home movie from birth through the endless comic and tragic scenes of growing up, tag teaming our roles as parents. When the kids were small, Joe took them on trips to explore caves and look for artifacts in New Mexico and to remote mountain lakes to dig for salamanders. When they turned twelve and the hormones kicked in, their wild and unpredictable energy became too much for him, and he handed them over to me. I took my responsibility seriously, cheering loudly at Nick's high school football games and binging on *Melrose Place* with Julia.

So much of our marriage was an elaborate form of tag teaming. I spent weeks on location, filming on the Navajo Nation, on the Wind River reservation in Wyoming, in Yuma, Arizona, and Los Angeles. We rarely did things together, except for our annual family Christmas pilgrimage to the Piedra Blanca, a funky hotel on the beach in the fishing village of La Cruz de Huanacaxtle, Mexico. For two weeks, the family relaxed together, lounging on the beach, body surfing, eating barbecued mahi-mahi and watching the pelicans swoop in a line skimming the tops of the waves. When New Year's came, we would return to our lives, and the ease would fade along with our tans, the kids would go back to locking their doors, and Joe and I would fall back into our dance of resisting each other, each wishing the other was somehow different.

As we inched our way toward becoming empty nesters, the thought of a movie starring just the two of us was terrifying. We needed a project. Joe was having back-to-the-land fantasies of growing fruit trees and tending vegetable gardens.

I had started dreaming of horses galloping through waves and racing across wide-open spaces.

Somehow it all added up to the brilliant idea of buying a ranch.

That's when I saw the ad for a 130-year-old homestead in the Wet Mountains and read the description to Joe, and he took the paper from me and asked, "Where the hell are the Wet Mountains?"

And I said, "I haven't a clue. Somewhere rainy. Or probably snowy." But Joe was no longer listening. He was heading back into the kitchen to call the realtor.

The Drive Down

"Isn't that where Timothy McVeigh lives?" I pointed at a vast federal prison complex along a barren stretch of cactus and sagebrush just outside the town of Florence. Joe glanced over. He wasn't biting. "Jesus, it's huge," I continued. "How great—five thousand convicts as neighbors."

It was Sunday, a week after seeing the classified in the *Denver Post*. We had been on the road for two hours and were now heading up into the Wet Mountains, on the last leg of our trip to Lookout Valley Ranch. I couldn't stop commenting on everything. Joe had gone silent.

We had left our house early and, after fueling up on coffee, had driven south toward Colorado Springs, with Joe at the wheel. "Did you lock the door?" he asked as we sailed out onto I-25. "Julia's home, sleeping; she must have gotten in really late," he continued in a voice that seemed to say it was my fault she was a teenager.

"She's fine," I replied, staring out the window as the highway opened up south of Denver.

I was getting a kick out of seeing Julia as a full-fledged teenager. The manic energy, the despair, the laughter and anger—all happening in a matter of minutes. It was amazing to watch both my children enjoying their years as teenagers, not enduring them, miserable and numbed out, dressed in black turtlenecks, hiding in their rooms reading Sylvia Plath and smoking Parliaments, which was my experience of those years. But Joe was not happy with the idea of his perfect little girl running wild in the streets of Denver.

It was one of the sore spots between us that we visited regularly. Another was Buddhism: specifically, my wanting him to become a serious, practicing Buddhist like me. He did try, but his heart never seemed in it. And he wasn't impressed with my progress on the path. "I don't see that you have changed at all," he told me once in a moment of bitterness. I didn't have much of an argument to present in my favor, just small, imperceptible changes only I could see. But the cold blue of his eyes and the meanness in his voice knocked the breath out of me. My body and mind went numb. Without a word, I stood up and left the room, a reaction increasingly common in our relationship.

When I met Joe, I was already a student of Chögyam Trungpa Rinpoche, a brilliant and outrageous Tibetan Buddhist teacher who had settled in Boulder. I had met Rinpoche in January 1972 at Tail of the Tiger, the retreat center he first established in an old farmhouse in Vermont. I was home for Christmas from London, where I was studying at the London Film School. I had begun meditating, but I wasn't sure I wanted to continue. I wasn't in Vermont to see Rinpoche; I had gone there to visit my best friend from college, Joanie. She had become a Buddhist nun, changed her name to Tsultrim, and was living at the retreat center.

I took the bus to Vermont from Washington, DC. I remember it was snowing when I arrived at Tail. A meditation program had just ended, and only a few close students were still there. Everyone, including Tsultrim, seemed to be just hanging out doing very little. I was at loose ends, not sure what to do with myself.

One afternoon, I was sitting on a couch in the library nursing a headache I had had since arriving three days before and trying to read an article called "Working with Negativity," when a man came in and told me it was time for my interview. I hadn't asked for an interview, but I went. Rinpoche was in his room, sitting in a straight-backed wooden chair next to a small desk. He was wearing a plaid flannel shirt with suspenders holding up his jeans. The light in the room was dim. I sat down in a matching chair, facing him, and he offered me a Marlboro. We smoked in silence for a while; I had no idea what was supposed to happen. Finally, I began to describe the confusion that arose in me when I tried to meditate. He put out his cigarette in his slow, deliberate way and said, "Open your eyes. It will make a big difference." I had not told him I was meditating with my eyes closed. Rinpoche then said that he was moving to Boulder, Colorado, and I told him that I was living in London but I owned a house in Boulder. "I will see you there," were his last words as I left the room, my headache miraculously gone. Karma or coincidence, a year later I was living in my house in Boulder, I had joined the community that had sprung up around Trungpa Rinpoche and begun studying Tibetan Buddhism.

I met Joe the following year, 1974, on Halloween. We spent a long and drunken night with two friends polishing off a bottle of whiskey. By the end of it, Joe was infatuated, and I was intrigued. The glitch was he was still married to his second wife. "I live upstairs. I have my own room in the house," he said. "We just work together in our stained-glass business—that's all our relationship is, really," he went on, trying to convince me that the marriage was over, that they were just business partners.

"I am not going to sleep with you until you move out," I said.

A week later he called and said, "I moved out." By the time my birthday rolled around a month later, I had given in.

Soon after, we drove up to Glenwood Hot Springs for the weekend in his old red Volvo. Joe was at the wheel, the sun flickering on his face, picking up the gold in his thinning hair. He had the body of a Lithuanian truck driver, sturdy and built low to the ground. I was watching his hands on the wheel. His hands were those of an artist—strong with surprisingly long, perfectly shaped fingers. He was downshifting as we climbed higher when suddenly I had the thought, *I am going to marry this man. I want him to be the father of my children.* I didn't say any of that to Joe. Instead I said, "How much longer to Glenwood? I'm starving."

Back in Boulder, I checked in with Trungpa Rinpoche. In those early days, his students asked his advice on everything, from marriage partners to whether to cut their hair. "He's not a Buddhist," I said. "Is it okay for me to get involved with him?" I had stopped Rinpoche in the hallway just outside the shrine room on Pearl Street.

He looked at me intently and asked, "Is his allegiance to sanity?"

I had no idea, but I wanted it to be true, so I said, "Yes," and then added, "I think." I didn't want to lie to my teacher.

He smiled his enigmatic smile and said, "Then, of course it's okay." As he headed into the shrine room, he stopped, looked back, and said, "Good luck, madam."

Sane or insane? After twenty years of marriage, I still couldn't say for sure.

I had drifted down memory lane as we drove. When I came to, we had passed the prison and were heading up into the mountains. The road climbed up and up, along a rock canyon wall. It was real mountain driving. I couldn't imagine sailing down it in winter. "Do you think Florence has the only grocery store nearby?" I asked.

Joe looked over at me as though I were speaking a foreign language. The practicalities of life in the Wet Mountains didn't interest him. "Probably," was his only answer.

Then the turn to Highway 165 appeared suddenly as the road curved to the right. Joe slammed on the brakes, steered left, and we were heading south along the spine of the Wet Mountains. We were only two hours from Denver, but it felt as though we had entered another world. The road was empty, no more cars coming toward us. We traveled alongside ridges covered in aspen trees just turning gold and open meadows dotted with boulders. In one was a herd of elk grazing alongside an abandoned cabin. "Look at the wood on that old building!" Joe exclaimed. "There's a creek down there," he pointed to the right, "a lot of water around here. Good for growing."

"They *are* called the *Wet* Mountains," I let slip. My sarcasm didn't faze him.

"Makes sense, doesn't it," he said cheerfully.

Staring at him, I thought, *Was there really a time when this man and I danced to the Allman Brothers, heat rising, late into the night?*

As Joe became more and more animated, I got quiet and still. His eyes darted from one side of the road to the other, lingering on a broken-down sawmill here and another abandoned cabin there. I kept my eyes straight ahead, willing the car to stay on the winding road.

We were following a fence line along a grove of trees when suddenly the road opened to a wide valley bordered by brilliant gold aspen. Nestled amid endless grassy meadows, crisscrossed by a meandering stream, was a butter-yellow stucco house, a big barn, a log cabin, and an old wooden corral, all glistening in the late morning sun under a deep blue September sky. Three horses—a bay, a chestnut, and a palomino—were grazing along the creek.

My heart began pounding like a drum. I glanced over at Joe. I knew the look on his face. *Oh, shit, there's no stopping this train now*, was my first thought. I could feel myself contracting, steeling myself against the rushing tide of his excitement, pushing down the unexpected seeds of my own. John, the realtor, was waiting at the gate, a sandy blond Robert Redford look-alike, recently transplanted from Pasadena. "You couldn't have picked a better day for this, could you?" I said grumpily as we walked up to him.

He smiled at me. "That's the Wet Mountains in September." Then, pumping Joe's hand, John guided him down the driveway. He knew he had a live one from the look on my husband's face. I followed slowly behind, every bone in my body resisting. But something inside me was fluttering like a moth trapped in a glass.

Who knows, it seemed to be saying with each flutter, *could doing something this radical yank our marriage off life support? Could we turn up the Allman Brothers one more time and get down?*

The First Visit

There was no denying the ranch was picture perfect. If I had been alone on a road trip, driving through the Wet Mountains, my heart would have skipped a beat at how scenic this rustic hideaway was. I would have slowed the car down for a moment to watch the horses grazing in the valley and marvel at the soft yellow of the quaint ranch house. The meandering stream glistening in the sun would have tugged at my heart. *I wonder who is fortunate enough to live in such a perfect place,* I would have mused as I sped up to take the curve up the hill, carrying a hint of longing for the imagined life now receding in the rearview mirror.

I had traveled through many places in my life and watched lives unfold from trains in India, from cars crossing the Navajo Nation, from buses in Catalonia. The familiar pain of beauty seen in passing, the longing stirred by fantasies of living another life, had always been part of me, a parallel storyline of lives not lived.

I got out of the car and followed John and Joe down the long driveway. As we approached the corral, an older couple, the man lean and wizened in full cowboy gear, and the woman with the reassuring look of a retired elementary school teacher, came forward to greet us. "This is Art and Paula," John said, introducing us. "They own these fine horses in the pasture."

"Beautiful," I murmured. I stayed by the corral while the men headed for the house.

"That chestnut there's mine," said Art. "Name's Red. He's a good horse." He was a good-looking horse, but it was the large bay that attracted me.

"Who's that?" I asked, pointing at him.

Paula answered this time. "That's Rain; he has been my horse. Handsome big boy, isn't he?"

"Handsome for sure," I agreed, and we stood together admiring him. Rain was keeping his distance, but I could tell he knew we were talking about him. There was something about him. He was the bad boy in high school I would never have approached.

"Too much horse for her," Art piped up.

There was one more, a small, older palomino. "That's Peanuts. More appropriate for this old broad." Paula laughed.

Joe and John had gone through the house already and were back out on the front porch, talking conservation easements and water rights. Joe had already broken the first rule of home buying; even the dumbest realtor in the world could tell he would pay anything for the place. I joined them on the porch. "Wait 'til you see the cookstove; it's original," Joe started in. "The place needs some work, but with a little care, maybe another bathroom and fireplace, it wouldn't take much to bring it back to life." He was away and running.

"Let me take a look." I stopped him and slipped in on my own.

The deep turquoise stove sitting majestic against the wall was the first thing I saw. It faced a picture window framing a view of the grassy hillside that flanked the valley rising up to a deep evergreen forest. Willows bordered the creek in the foreground. Standing in the room, empty of furniture except for a burnt orange recliner, I could feel the space breathe, calm and quiet. Dust motes danced in the light flickering on the scuffed wood floor. A small window over the kitchen counter revealed a mountain at the end of the valley. I opened the stove, the enamel cool to the touch, and could almost smell the bread rising.

I could tell that the house had once been loved deeply and was just waiting to be loved again.

"The owners haven't been living here," John volunteered when I found them out by the big barn. "They never did settle in. Art and Paula keep an eye on the place, and they graze their horses here."

"Can we walk around?" I asked. "Of course," John replied, leading the way.

Joe was talking as we walked. "It's wet enough up here, we could have a garden, grow apple trees or herbs." He could barely contain himself.

We walked away from the house up a long dirt road toward the mountain. The road had its own gate off the highway.

"Is there another house up here?" I asked John.

"Yes, yes, I was going to tell you about that. There is a house up there; the road here is grandfathered in. A doctor who lives in Pueblo owns it. I heard he's from Bulgaria. He isn't here much. Just hunting season mostly."

"When is hunting season?" I asked.

"Starts soon, but it wouldn't be any bother down here. It's elk farther up they're interested in."

I took a deep breath and tried not to think about hunting season as we kept trudging up the grandfathered road.

We were walking alongside a ridge that looked like the spine of a dragon. "I kinda wanted some rocky outcroppings," I said. "I only see one little one on that ridge."

"What do you need rocky outcroppings for?" Joe asked distractedly. He was kicking at a six-foot-high Russian thistle. The valley was dotted with them standing tall like sentinels.

"To hide behind when I need to shoot the bad guys. Or jump off if I can't take it anymore."

"There was a Western shot here in the early fifties," John chimed in. "*Vengeance Valley*, it was called."

"Wow, that sounds promising," I said. Even Joe laughed.

By then we had turned around and were heading back toward the cluster of buildings at the center of the valley, walking through the meadow along the creek, which we later learned was called Hardscrabble. Near the house, there was a small pond, clogged with green slime, and just inside the wood fence that created a yard, a root cellar with rock walls and a sod roof built into a small rise. The creek was wider as it passed near the house, and there was an island in the middle covered in peppermint, its sharp smell faint in the warm air. By the road to the south of the house was an old cabin made of rough hand-hewn logs. "Look at that," Joe said in the kind of awestruck voice tourists use in cathedrals as he ran his hand along the perfectly hewn corner. A corral that had seen better days joined the cabin with a newer, large barn. In between was a small ramshackle building—a blacksmith shop. An old but functional outhouse stood in the middle of the yard, its open door facing the woods.

There was a small hill at the farthest corner, where the valley made an L-shaped turn to the right. Even from a distance, you could tell it was the perfect lookout with views north, east, and west. We huffed and puffed our way to the top. "Hey," I cried out, "a rocky outcropping!" It was a large boulder surrounded by smaller ones framed by a grove of aspens, their gold leaves fluttering in a light breeze.

In the middle of a clearing in the trees was a campfire site that looked like it had been there for hundreds of years. Joe reached down and picked up a rock streaked with green. "I bet you could find some arrowheads up here," he said.

"I think there is some Indian story about this spot—a sad one, as I remember," John said.

"Yeah, it's pretty obvious it was a camping spot, probably traveling bands, maybe Ute," Joe went on.

I was barely listening to their conversation, all my attention held by the view down the valley. From where I stood, I could see clearly why it was called Lookout Valley Ranch. The ranch house and barns and corral, small from where we stood, were nestled in the heart of the valley. The stream zigzagged from one end to the other, etched into the green and gold of the late summer grasses. The horses, their heads down, were barely moving as they grazed alongside it. Then, suddenly a wind stirred and something spooked Rain, and he took off galloping toward us, the others following. My breath caught in my throat at the sight, my heart racing.

"Imagine," Joe said, coming over to stand beside me, "everything you can see from here would be ours, this whole valley and mountain, even across the road."

I wasn't listening. It would be a few years before that idea would mean anything to me. At that moment, something else was speaking to me. Something more intangible, deeper, a faint memory, a longing, for what I wasn't sure.

I shook it off. "Okay, we should think about getting back to Denver before dark," I said, heading down the hill.

Back at the ranch house, I turned to John. "How are the winters here?"

He laughed. "They don't call them the Wet Mountains for nothing." I looked over, but Joe wasn't listening. He was fingering a handful of dirt from the weedy flowerbed next to the porch. As we walked to the car, Rain sauntered over to the corral fence. I stopped and stroked the white blaze on his forehead, his deep, earthy smell enveloping me. I felt like wrapping my arms around his neck but held myself back. "What are you going to do with Rain, if Paula isn't riding him anymore?" I asked Art.

"Guess I'll just have to sell him." He chuckled. "Look at that, I think he likes you."

I moved away from the fence. "Good meeting you both," I said and headed up to the car.

The afternoon light lay soft on the valley as we drove away. We traveled in silence for a while, lost in our own thoughts. I could have objected. I could have rained on Joe's parade. I could have harped on the winters and the snow and the isolation, but something kept me quiet.

Not long before I had read a teaching by Pema Chödrön, a well-known American Buddhist nun. A simple instruction in the middle of a page jumped out at me: "Do something different." When you are faced with something that pisses you off, that scares you, something that pushes some old button, there is always a split second before you launch into your habitual response—blowing up, grabbing a cigarette, running a mile in the other direction. In that moment, you can do something different. Anything. Even something as simple as saying "yes" when your knee-jerk reaction would be to say "no."

I had tried to follow these instructions and failed too many times to count. But at that moment, I thought, *What the hell. Why not go for it? What do we have to lose?* Maybe Joe and I could find a way to get real with each other alone in this remote place. Maybe my head and my heart could somehow find a way to meet.

My whole life I had seesawed back and forth between longing for the perfect home and flinging myself into the unknown. This time, as we drove up I-25 back to Denver, I had the strange sensation of both impulses operating at the same time.

"I think we found it," I said, looking at Joe.

It took him by surprise for a moment, then he nodded. "I don't think we'll find anything better. I know I can make it perfect."

"I want Rain too," I added.

"I don't think you need to worry about rain," Joe answered. I felt a familiar wave of irritation wash over me. Joe felt it too, finely tuned as he was to my disapproval. "What?" he said, confused, as I glared at him. I was about to keep going with, "What the fuck is the matter with you, I am talking about the horse," when suddenly the words *do something different* appeared in my mind.

"Yeah, what else would you expect in the Wet Mountains," I said. "Rain, and lots of it." I laughed. It was so easy. I could feel Joe relax, and he smiled. Not for the first time, I thought, *Why is it so hard for me to be kind to him?*

I reached over and lightly rubbed the back of his neck, letting my hand rest there as we cruised down the canyon to Florence. We had just stepped out of our comfort zones into the unknown. It was scary as hell and completely exhilarating.

Buying the Ranch

It was 1965 when I started college, but for most of us, the sixties hadn't begun. I was still pretty straight—and fearful. When I think about it, I ended up going to the University of Colorado in Boulder only because it was familiar. I could have gone to Stanford or Sarah Lawrence, but I had no history with either of them. My father had gone to the University of Colorado. I had spent summers in Boulder. I chose it because I was exhausted with having to deal with so many unknowns my whole life.

All that changed after I met Joanie our freshman year at CU, when we found ourselves living in the same girls' dorm, Sewall Hall. She was from New Hampshire, born into a family of intellectuals, liberals with old money and good values. She grew up in a stable home with siblings. Her private school had been co-ed and way more progressive than Holton-Arms School for Girls. I was in awe of her self-assurance. She was voluptuous, with wild, wavy hair. She skied and had a ski bum boyfriend in Vail. I was skinny, verging on anorexic, a sedentary smoker, dressed all in black except for my WWI brown combat boots. Tortured. On the surface, we couldn't have been less alike, but we soon discovered that we shared a raunchy sense of humor and a longing for something deeper in our lives. We started smoking weed and getting in trouble.

Our first encounter with the law happened when we decided that the cream-colored stone walls of the chemistry building were crying out for pastel flowers. It took an hour to decorate one side of the building and a long, hard day to scrub it clean. At the end of our freshman year, Joanie and

I were caught in a middle-of-the-night sweep by the dorm patrol who found our rooms empty. On the sign-out sheet we had scrawled the names T. Leary and R. Alpert at a nonexistent address. Nobody else thought it was funny. We were sent before the disciplinary committee.

After we were put on probation, Joanie took off for San Francisco. I tried half-heartedly to keep going, but in the spring of 1967, I dropped out and moved into a ramshackle farmhouse on the edge of town and started tripping on LSD every week.

That summer, Joanie and I met up in San Francisco and headed to India, where my father was consul general in Calcutta. We pretended we wanted to do good works, but really, we were spiritual seekers following Richard Alpert on the hippie trail to Kathmandu. We dropped acid the night before getting on a plane to Hong Kong, where we loaded up on books by Hermann Hesse and Alexandra David-Néel at an esoteric bookstore and then set sail on the Italian liner *Leonardo da Vinci* to Bombay. The night after we arrived by train in Calcutta, we bookended our journey by dropping acid with two Peace Corps volunteers and dancing to the newly released *Sergeant Pepper's Lonely Hearts Club Band* in the garden of the consulate. After putting in our time volunteering at Mother Teresa's orphanage, we took off. By the time we reached Kathmandu, Richard Alpert had left to find his teacher. He was soon to begin his new life as Baba Ram Dass.

Those were wild and unpredictable times, living on the edge with no safety net. I rarely planned my trips: the moment would arise, someone would offer me a hit of acid, or there would be a gathering, and we would all drop together. I loved the quality of reckless abandon, of not having control, of the possibility of danger. I loved saying yes to whatever arose and seeing if I could get through to the other side in one piece. It was the flip side to my longing for security, and I seesawed back and forth between the two with abandon.

Thirty years later, that kind of seesawing felt insane.

After the giddy moment when I said yes to buying Lookout Valley Ranch, I plunged into a long stretch of low-level anxiety spiked with panic attacks as we went through the arduous process of making an offer and working out the financing, the conservation easement, water rights, and the millions of details involved in purchasing a 160-acre property. It took a year. Throughout those endless months, my mind kept coming up with analogies to describe the roller coaster I was on: I was told I had a terminal disease; I was a prisoner given an execution date; an astronaut about to launch into space.

There were many times when I could have stopped the process, but I couldn't. I felt like I was a child once again, paralyzed by the fear of a future over which I had no control in a place I couldn't recognize. At night, lying in bed in our Denver home, waves of panic would sweep through me, shattering whatever fragile sense of self I was hanging on to. The feeling was so harsh and so familiar, as though I had spent a lifetime in rough seas pummeled by waves of anxiety. I could see it in the fear and defiance on my face in childhood photographs, in pictures of myself as a painfully thin teenager, throughout my adult life as a filmmaker, a wife, a lover, and a mother. There would be times of smooth sailing, and then, without warning I would be lost once again, breathless in a sea of anxiety. In those months spent buying the ranch, I felt like my very being was being blown apart. Night after night I dreamed I was stranded somewhere scary, trying to stuff all my belongings into a small suitcase, desperate to gather my world back together.

In the meantime, I turned fifty and—as if the moving anxiety weren't enough—I was wracked by hormonal changes, veering wildly from rage to the verge of tears.

Then, out of the blue, a lifeline appeared. One day, standing in line at our neighborhood post office, I picked up a copy of a Denver continuing education brochure from the counter and opened it at random to a page that offered a class in natural horsemanship. It was a sign from above. I signed up.

The class was taught at a ranch east of Denver by a woman named Janice, a lean, no-nonsense, former Westernaire rider who had once graced the cover of *Western Horseman* flying across an arena standing on the back of a palomino. After two classes of the basics—catching and haltering, tying a proper knot, brushing the horse, picking up each hoof and cleaning it, lifting an incredibly heavy western saddle onto the horse's back and tightening the cinch—our class of four middle-aged women was ready to mount up and ride.

That first day, Janice stood in the middle of the arena and, as we circled slowly around her, perching awkwardly on our saddles, she said in her clear, decisive voice, "Okay, now I want you to visualize your legs melting down the sides of your horse all the way into the earth." It was like being hit by lightning; my whole body was electrified. I had spent so many years living in my head, cut off at the neck, and now I was being asked to be fully in my body. It was terrifying and exhilarating, and I was smitten.

Once the group class was over, I kept going, faithfully turning up at Janice's place for lessons twice a week, fearful and awkward. It was a tall order, but I was determined to find a way to connect my head with my body, to feel my legs melting down the sides of a horse.

Come spring, the deed to the ranch was signed, the key was handed over, and we became the owners of a 160-acre 1870s homestead in the Wet Mountains. It would be another year before we could move in. Julia still had her last year of high school, and I was deep in production on a drug prevention video series on cocaine, meth, and heroin. We entered a transition period: one foot in Denver, one in the ranch.

Joe took on the project of bringing Lookout Valley Ranch back to life. It was his fantasy come true. He began to spend weeks there, happily tearing things down, building things, weeding, and planting. His first project was to install a second bathroom, complete with a salvaged claw-foot tub and a view up the valley. He carved out a little alcove for TV viewing. Using bits and pieces of old Tiffany glass from his years as a stained-glass artist, he created a window for the dining area. He installed kitchen cabinets made from the sugar pine floors of an old church. He planted a vegetable garden, built a gazebo, and cleaned out the barn to turn it into his office. Answering an ad in the *Denver Post* offering an original redwood hot tub for free if you would haul it away, he spent a week dismantling and removing it from the basement of an old Denver Square home and another week putting it back together piece by piece in the yard at the ranch.

His sidekicks were our dogs Bronco and Abby, mother and daughter blue heelers. They kept an eye on everybody and everything, especially the cows that were leasing pasture for the summer. The first time Bronco saw cows grazing, she took up a position of vigilance and watched their every move intently for two hours, downloading the "cow program." From then on, all you had to say was "get the cows," and she would start herding.

I came and went, visiting on weekends, driving from Denver, listening to classic country on the radio, trying to imagine our new life as ranchers. Everything about it, even the language, was foreign. The man who came to install our carpet said "dadgummit" when he dropped his clipboard. When Art said I needed to "watch out for the bars," I thought he was warning me away from the Alibi Lounge in Florence.

Bears loomed large in my overactive imagination. I read everything I could find about bear attacks and posted instructions for dealing with bear encounters on the refrigerator: stand your ground, make yourself really big, and DON'T RUN AWAY. Right. Running away was high on the list of things I wanted to do.

Meanwhile, my life in Denver went on as though nothing were about to change. My days were spent interviewing crack addicts, going to yoga, running to Spinelli's for take-out lasagna, and watching Julia and the cheerleading squad do something just this side of bump and grind at the basketball games. It was a juggling act, keeping track of all the plates circling in the air above me. At any moment it felt like they could come crashing down on my head.

When we took possession of Lookout Valley Ranch, I also took possession of Rain, as I had requested. It turned out that Rain wasn't just any old bay gelding; he was a registered Appaloosa whose name was Might Rain, a name I would soon learn perfectly described his personality. He was obstinate and manipulative and funny and willful and very smart. He was my first horse. I had no idea what I was getting into.

That last winter in Denver, I brought Rain to board at Janice's and began taking lessons on him. Right away, I could see why Paula had given up. Rain was a big horse with a mind of his own, and I was a fearful, middle-aged woman. The more I tried to do the right thing, the tighter I got. My paralysis would feed his reluctance, and the cycle was set. We weren't going anywhere. We were just stumbling over each other's feet on the dance floor, desperate for the song to end. "What are you afraid of?" Janice would ask, and when I couldn't answer, she would tell me, "Stop paying so much attention to what could go wrong; focus on where you want to go." I'd have to have been dumb as a brick to not see how everything she said was applicable to my whole life.

By the time spring rolled around, I was gaining confidence in the indoor arena—walking, trotting, even cantering. It was time to move to the outdoor arena. Our first time out, we made it halfway around the arena before Rain saw a mower abandoned by the fence and took off at a gallop, hell-bent for the half-opened gate, with me yanking on the reins as hard as I could. Just before he hit the gate, I bailed off him, landing on my butt in the dirt. After I limped back to the barn, Janice sat me down and said, "Here's what you do next time a horse takes off with you: loosen your grip on the reins, let go, and relax. Now get back up on him and show him you're not afraid." At that moment, nothing she had said made any sense, but over time, "Let go, relax, don't give in to fear" became words to live by, and not only for riding a horse.

The clock was ticking, each day bringing closer the inevitable, irreversible end of our life as a family in Denver and the beginning of our life as empty nesters in the Wet Mountains. Julia graduated from Manual High School and began preparing for her new reality as a freshman at Occidental College in Los Angeles. We sold the house in Denver and completed the ranch remodel. Most of our furniture and clothes had been moved piece by piece, sold, or given away. All that was left was our video editing equipment, a couple of suitcases, the two of us, and the two dogs.

I was determined to keep it together if it killed me. *Change is good*, I told myself over and over. But my chest hurt from holding off the demons of my childhood banging at the door.

Then one day, I woke up to the thought, *This is like dying. Dying is inevitable. I need to make this move into a practice for dying.* The thought didn't just come out of the blue.

At the ranch, death and the prospect of dying were everywhere. Rifle shots from hunters at Eustace's place cracked and reverberated off the hill. A hawk rose slowly from the field, its belly glinting in the sun, a rabbit in its claws. Coyotes yipped and howled on the hillside, trying to entice the dogs into the woods. The cows grazed in the tall grass, blissfully unaware that their days were numbered, that the feedlot was just around the corner.

The more I was confronted by death, the more obvious it became that all the panic in the world wouldn't make it easier. I needed to figure out a better solution.

I've always thought Buddhism does dying better than any other religion. There are pages and pages of Buddhist texts devoted to how to die, the most famous being *The Tibetan Book of the Dead*. What I understood of these teachings is that everything, including living and dreaming and dying, can be viewed as a transition from one state to another. The only way to work with that reality is to make a relationship with our own wild and intractable mind during this brief period of living, to tame our minds now so we don't panic at the moment of death.

One morning, with a wisdom I didn't know I had, I came to the conclusion that the secret to learning how to live with ease at the ranch was somehow connected to these teachings about learning how to die with ease. In order to figure that out, I needed to do things differently. I needed to learn how to let go and relax with whatever came my way.

When Things Fall Apart

In August, before Julia left for college and Joe and I left Denver for good, I spent ten days at Rocky Mountain Shambhala Center assisting at a retreat being led by Pema Chödrön. The name of the retreat was "When Things Fall Apart," after her most recent book.

I was helping with the cooking at the house where Pema was staying and leading discussion groups and meeting with participants about their meditation practice. Four hundred people were there, most of them women, many of them grappling with their own version of falling apart. I had known Pema since I first became a student of Trungpa Rinpoche, long before she became a well-known teacher and author. Her books had been road maps for me on my path, showing up exactly when I needed them. I had read *The Wisdom of No Escape* when I was grappling with a very old depression and years of dissociating through alcohol and meaningless sex. Simply reading the title set off a panic attack in me so intense I thought I was having a heart attack.

The timing of a retreat about things falling apart was perfect.

Every few days, all the meditation instructors would meet with Pema as a group. It was supposed to be a time to talk about the students we were seeing, but of course most of the time we talked about ourselves and what we were going through. At one meeting, my friend Helen spoke about her struggles with meditation practice. "When I sit, all I experience is numbness. Nothing else, just endless numbness," she said.

I was sitting opposite her in the circle, and her words hit me like a javelin. I knew exactly what she was talking about. I suddenly saw that during all the years of sitting on my cushion, congratulating myself on how calm I was becoming, most of that time I was just numb. I was checked out, and it was no different from when I drank too much, only without the remorse and the hangover. Joe was right. Meditation practice hadn't penetrated all the membranes, all that thick flesh that had grown around my heart. Fundamentally, little had changed.

Toward the end of the retreat, I could feel my anxiety growing, with the big move coming up when I got back to Denver. Nights of little sleep and days spent with four hundred people all going through their own roller coaster ride of insights and breakthroughs and despair and panic were taking their toll.

The day before the retreat was to end, Pema was performing a Refuge Ceremony for a group of participants who were new to meditation and now felt it was time to give up searching everywhere for the perfect solution to their suffering and instead make a commitment to a practice of Buddhist meditation and teachings as their path to freedom. At the end of the ceremony, they would receive a refuge name—traditionally given as a reminder of who we fundamentally are, stripped of our conventional identity.

The afternoon before the ceremony, we set up an assembly line on low tables in the house where Pema was staying. Our job was to create the piece of paper that each person would receive with their refuge name written on it. It was an arduous and time-consuming process. Each name was first written by Pema in Tibetan calligraphy, then by one of us in English, and finally two seals were stamped in deep red on the bottom. Three of us sat on cushions at a low table. I was given the easiest job: stamping a simple lotus, *pema* in Sanskrit, under each name. Time dragged on. There must have been a hundred names, and we were exhausted and hungry by the time the end was in sight. The light was fading, and no one wanted to get up to turn on a lamp; we just wanted the ordeal to be over. Finally, we were down to the last one, waiting for the piece of paper with the name to emerge from Pema's room when, for some reason, everything stopped. After a moment of sitting at attention, we all slumped down on our cushions, drifting off in the twilit room. I put my seal down on the table and rested. Then suddenly the last page was delivered, and we started up again. I picked up the lotus seal and stamped it hard on the page, and then, seal still in my hand, I saw in horror what I had done. I had stamped the lotus upside down.

I was going to have to go and tell Pema Chödrön that she had to pen the last name again.

Suddenly, I was five years old at Miss Ironsides School for Girls, and I was in trouble. My heart was pounding. There was no way out. I dragged myself up off the floor, clutching the messed-up paper, and knocked on Pema's door. She was sitting at the end of a long dining room table in the dusky light, looking small and very tired. I hovered in the doorway, took a deep breath, and gave her the bad news. In my mind's eye, I still see that moment when she looked up at me and daggers seemed to shoot from her eyes. Then, out of the blue, I blurted out, "I just want to be loved." Time stopped, *I just want to be loved* hanging in the space between us. And then we both dissolved into laughter, and we laughed and laughed until finally we stopped, and Pema took a fresh sheet of paper from the stack and wrote out the last name one more time.

A day later, the meditation retreat was over, and it was time to get back to my life. As soon as I got back to Denver we would be leaving for our new home in the Wet Mountains. I felt stronger, armed with new insights and ready to confront the move, my fear, my numbness, and the big one, Joe and me. After twenty-two years, our marriage was struggling to survive; it needed a lot of work or a miracle to revive it.

The Commitment

As I drove back to Denver, the words *I just want to be loved* kept gnawing at me. The phrase seemed to have come out of the blue, but I knew it hadn't. As I cruised down the highway, I suddenly remembered a conversation I had had with Nick a few years before.

"Why don't you guys ever say, 'I love you'?" Nick had asked me one day as we were driving across town. He was sixteen. Not long before, he had begun draping himself on my shoulders while I was at the sink or chopping vegetables, and saying, "I love you." A six-foot-four linebacker smothering me in an awkward show of affection.

"What do you mean?" I asked, more defensively than I meant.

"Like other parents, you know. When they leave for work the dad and mom say, 'I love you.'"

"We both work at home," I said, trying to make light of it, but I knew he had been observing a friend's family, and he wanted ours to be like theirs.

Growing up, nobody in my family of three had ever said "I love you." I had no pictures of my mother holding me, no memories of being cuddled. When Nick was a baby and I handed him to my mother, I watched her hold him with her arms outstretched as though she were delivering the Thanksgiving turkey on a platter. In that moment, my whole childhood flashed in front of me with horrifying clarity. It hurt to hear Nick ask the question, but the answer was clear. "I didn't have the most loving of childhoods. Nobody ever said those words growing up, so I didn't know people did that on a regular basis," I told him and kept my eyes on the road.

Later, I brought up the conversation in one of the few marriage-counseling sessions Joe and I had, and the therapist made the suggestion: "Why don't you and Joe start by finding a time each day to sit and talk and listen to each other?" The problem was that Joe and I talked all the time. We talked about everything. We shared opinions on movies and paint colors and people we couldn't stand. But really talking, and more to the point, listening, to each other was above our pay grade. We tried, but inertia is a strong force. We were two wounded, self-conscious people, pushing a heavy rock uphill.

From the start, our marriage had been confusing. We did everything backward. When Nick was born, Joe was still legally married. Nick's birth certificate identified him as "baby boy Hitchcock." We had to petition to have that changed after our wedding, six months later.

Trungpa Rinpoche officiated at the ceremony on a sweltering day in August 1976, in the shrine room at 1111 Pearl

Street. We had a full house of friends and family and friends of family. I was wearing a hideous, long, burnt-orange cotton dress that looked like a sack held together at the waist with a green woven belt. My hair was styled in tight curls with a gardenia pinned behind my ear. I hated how I looked. Nothing about how I looked matched how I envisioned it. Three weeks before, I had gone wedding dress shopping with a friend in Denver, trudging from department store to department store until arriving at Nordstrom's, our last chance to find something for me to wear. After striking out in the women's department, we decided to go to the designer floor. It was a long shot. We imagined rows of matronly, satin cocktail dresses. But there, hanging on a rack, was the perfect wedding dress: cream, draped silk, light as air, with hand-painted Japanese-style flowers in blues and greens scattered across it. It was elegant and simple, and I loved it. It was also $400, way more than I had planned on spending. I bought it anyway. When I brought it home, Joe looked at me, incredulous. "Are you nuts?" he said. "We could buy a couch with $400."

The message was loud and clear: How could you be so selfish? This is just a dress for you. We need a couch for us.

Joe enlisted my mother on his side. After all, it was her $400. The next day, the two of them went out together and bought a couch. I gritted my teeth and took the dress of my dreams back to Nordstrom's.

I was shattered, and I was angry—at losing the dress, at Joe not understanding, at how powerless I felt, and at how I had shut down completely, unable to say, "NO, this is the dress I want to wear. This is my wedding day. I don't want to settle for some cheap piece of shit." I hadn't said any of that.

I hadn't called off the wedding. I had swallowed my feelings and kept quiet.

Even as we knelt in front of the shrine and Trungpa Rinpoche led us in reciting our wedding vows to practice the six virtues of generosity, discipline, patience, exertion, meditation, and insight, I felt heartbroken and sick. At the end of the ceremony, Rinpoche told us that in marrying each other we were marrying the world. I had no idea what he meant. Where was the part about having and holding until death do us part? Where was the promise of eternal love?

For the next four days, trapped in our honeymoon cabin with a sick, fussy, six-month-old baby, I paced back and forth, hungover and freaked out, haunted by the memory of another red flag I had ignored early in our relationship.

It was Thanksgiving dinner at my house, soon after Joe and I had gotten together. We were a small group, seated on the floor around a low table in the living room. We all drank a lot of cheap wine and ate a lot of turkey and stuffing, and it was getting late when I looked up and saw that Joe and a woman I barely knew, and he had only just met, were by the door putting on their coats. At first, I couldn't understand what was happening, and then, just like that, they walked out and shut the door behind them. I could see them through the picture window getting in her car. His Volvo stayed parked in front of my house for two days. When he walked back in looking sheepish, I didn't say anything, and we went on as though nothing had happened.

It was the first imprint of a pattern that became woven into our lives for the next twenty years—a pattern of holding our feelings tight and willing ourselves not to see what was going on in front of us. Our vows of patience and generosity and the other virtues were relegated to the realm of the theoretical. We were too busy with work and family and friends and love affairs to make them part of our real, everyday lives.

Our first night at Lookout Valley Ranch, sitting in the hot tub, I told Joe I wanted to spend our first year in our beautifully renovated ranch renovating our marriage. "Don't you think it's kind of now or never?" I asked, staring at the stars, too nervous for eye contact. "I mean, what's the point of all this if we can't find a way to crack this big iceberg that's grown between us?" He didn't say anything. After a long moment of silence, I looked over at him. From the light filtering out from the kitchen, I could see his face, a face I knew so well. His fear, his exhaustion, his skepticism were all on display. *Couldn't we just get along and not have to talk about it?* I could almost hear him thinking.

I felt myself deflating, my courage draining out into the hot tub, when he said, "Maybe you're right. I guess it does kind of feel like the end of the trail. All right. If you think it'll help, let's give it a try."

We decided to give the marriage nine months. Come spring, we would make the decision of whether we wanted to be together for the long haul or give up and go our separate ways. For the next nine months, we would try doing things differently. That night, under the vast sky of our new home, we made a commitment to start by spending an hour each morning talking and truly listening to each other.

PART 2

First Year at the Ranch

Practicing Patience

The days of late summer were breathtaking. Joe's vegetable garden was overflowing with squash and carrots and peas. The sun was warm during the day, with just a touch of cool in the air. Nights were cold, clear, and star studded. The space and the silence were all-pervasive. I could feel myself settling into a slower rhythm, finding it impossible to keep my usual frantic pace.

My whole life, ever since I could remember, I had been impatient. I got antsy slathering my body with lotion after a shower. Impatience was in my blood, a legacy from my mother and my grandmother. I decided this new, slowed-down world was a perfect place for me to practice patience. It was one of the six virtues Joe and I had recited as our wedding vow. With our new commitment to doing things differently it seemed like a good time to dust it off and give patience a try.

One afternoon on my way home from Florence, I pulled over by a stand selling Palisade peaches and, on a whim, bought a full box. That's a lot of peaches. I decided as my first exercise in patience to peel them and can them. As a hippie, I had canned things; that's what you did in the sixties. It couldn't be that hard.

I set the box down on the porch and, surrounded by buckets, I picked up my paring knife and started peeling. The peaches were a deep gold with splatters of rose in their hearts. For two hours, I peeled, peach juice dripping through my fingers, peach juice everywhere, my fingers aching. For two hours, I found myself on a battleground. On one side, my mind harped on about what a useless waste of time this all was; I could go to Safeway and get peaches for $1.25 a can. Then, the mind chatter would lift, and I would encounter a moment of pure joy—warm sun, blue sky, soft breeze, hummingbirds hovering. In the end, I abandoned the canning, made a peach pie, and froze the rest, but a start had been made and at least I had something to show for it.

My next project was staining the two pine rocking chairs we had found in the dim recesses of the unfinished furniture store in Canon City. Driving home with them, I had had a vision of sitting with Joe, rocking together side by side into our dotage. The next day, I set the chairs up on the porch and began staining and sealing them. It took a while for me to settle down, to not jump up and get a glass of water or smoke a cigarette, but gradually, as I moved the paintbrush back and forth slowly darkening the unfinished wood into a deep copper, I began to feel an unfamiliar sense of ease settle into my body. The sun was just dropping behind the mountain by the time I finished. "Look at what I just did," I called out to Joe as he made his way out to the hot tub in his dressing gown, carrying a bottle of beer.

He glanced over. "Nice," he said, which was not as much appreciation as I was looking for, but I let it go.

It was my first hint that there might be an element of one-upping Joe or at least showing off in my patience project. That became clearer when I decided to tackle a project he had been putting off for days: stacking rocks in the creek to divert water into the pond.

The week before, our neighbor from up the valley, Eustace, had arrived unannounced with fifty trout to dump into our pond. I guess it was a welcome-to-the-neighborhood gift. He parked his big truck on the lawn, lumbered up the porch steps, and banged on the door. He was a large man; the buttons of his black shirt were popping open, his face beet red from the exertion of climbing the four steps to the porch. His accent was heavy Eastern European. He introduced himself, then pointed at the truck and said, "That's my wife." The woman in the truck didn't look over. All I could see of her was a bouffant, peroxide-blonde head of hair. After his opening pleasantries, he said, "These are for your pond. They'll need fresh water," and nodded toward a large tank in the back of the truck. I could see fish tails flapping. "I need your husband," he added, and then he got in the truck, revved his motor, and drove across the lawn to the pond with Joe hurrying behind him on foot.

For days, Joe had put off dealing with getting fresh water into the pond for the fish and I was beginning to get worried we were soon going to find them belly up on its surface.

It didn't take long for me to regret my impulse to show Joe how diligent I could be. I bitched and moaned under my breath as I stacked rocks and dug into the black sludge and watched impatiently as the water pushed against the new wall, searching for a way through. Grumpily heaving rocks into the water, I told myself, *Just think of it as weight training.*

Gradually the rock wall in the creek grew. After a while, the chatter in my head began to fade, and I became transfixed by one large rock lodged under the flowing water. "This is just the one I am looking for," I said to the dogs who were hovering nearby, waiting for a stick to be thrown. Reaching into the icy water, I picked up the rock and placed it on top of the wall. Sweating and dirty, my sneakers soaked, I fell into a rhythm of picking up rocks and stacking them one by one. The wall grew larger and larger. The trickle of water kept searching for a way through until all of a sudden a full flow of burbling creek branched off and poured into the pond. I whooped and hollered and threw myself down on the bank, exhausted and laughing. The dogs joined the party and brought me sticks to throw into the pond over and over.

I lay there for a long while warmed by the sun, intoxicated by the pungent smell of peppermint growing along the creek. I had definitely done something different, I had slowed way down and it felt ridiculously good.

The next morning, I shared my struggles developing patience with Joe at what I had started calling our daily briefing. I began with the peaches and then the rocking chairs and then the grand finale at the pond. I could tell he was trying to be interested, but it wasn't convincing. Maybe the minutiae of someone else's torturous path of mind training was more than anyone should be asked to endure, but if I couldn't share those moments with Joe, what could I share? That morning, Joe had nothing he wanted to talk about. The past few days, he had mostly complained—about the slowness of the internet, about his endless battle with the thistles in the meadow, about Rain having stuck his head in the window of his office and pushed a large box of nails off the ledge, scattering them all over the floor. It was hard for me not to laugh at that story, but I could tell Joe was struggling to find humor in anything. Something was eating at him, and I wasn't quite sure what it was. I was trying not to get impatient with him, but it wasn't easy.

I also needed to be patient with myself as I struggled to overcome my fear of riding alone at the ranch. Just thinking about riding Rain out into the wide-open space of the valley would set off an intense fear that grabbed me in the chest and migrated down to my belly, my teeth clamping shut. I found that chewing gum helped some, but soon I discovered the magic formula for calming my nerves was singing—one song in particular.

Each day, I would bring Rain out of the corral, saddle and bridle him, get up on him, take a deep breath, and pop a piece of gum in my mouth. Then, as we took off, I would launch into "All of me, why not take all of me, can't you see that I'm no good without you," and gradually, I would start to settle into the saddle. It worked every time. Each day, we ventured a little farther on our expeditions. Then, late one morning, I decided to tackle riding across the creek. I was feeling confident. It was only a foot deep. I had watched Rain amble across it every day. What could go wrong? We headed toward the creek at a fast walk, got to the edge, and Rain stopped. He wouldn't budge. I backed him up and started again. Same thing. "Never give up," I heard Janice's voice in my head. "If you ask something of a horse, you can't do anything else until they do it." Again, I circled Rain around, we headed toward the creek again just fine, and then, at the edge of the water, he came to a halt. We sat for a while contemplating the valley on the other side. I tried again and then again. An hour went by. I started to panic. Were we going to be there until night?

After one more attempt, I began to sing, my voice a whisper, "All of me, why not take all of me . . . ," I felt myself start to relax.

As I sang, I could feel Rain's neck begin to soften. "Can't you see that I'm no good without you." I kept on singing, and then I nudged him with my legs and he took a step forward, and then, smooth as silk, he stepped into the creek.

The sun sparkled on the water as we splashed across and climbed up the other bank. I gave Rain another nudge and he took off at a trot, gathering speed as we neared the hill. My mind was no longer in charge, criticizing me or trying to get me to do something different. I was just there, riding my horse across a wide mountain valley on a cool afternoon in autumn. Tired and happy, my body knew exactly what to do.

Meeting the Neighbors

"The horses are gone," I yelled as I crashed through the door into the kitchen where Joe was pouring himself a cup of coffee. He stared at me like a deer caught in the headlights.

"What do you mean?" he asked.

"The horses are no longer in the corral," I enunciated overly clearly. Patience, I was discovering, was a lot harder with other humans, especially those with whom you have a history of impatience. "You need to get your ass out here and help me find them," I said, slamming the door on my way out.

I was in the driver's seat revving the engine when Joe climbed in, holding his coffee cup. I backed up before he got the door shut, coffee spilling down his T-shirt. "Aren't they just out in the pasture?" he said, trying to be helpful.

"How could they be out in the pasture? Look." I pointed at the corral gate hanging open to the driveway as I swung around, drove up to the road, and turned right. "Look in the trees," I ordered as I drove slowly down the gravel road to Wetmore. With the creek running alongside, this spot looked promising. But no dice. When we reached the sign saying we were entering the San Isabel National Forest, I turned around and headed back up the road. This time I kept my eyes on the trees. I could feel my need to blame someone for this disaster rising in my throat. The only person I could find was Joe. "You've been here for months. Why didn't you fix the gate?" I couldn't stop myself, even though I knew it was a stretch. Joe had no interest in the horses. They were my thing. Fortunately, he didn't respond.

Other than Eustace and his blonde wife, we hadn't met any other neighbors. I knew there were some across the road who came on weekends. We had seen their large truck arriving on Saturday mornings. Their driveway was across from ours, their mailbox said Trimble. It was Sunday, and their gate was open, so I drove in.

The dirt driveway was long, steep, and narrow. I could see fresh hoofmarks in the soft dirt along the side. At the top it leveled off, opening out onto a lush meadow. There, grazing nonchalantly, were the horses. They didn't even look up. A pale blue double-wide with a wraparound deck overlooked the meadow. A giant of a man wearing overalls and holding a large mug of coffee came out and stood on the deck, watching us arrive. He had a long white beard and hair in a ponytail down his back—a cross between Santa Claus and Willie Nelson.

"We were expecting you," he said by way of greeting as we parked and got out of the car. "How about some coffee? I don't think those critters are going anywhere soon." He ushered us into the house. "Name is Otis. That's Johanna." He nodded toward a heavyset woman with a faded blonde perm sitting in a recliner, wearing a velour bathrobe, a cup of coffee in one hand and a crossword puzzle book open on her lap.

She smiled up at us. "Take a seat; any of 'em will do." She indicated a ring of large couches and recliners in a semicircle, an amphitheater facing a huge TV set to the Broncos pregame show, the sound a low hum. I sat down on a couch next to her. Joe picked a recliner across the room.

"I'm Vicki," I said. "That's Joe."

"You take cream and sugar?" Otis called out from the kitchen.

"Yes, please," I called back. Joe seemed to be tongue-tied.

For the next couple of hours, we settled in for a long and rambling storytelling tour of the neighborhood. At one point, Otis brought out some doughnuts on a plate. We heard about one other semi-full-time resident named Greg, who lived up the road from the Trimble place. He had a heavy metal band and a janitorial service in Denver. "He did have a wife—a lawyer—but she ran off with someone last summer. Broke his heart," Johanna told us.

We learned that Otis had recently retired after thirty years at the steel mill in Pueblo. "Hated every damn minute of it," he told us.

Johanna was a nurse who now worked in the prison in Canon City. "I used to be down in Pueblo. Worked with Useless down there. Your neighbor—Useless, I call him." She launched into an impeccable imitation of Eustace telling a patient to spread her legs.

"You're kidding! Eustace is a gynecologist?" I asked, dumbstruck.

"Yep. I've seen him not even put on gloves when he was examining a patient." Johanna chuckled and glanced over at me. "I wouldn't let him get his fat fingers anywhere near my pussy." I grimaced in agreement, and we both took a gulp of coffee to seal the deal. Otis kept smiling benevolently as Johanna regaled us with more colorful stories of Eustace and the prisoners she now cared for. I was loving every minute of it. I had made a career of interviewing people for my videos. I could spend hours listening to stories, following people down the dark twists and turns of their lives. But I could tell Joe was getting antsy. We were on our second cup of coffee when a scrawny kid, maybe twelve, wearing boxers and a T-shirt, slouched into the room.

"He'd sleep the day away if he could. He only comes out for food." Johanna volunteered, "Our daughter left him with us."

"For the summer?" I asked.

"Nope. To raise. Name's Casey. Say hello to our new neighbors," she said, turning to her grandson.

"Hi Casey," I said, and told him our names. He raised a limp hand in our direction and continued shuffling to the kitchen.

"You all done a nice job prettying up your place down there," Otis said, clearly changing the subject away from Casey and his mother.

"Joe has been hard at work since we bought it," I said, jumping at the chance to engage Joe in the conversation.

"It needed a lot of work," Joe said. Otis nodded a couple times, and that was all the encouragement Joe needed. He was off and running, talking about the projects he had undertaken so far.

Johanna and I branched off into our own chat. "It's been a while since anyone took good care of the place," she said. "Treva was the last. She was a tough one, lived there alone. Fought off a bobcat on the porch trying to get her little dog.

With a broom." Johanna laughed raucously. "Not too many people can take living way out here. They go bat-shit crazy, like my brother. Jim Bishop is his name. You seen that death trap he's putting up down the road? His castle built single-handed with, in his words, 'no help from the criminals in Washington.'"

A light bulb went off at the word *castle*. "I read about that place, Bishop's Castle, in an airplane magazine," I said.

"Well, there you go." She chuckled. "Just don't visit in the afternoon when his meds wear off."

Joe and Otis's conversation was winding down. I could see Otis's eyes drifting toward the TV screen, where the Broncos game was gearing up for kickoff. I was jittery from coffee and doughnuts and worried about the logistics of getting the horses back to the corral. Otis, seeming to read my mind, yelled into the kitchen, "Hey, kid, come in here. Help these folks get their horses back down to their place." To my surprise, Casey got up from the kitchen table where he had been deep into a bowl of Honey Nut Cheerios and went to get dressed.

The horses were now well fed and lazy, their adventure over. They stood quietly while I put on their halters. "This one is Peanuts," I told Casey, handing him the rope. We started walking, me in front with Rain and Red, Casey, and Peanuts behind me; and Joe inching the Explorer along at the back as we made our way down the driveway and across the road. After the horses were safely behind the fence, I turned to thank Casey, who was standing watching them trot out into the pasture.

"I never rode a horse," he said, uttering his first complete sentence of the morning.

"We'll have to do something about that. Looks like Peanuts and you hit it off pretty good," I said, and he smiled, a sweet, shy half smile, and jumped into the car with Joe for a ride back.

"Boy, there are some interesting characters out here in the woods," Joe said, opening his first beer later that afternoon. I looked over from where I was chopping onions.

"I liked them," I said. Somehow, I felt protective, like I didn't want our neighbors to be just "interesting characters" for us to talk about. "I think they could be friends," I added and scraped the chopped onions into the cast iron skillet.

An old memory was stirring inside me. A memory of being a child in a new school in a foreign country and another child reaching out, offering me a piece of orange or handing me a ball to throw. Throughout my childhood, there were always moments of connection that penetrated the self-conscious fear I carried with me everywhere. That morning with Otis and Johanna and Casey felt like another of those moments of being welcomed into a new life.

Joining Fantasy and Reality

"Shit, we are out of milk," I said as I peered in the refrigerator. Until we moved to the Wet Mountains, I had never lived more than a ten-minute walk from the nearest carton of milk. Growing up, I had lived in cities—London, Paris, Madrid, and Washington, DC—where people traveled in buses and subways. Even after moving to Boulder for college, I walked everywhere. I didn't learn how to drive until I was twenty-five.

From the ranch, everything was twenty-five miles away: food, gas, liquor, milk, a doctor, yoga class. Twenty-five miles of winding mountain roads, trees, and more bears than people.

To get to either Westcliffe, a small mountain town in the Wet Mountain Valley to our west, or Florence, the larger town to the east, we had to travel up Highway 165 for eleven miles then go east or west on Highway 96. One thing I realized quickly is that those kinds of details become important when you live in the middle of nowhere. You had to be able to locate yourself in an emergency, and a street address was useless.

I began taking road trips in my Explorer to get to know the lay of the land, traveling the back roads, checking out old ranches and abandoned buildings. Down the gravel road to Wetmore was a place that intrigued me: nestled in scrub oak was a sign with the words Stillpoint Center. Each time I drove by, I would check to see if anyone was there, but the place was always empty. Traveling north on Highway 165, only a few places appeared inhabited. One sat right on the edge of the road, a dilapidated white farmhouse with a couple of outbuildings. Johanna Trimble had told me it was owned by an old couple named Miller who spent most of their time in Denver.

One day, cruising down the road on my way back from the market in Westcliffe, I saw a beat-up truck parked next to the house. I screeched to a stop and pulled off the road. As I walked across, an older man emerged and slowly ambled toward me. He was wearing ancient overalls and a dark gray, misshapen felt hat that looked like a dirty mushroom on his head. "Howdy," he called out.

"Hi there," I answered.

"You lost?" he went on, not unfriendly. By then I was all the way up to where he was standing.

"I'm your new neighbor." I introduced myself and reached out my hand.

"Well, isn't that just fine." He smiled and shook it. "Harold Miller's my name."

It was a warm day with just a hint of fall. Perfect weather to stand around talking about this and that. At one point, Harold said, "You had any dealings with your neighbor Eustace?"

"He's not around much," I said.

"Just watch out, he's a slippery son of a bitch," he went on, and then launched into a story about Eustace moving the fence between their properties in the middle of the night, giving himself a few more feet of their land. "The missus and I, we walked the whole damn thing, pulled up his new fence, rolled it up, drove down to his fancy house in Pueblo, and dumped it in his yard early on a Sunday morning." He chuckled.

"What did he do?" I asked.

Harold was a good storyteller; he knew how to keep his listeners at the edge of their seats. "He came out, still in his pajamas, face bright red, yelling up a storm. Mad as hell. Wanted me to get the fence and myself off his lawn. When I wouldn't do it, he hollered, 'I'll see you in court,' and slammed the door in my face. I saw him in court, sure enough." He dragged out a long pause, and ended with, "And I won!"

I clapped my hands. "I bet he hasn't messed with you since," I said, delighted. It was a good story and a prophesy. The next spring, Eustace pulled the same trick on us, but by then I couldn't bring myself to fight him.

It was getting late; I had almost forgotten the groceries in the car and the dinner I was supposed to be cooking. I got ready to leave, and then said, "Would you like to exchange phone numbers? Just in case?"

"I would like that very much," Harold answered. He pulled out a little notebook from the pocket of his overalls and started flipping the pages covered in illegible scribbled notes until he got to one that said, in large capital letters: "FUCK!"

It filled the whole page. Harold gave me a sideways glance. "I guess you shouldn't have seen that one." He chuckled, and I giggled with him.

"You are a man after my own heart, Harold Miller," I said as we wrote out our numbers and handed them to each other.

"You are just flattering an old man," Harold said in parting, "but I'll take it."

"It was a classic moment; I couldn't believe it. So good," I told Joe the next morning, describing my encounter with Harold. I had been sharing about how I was beginning to feel at home in our new life. "I like that people are who they are here. There's no bullshit." As I spoke, I saw a look on Joe's face I can best describe as wistful, as though he was remembering a feeling that he had forgotten.

When I finished talking, he sat quiet for a while and then said, "I wish I felt that way. Comfortable. I look around, and I can see how beautiful it all is, but I don't feel anything." I had no idea what to say. We sat there for a long moment. Then he went on, "I guess what they say about our minds coloring our perceptions is right. I look out there and it just looks flat, colorless. I can't seem to enjoy any of it."

It hurt to hear him open up about his distress, his disillusionment with life at the ranch. "It'll be okay," didn't quite cut it. There was no guarantee. For me, moving to the ranch had felt like getting used to being in an arranged marriage, but I was growing to love the place and my life there. Joe, who had started off in a state of wild infatuation, was now hitting the skids. For him, the honeymoon was over.

The year before, I had seen the Dalai Lama give a talk to a sold-out audience at Macky Auditorium on the University of Colorado campus. Afterward, someone asked a question.

"Why," the translator read from a scrap of paper, "are intimate relationships so difficult?" You could hear the room collectively suck in its breath. Why on earth would anyone ask such a question of the Dalai Lama, a monk? We all squirmed in our seats and stared hard at the floor as His Holiness looked calmly at his hands resting in his lap. Finally, he looked up and said, with a slight smile, "Because of the difficulty of joining fantasy and reality." We all let out our breath. He went on to say that bringing fantasy and reality together is our life's work, not just in intimate relationships, but in every aspect of our lives.

Remembering that exchange got me thinking about the nature of relationships and about how everything in our life is an intimate relationship—not only with our partner but with the place we live, with our friends, our animals, even with ourselves. We were in a continual process of joining fantasy and reality. I began to see how for Joe, his fantasy of living on the ranch had worn thin, and he was having a hard time accepting the reality of daily life in the middle of nowhere.

When I was young, I thought things just were the way they were; a relationship was good, or it was bad. A place was right or wrong. It was a good day or it sucked. I took me a long time to understand that "be here now" meant be here with the constantly changing reality of each moment, not trying to nail down each moment with an opinion and pick the good ones. It took a lot of patience to let things reveal themselves. I knew that if I was going to find my way in our new home, I had to slow down and pay attention to each moment and try not to rush anything, including Joe.

Seesawing

One thing in life you can count on is that whatever goes up, comes down. As the weather cooled and I began to worry about the snow I knew was coming and where to board Rain for the winter, a new wave of anxiety capsized my easygoing boat. So many scary possibilities loomed in my unsettled mind—days of frigid isolation, running out of food, no power, no water, just me and Joe alone, going crazy. Sometimes my throat would seize up and I could barely breathe. On those days, I would climb back into bed and try to ride out the stormy waves. I felt like a child again, living in another unfamiliar place, surrounded by strangers speaking a language I didn't understand.

I would watch the dogs for clues; for them, every day was an adventure. They explored the creek and hillsides and woods. They lay in the sun and shivered with dream excitement. They were ready to join us whenever we set foot out of the house. They didn't worry about whether they belonged here or how they were going to weather the approaching winter storms.

Joe had rallied as the weather began to turn. He had his new office in the barn and a new video project to work on, and it probably helped his state of mind that I was no longer having a jolly time making friends with the neighbors.

Each morning, I would drag myself into my office, a small space jutting out from the dining room that had been the original post office for the area. I would start each day determined to work on the script for a program on addiction I was producing. I would sit down in front of my computer ready to write and, before I knew it, I had veered off course and was trapped in a game of computer solitaire. The cards would magically appear on the screen, and I would feel the anticipation rise, the hope of winning bubbling in my chest as I began to move them from one row to another, stacking them into piles at the top, each game a new opportunity to win. I would set up the next game and then the next one, losing again and again. I would feel the gnawing begin in my belly, my breathing becoming shallow. *Just one more game*, and then, *I'll just play 'til I win.* Then I would win, and the need would shift to two wins, or maybe five would satisfy this craving. I began to feel an unbearable revulsion as the minutes and hours clicked by on the bottom of the screen. But I couldn't stop. The need to numb the panic was too great, and by then my shame was too overwhelming to stop. If Joe came in the kitchen door, I would quickly switch screens to the addiction script and start writing about the very stages of use, abuse, and dependence that I was experiencing in my own cycle of addiction.

I had been in this space before. The summer I was twelve, we left Madrid and returned to Washington, DC. I was heartbroken. For weeks, I sat day after day in the darkened TV room watching baseball games and laying out game after game of solitaire on the ottoman in front of me, trying to hold at bay the grief I was carrying from leaving a place I loved and the fear of entering a new, harsher reality when the school year began.

To make the anxiety worse that first autumn at the ranch, I had, for some incomprehensible reason, decided to quit smoking. I was not a heavy smoker; I kept a pack of American Spirits stored in the freezer and smoked one or two a day, usually in the late afternoon sitting on the porch.

A few days into my resolution, I was at my computer playing solitaire when I looked out and saw smoke drifting up from the chimney of the blacksmith shop, exactly like smoke curling off the end of a cigarette. I wanted a cigarette so bad I could taste it. The sadness I was trying hard to keep from feeling was right there, ready to overwhelm my flimsy defense. Lungs, they say in Chinese medicine, hold our grief; smoking had helped me keep sadness at bay for years.

Splashes of autumn orange and gold were splattered across the forest, random and messy. I wished it would grab my heart and make it sing with its ephemeral beauty, but I was too busy holding back the sadness to feel anything. In a last-ditch effort to pull myself out of my trance, I decided to try compassion practice.

Trungpa Rinpoche once said that if you are having a hard time generating compassion, imagine a starving dog being beaten. That morning, a starving dog was more than I could handle. But a fly was dying on the windowsill, so I picked it up and held it on my hand, and tried to generate compassion. I breathed in its suffering and breathed out whatever I could imagine a fly might want—peace, a swift death, a warm pile of dog shit. It was taking a long time for him to die. He would stop his indignant buzzing for a moment and then, just when I thought he was done, he would start up again. I was getting more and more impatient until finally I gave up and put him back down on the windowsill to take care of his own dying. I was done being Mother Teresa.

It had started to rain, and the day was turning even gloomier. Immersed in melancholy and remorse, I decided to light a fire in the fireplace next to my desk. I crumpled up newspaper, stacked the wood, and held a match to the paper, and then, just as it lit, I remembered the damper. I grabbed the chain and pulled. Nothing happened. Smoke began to fill the room, and I ran to the front door and yelled for Joe.

"What the hell did you think you were doing here?" he barked at me when he came in and began yanking at the dangling chain, swearing under his breath. The damper wouldn't budge. Finally in exasperation he smashed the thing with a hammer and it flew open.

"Jesus. I fucking can't do anything right," I shouted. Grabbing my wallet and the car keys, I stormed out of the house.

A half hour later, I was buying a pack of American Spirits at the Conoco station. Back in the car, the window cracked open, I lit up. As I exhaled a long tendril of smoke, the line "All of me, why not take all of me" began to play in my head. I started to sing, the lyrics rolling out, gathering steam, louder and louder, as I cruised down the curving road:

"You took the part
That once was my heart
So why not take all of me?"

By the time I got home, I could feel the sadness I had been trying so hard to keep at bay had burst through and filled my chest, softening all the edges.

Joe was in the kitchen, cooking. He didn't comment on my disappearance; he just poured me a glass of wine, and I sat and watched him cook and half listened to him talk about his work and the movie he wanted to watch that night, and everything was open and easy. It felt good to let go of trying to keep the sorrow out and welcome it instead, keeping it close as I would an old friend.

Meeting Berna

The next morning, we woke up to a breezy, bright blue fall day, everything clear and fresh after the rain. "If you don't like the weather in Colorado, wait five minutes," was what the old-timers always said. I had hung a load of laundry on the line by the vegetable garden, and that afternoon I was out taking down the clothes. As I walked back to the house, I saw a white Toyota Camry driving slowly down the driveway. I waited by the porch, holding the laundry basket, to see who it was. The car came to a stop and a woman emerged from the driver's side.

She was small and very thin, in her sixties, her brown hair cut into a bob at her chin, with bangs straight across her forehead. If she were a bird, she would be a finch, one of the brown and gray ones, unassuming and bright. She introduced herself—Berna Finley—and told me she had been born on the ranch and lived there for the first ten years of her life. She had just come from her home in Massachusetts to attend her mother, Angelica's, memorial down in Florence.

"I didn't really expect to see anyone here," she said. "I just wanted to take a look. I have so many memories of this place." I could see she was barely holding back tears. I invited her in for tea.

"This is very kind of you, I wouldn't want to trouble . . . ," Berna was saying as we came into the kitchen. She stopped midsentence, transfixed by the turquoise enamel cookstove. "Oh my," she said, "it's still there, right where it has always been."

"It was definitely one of the selling points." I smiled, putting down the laundry basket and filling the kettle.

"Before the outside was stuccoed, the wind would whistle through the walls," Berna said, nursing her cup of tea. "That stove was a lifesaver. Of course, I also lost my eye when a live round went off in the coal bin. But that was later." I had noticed one of her eyes looked odd, like a wandering eye.

I was mesmerized, listening to her talk, feeling the deep roots that connected her to the ranch. "My first love was a horse named Lindy," she told me. "I rode all over this place on Lindy. It was a very sad day when we moved to Florence and I had to leave Lindy behind."

"I have so many questions," I told her. "Like are those your initials carved into the wall in the blacksmith shop?"

"That's right, I carved them myself. BJ. Berna Jean is my full name." She went silent for a moment. "Those were good years," she added, looking sad.

"It's nice to hear you talk about the ranch . . . your ranch. I don't know if I'll ever feel that strong a connection. I can't seem to figure out how to be here," I confided in her. "There are moments when it makes sense. And then I feel lost. It's kind of a seesaw."

The afternoon had slipped away and the sun was getting low in the sky. Berna needed to get to Denver to catch her flight to Massachusetts. "I am a writer by trade," she told me. "Do you know what Flannery O'Connor said about writing?" I shook my head. "I write to discover what I know." Berna looked at me with her kind eyes. "That's what I'm doing these days: writing some of my memories down. It's helping me with the sadness. You could try it. You might find it helpful too." She smiled and then added, "We could share our writings about the ranch."

I felt a tingling in my body, that kind of tingling when you know something is right. I smiled at her. "That sounds just right, as long as you don't read what I send." She laughed and then, in a gesture strangely intimate and totally natural, she reached out and took my hand and held it for a long moment.

Before she left, we made a pact. She would send me reminiscences of her years growing up on the ranch and her heartbreak at having to leave. And I would send her writings about the ups and downs of my journey settling into my new home. It felt like the start of something real, a true connection.

A week later, her first piece landed in my inbox.

Hi Vicki,

Here, as promised, are some thoughts on our meeting last month:

The autumn air kisses my elbow as I pass the Wetmore Post Office, my eyes searching for familiar landmarks. I am driving to the ranch where I spent the first decade of my life. Sometimes the thought of coming here fills me with a sad longing and I close the doors to childhood memories. But today, still fragile from revisiting my mother's death and her passionate love for this corner of the Wet Mountains, a strong feeling of at-homeness envelopes me.

The once washboard road is now paved and as smooth as the cloudless blue sky that hangs above. The landscape has changed hardly at all. And there are sights along this route that pull thoughts from the bottom of my mind where they have lain unexamined for more than half a century.

I steer the Camry around a sharp bend in the narrow road and without warning dead ahead is a gigantic bullet shaped rock shooting out of the hillside. "That's it.

Right there," I hear myself yell, a five-year-old squished between my parents in the cab of their logging truck. Then I hear my mother's voice tell me the story of the Indian boy and white girl who, forbidden to express their love for one another, climb to the pinnacle of the rock and jump hand-in-hand to their death. Fact or fiction, the legend of "Lover's Leap" was my own sweet love story. Even now I feel little spasms of pain looking at the rock and imagining their plunge downward.

The hills fold around me as I near the ranch. I turn into the drive and stop in front of the house. The yellow tinged aspens, the creek, the rough stucco house, the soft breeze all stir sadness in my heart. A woman is standing in the yard, holding a laundry basket under her arm. Her name is Vicki and when she welcomes me with a smile and ushers me into the kitchen where that same old blue enameled stove still sits, I feel a hint of the possibility of healing the past. And for a moment, I feel I am finally home.

Yours truly, Berna

Learning the story of Lover's Leap from Berna and follow-ing the trail of her feelings of sadness and fragility when she wrote about the ranch stirred something inside me. I felt a resonance with her experience of longing and grief and the desire to heal, as though I had found a soul sister.

That afternoon I went for a ride up a trail I had never rid-den on before, along a small creek that meandered through an aspen grove near the road. The leaves had all turned and were beginning to fall. The ground was blanketed in gold. The afternoon sun flickered through the almost bare branches.

I stopped for a moment in a clearing, letting Rain graze on a patch of grass. Closing my eyes, I listened to the slight rustling of leaves and the murmur of the creek. When I opened them, I was looking at a tree, illuminated by a brilliant ray of light. Two letters were carved in the trunk, cut deep into the bark, decades old: the letters V.H. My mind stopped. V.H. Victress Hitchcock. My initials. Here in this very spot.

Had somebody with those initials lived here? As soon as I got home, I turned on my computer and added that question to a piece I had started writing that morning.

Dear Berna,

It was so good to meet you and to get your email. I have been following your advice and writing. I just wrote this piece today:

These past few days, I am feeling the vastness of the space here, and how there is nowhere to hide. If I try to shut down, I run into an unbearable darkness inside. Then, I catch a glimpse of happiness, and I know that I have no way to get there except through the darkness, and I hesitate, perched on the edge, unable to jump.

Malidoma Some, an African healer, tells of a custom in his tribe. When a woman gives birth, she goes to a hut and all the children of the village are invited to surround her. As the baby comes out and utters its first cry, the children call out the baby's name, welcoming it. This is how the newborn child knows it has arrived at the right place. Without that answering call, Some tells us, we can spend years in wandering, trying to arrive at where we are supposed to be.

Just this afternoon, riding Rain through a grove of aspen, I came upon an old tree with the gnarled initials V.H. perfectly carved into its trunk years ago by someone long forgotten. The shock of recognizing my own initials woke me up. I was struck by the thought that, in time, maybe I will feel welcomed here, that this is where I am supposed to be.

Do you know who might have had my same initials? I am so curious.

With warm regards,

Vicki

When Berna wrote back a few days later, she was unable to solve the mystery of the initials, and I realized how much I had been counting on her to make sense of it. Reality suddenly became shaky, and that afternoon I rode back down the trail into the grove to make sure I hadn't been hallucinating.

The afternoon light was flickering. The aspens were now completely bare, and the grove was redolent with the smell of leaves decaying into the earth. The tree was still there, the initials carved deep into its trunk.

The Prison

The phone was ringing as I came into the kitchen. Wiping my hands on my jeans, filthy from mucking out the corral, I grabbed it. "Is this Vicki Hitchcock?" a man asked.

"Yes," I said, trying to figure out if I knew this person. He told me his name, and said he was calling from Boulder.

"I'm calling," he said, "because I heard you were living down near the federal prison in Florence."

I wouldn't have described where we lived that way, but I was intrigued. He went on to say that he was part of a group called the Shambhala Prison Community and that they had been invited into the prison to teach meditation and was I interested in doing that, since, by some auspicious coincidence, I was living nearby. I didn't have to think about it too long, in fact I didn't think about it at all. Right away, I said yes.

I had spent years filming incarcerated teenagers in juvenile prisons and men in county jails and state prisons as part of my work producing what, in those days, were called "guidance videos." I was also, during those same years, a meditation instructor for students at Naropa University, meeting with them regularly as they made their way through the contemplative psychology program at the university started by Trungpa Rinpoche. I loved being challenged in both of those worlds. It was a gift to have something in my life that penetrated the neurotic self-preoccupation that was more my default position. Having the two come together did seem auspicious.

A month later, I was sitting in a windowless room at the federal prison, along with Christian pastors and Siddha Yoga volunteers, being trained by a group of wardens and chaplains. "Remember, these men are all master manipulators. They are con men. They are not here because they are good people." The trainers, who were all guards in uniform, kept repeating this refrain over and over in different ways. I looked around the room at the faces of the new volunteers and could tell the message was getting through. But I also knew that in all the times I had interviewed offenders, spending hours in small visiting rooms with marginalized, violent, abandoned-as-irredeemable individuals, I had always felt a strange calm. I had never been afraid.

After a few weeks, my training was finished. I was asked to give a short introduction to meditation in the medium-security wing of the prison the following week.

The morning of my talk, I dressed in my most conservative clothes. The handbook was very specific: "no see-through clothing, tube tops, tank tops, halter tops, crop tops, sleeveless clothing, backless clothing, swimsuits, sweatsuits, mesh clothing, breakaway pants, open toe shoes, and no khaki." I turned on the radio, trying to keep any anxious thoughts at bay on the way down the mountain. The dial was on talk radio, and soon I found myself lost in the world of Rush Limbaugh. He was fielding calls about Y2K, the catastrophe predicted for the end of the century, New Year's 2000, an event that was over a year away. By the time I pulled into the parking lot, I was so anxious about the inevitable end of the world, I had to spend five minutes sitting in the car deep breathing.

Taking a final breath and a last look at myself in the rearview mirror, I stepped out into the parking lot. My instructions were to proceed to the front entrance of the medium-security facility. I was standing in the parking lot surrounded by large brick buildings, one of which was the right one. The Super Max was set back, away from the road, built into the ground like a bunker. I picked the nearest building and, clutching my bag with the notes for my talk, walked up to the front door. On this breezy fall day I could hear the flags flapping against the poles. My belly was fluttering with nervous excitement.

The chaplain was there to meet me in the waiting room. She was a no-nonsense person, friendly but not forthcoming, her hair pulled back in a tight bun. I hadn't been sure what kind of reception to expect, being a Buddhist, but she didn't seem concerned. We left the waiting room and were buzzed through a gate in the fence surrounding the main facility. Looking up, I could see the guard, holding a rifle, watching from the tower. Inside the building we had to walk down a long corridor, large windows on one side facing into the courtyard, doors into offices lining the other. I didn't expect to see so many men in the hall. Men of all shapes and sizes and ages, dark skinned and light, all wearing khaki uniforms, some leaning against the wall, some just standing there, for no apparent reason except to watch us walk by. It felt like a perp walk, with all eyes on me. The corridor seemed to stretch for miles. All I could do was focus on putting one foot in front of the other. The chaplain greeted a few men here and there, perfectly at ease. Finally we turned into the education area, a warren of small offices with a large room that served as the meeting space for the non-Christian groups.

In the manual they handed out at the training, I had read these encouraging words on the religious offerings available: "There is a remarkable interest in spiritual life among the population at FCI Florence. We invite you to come and investigate matters of faith for yourself." I was amazed at how many men turned up to that first talk—fifty at least. Either there really was a strong interest in spirituality or they were desperate for any kind of entertainment. The group was not diverse; most were middle-aged and white. For the introductory talk, they all sat on chairs that had been set up in the meeting room. The chaplain gave me a buzzer to have nearby in case something got out of hand, and then she left me alone in the room with fifty "predators."

My memory of that first talk is a blur. I forgot my notes—they were safely tucked away in my purse stored in a locker in the waiting room—so I had to wing it. I gave the "Buddhism is a non-theistic tradition, which means it's up to us to work with our own minds, no one is going to save us" talk. Then I led them in a short meditation. "Sit up in your chair, drop your shoulders, soften your jaw, and relax your neck. You can close your eyes, place your hands on your knees, and take a few deep breaths. Inhale, exhale." Most of the men sat up straight in their chairs with their eyes closed; a few continued lounging, watching me. I guided them through a simple "focusing on their breath" meditation for ten very long minutes.

At the end, I thanked them for coming and invited them to come to the weekly meditation group starting in two weeks. On my way out, I asked the chaplain if there was a way that people could sit on cushions; she said that would be fine, but I would have to bring them with me.

"It was terrifying, but really kind of exhilarating . . . it's hard to explain," I told Joe over dinner that night. I had been talking for a while in that hyped-up state of having just gone through something intense, and I was starting to describe some of the men when I realized he wasn't listening. His mind was somewhere else. His eyes had a blank look that was happening more and more often. I could feel resentment churning in my belly, ready to spew. I breathed and took a drink. Joe was still eating, silently. Okay. *Do something different.* I changed the subject. "Did you call John Watson back about joining the board of the conservation group?" The San Isabel Land Protection Trust, that held the conservation easement on the ranch, had invited Joe to join their board.

"I don't know. I've got a lot of work to do on my new program. I don't think it's a good time for me to take on anything more," he said and poured himself another glass of wine.

"I wasn't talking about another job, I was talking about making connections with interesting people," I said, my voice brittle, "in this place where we now live. But have it your way." Clearing the table, I dumped the dishes in the sink and turned on the water to stop any further conversation.

I was sick of Joe working all the time. I was sick of him feeling sorry for himself. I was sick of his doom and gloom. But I was worried, too. The expenses of living at the ranch were mounting. Our income from royalties on our video programs had inexplicably plummeted. The weather was getting colder. We were well into October, and the pressure was mounting to find a place to board Rain for the winter. The one place I had found fell through when the owner picked up and left her husband, taking her horses, goats, and ducks with her. What did I expect when I picked a stable called Chaosland? Maybe our neighbor Johanna was right when she told us that most people couldn't handle living in the Wet Mountains. In her words, "You had to be tough as nails, or you could go bat-shit crazy."

Death Is Real

Joe was already at work in his studio when I woke up from a disturbing dream of being trapped in a room full of strung-out heroin addicts. The weather was unseasonably warm, so I took my tea out onto the porch and sat on the glider. I wanted to clear my head and contemplate what I needed to do that day.

A moment later, I saw a pickup truck careening down the road toward the ranch. It turned into our driveway and screeched to a halt in front of me. "I need to use the phone," Vernon, a neighbor from up the road, yelled. "Been an accident up on the Bigelow Divide."

I showed him the phone in the kitchen and pulled on my boots while he gave directions to the dispatcher, then we climbed into his truck and took off. I had never seen Vernon drive over twenty miles an hour; that morning he was hauling ass up the hill. "I seen a flash of light hitting something silver off the road on my way up to check on the cows above the Divide. I pulled over here on this bad curve and climbed down through the fence there," Vernon told me as he parked the truck. "Son of a bitch, if he had only crawled up instead of down," he said, pointing at the overturned motorcycle hanging off the edge of the road.

We climbed through the barbed-wire fence. I had a sick feeling in my stomach as I saw what he meant. The drag marks in the sandy dirt led us through scrub oak, and then out into an open space in the trees. The rider had crawled a long way— fifty feet or so—away from the road. He was lying flat on his back in the dirt, the sun beating down on him, one shoe missing. His overalls were the same orange-brown as the dirt that matted his hair and caked his sunburned face.

I took a deep breath and walked over to where he was lying. Sitting down beside him, I gently eased his head onto my lap. His breathing was ragged, with long intervals between each breath. "You're going to be okay," I whispered, shading his face with my hat. "Just hang on; help is coming." He was a young man. His eyes were closed and his mouth open, his lips and eyelids blistered. A hill of dirt had formed around him.

It took me a moment to realize he had probably been flailing and kicking in the night. Vernon was slowly circling the area, looking for anything that might help us identify him. A few feet away, he picked up a wallet and took out his license. "Looks like his name is Eric," he said and handed it to me.

Eric was from Trinidad, a town south of us. He was twenty-two years old, born in 1976, the same year as my son. They had the same sandy blond hair. "Hang on, Eric, I'm here with you," I told him, stroking his burning forehead with my cold hand. He took a long breath, shuddering slightly as he exhaled.

"How long do you think he's been here?" I asked Vernon.

"If I had to guess, I would say around dusk last evening," he answered, "when the rain started." Sixteen very long hours.

"I can't believe no animal found him, a bear or mountain lion," I marveled.

"Just lucky, I guess." Vernon said, and sat down beside me.

"I hope his luck holds out awhile longer," I said, dripping a little water in Eric's mouth.

It had been a good half hour since we called for help, and I started to pray. *Please, let Eric live, please keep him safe.* Over and over in my mind, I prayed to the universe, to whatever dispensers of good fortune I could imagine. I began doing the same Buddhist practice of "sending and taking" I had tried with the fly just a few days before. I breathed in his fear, his body wracked with pain, and tried to breathe out peace, ease, the breath of life itself, anything to help this young man, who could have been my son, live. An ambulance would have been good.

When we heard a siren in the distance coming closer, I began to feel a little hope. But it was only a sheriff's deputy. He sat down with me and began to pray as well. "Lord, keep this young man, Eric, safe." We prayed in silence for a while, and then the deputy, whose name was Luis, crossed himself and said, "Thank you, ma'am, for being here." I had kept it together until then, but it took a lot to not break down in that moment.

I shook it off and asked, "Why is it taking so long for an ambulance to get here?"

"Unfortunately, ma'am," Luis answered, "this area right here is called the 'dead zone' because no one seems to be able to figure whose jurisdiction it is under . . . which county services should respond." He stared hard at me and said, "It's a real goddamn mess."

By the time an ambulance arrived, Eric was barely hanging on. The gaps between each tortured breath had become interminable. The EMTs gently moved him onto a stretcher, slowly carried him up the hill, and loaded him into the back of the ambulance. After they left, Luis and Vernon and I stood together by the side of the road listening to the wailing of the siren become fainter and fainter. "All we can do now is hope the prayers helped," Luis said as he got in his cruiser and took off down the road.

"You want to know where we are now living?" I said to Joe after Vernon dropped me off at home. "The dead zone. Can you believe it?"

He shook his head and asked, "Where on earth have you been this morning?"

"I'll tell you about it later," I said, suddenly bone tired. "I need a bath."

Early the next morning, my hands shaking, I dialed the number for the hospital in Pueblo. "I am calling about the young man they brought in yesterday. A motorcycle accident," I said.

"Are you family?" the woman at the desk asked.

"No," I said. "I was there with him. I sat with him while we waited. His name is Eric." I pleaded, "Please, can you tell me how he is?"

There was a long silence. "I'm sorry, ma'am, Eric didn't make it. He died last night."

"Was someone with him?" I asked, my voice trembling.

"I'm afraid I don't have that information," she answered.

"Thank you," I whispered and hung up.

The kitchen was still and cold. I stared out the picture window at a flutter of yellow cottonwood leaves stirred up by a gust of wind. A deep melancholy enveloped me and extended out, gathering the surrounding hills, filling the pale early morning sky.

What on earth was I thinking when I decided to use my fear of entering this new world as practice for dying? What hubris. Did I have any idea what dying was really like, of the real pain and fear and suffering of those last few moments facing death? Every morning, I began my meditation with the words:

Joyful to have such a human birth,
Difficult to find, free and well favored.
But death is real; it comes without warning.
This body will be a corpse.

How many times had I rattled those words off, racing through the recitation? How many times had I sat and let their meaning penetrate my heart?

Standing in my kitchen that morning, I vowed to spend more time contemplating the meaning of the words I recited about the reality of death and remembering the joy available to me every day. I walked slowly to the sink and filled up the kettle, my mind empty and clear. Then, just as the water came to a boil, I remembered it was the day of my second weekly prison group. In two hours. There was no time to reflect on matters of life and death. I had to get a move on. I had no idea what on earth I was going to talk about.

Medium Security

As I drove the twenty-five miles to Florence, I went over in my mind what had happened at the prison the week before.

I had been surprised by how many men showed up for the meeting, the first one after the introductory talk. There must have been twenty-five men waiting for me when I arrived with a trunk full of meditation cushions donated by the Buddhist center in Boulder. Most of the men stayed on their chairs, but a few of the younger ones tried sitting cross-legged on the ground.

I guided them through a basic meditation, following their breath, coming back when their mind wandered. Then I introduced the first teaching of the Buddha, the Four Noble Truths: the Truth of Suffering, the Cause of Suffering, the Cessation of Suffering, and the one they were most intrigued by, the Path out of Suffering.

For that first talk, I had focused on the Truth of Suffering. "We're not just talking about the suffering of hunger and illness and war; it's about the suffering we all experience each day. The suffering of things not working out the way we want them to, of losing people we love, of being trapped in our resentments and anger and fear."

"I don't think any man here has a problem understanding suffering." The speaker was an older, gaunt man named Roy with thinning hair that had once been red. Most of the men had an air of being defeated by life. Very few were young.

"Try spending a few months in solitary—no windows, no nothing, just your mind," Jake, one of the younger men, added.

More and more men weighed in on the truth of their own suffering, until Duane said, just as we were reaching the end of our time, "So you're telling us there's a path out of this shit hole?" All the men laughed, some louder than others. I felt like something in the room shifted.

At the end a few men stayed behind to help stack the cushions. I left feeling good about the meeting and eager to keep going.

The timing for this second meeting couldn't have been better. It was good to be in the car, to have something to do, to get my mind off Eric. It was even perfect that the subject for the day was to be the Cause of Suffering, which ironically starts with trying everything we can to avoid suffering. As it turned out, talking about the causes of suffering was just as difficult as talking about the truth of suffering when your audience is incarcerated.

"One of the reasons I meditate," I started off, "is to be able to be with what is going on in my mind, to be present with what I am feeling, my fears, my sadness. If I can do it sitting, maybe I can find a way to be more present in my life."

"Why the hell would I want to be present in this life?" John, a middle-aged man with mousy brown hair, said. "Present is the last place I want to be."

"Yeah," Roy said, "but whatever I do to not be present isn't working that well." Most of the men had something to say about what made them suffer. Addiction, bad choices, shitty relationships were all on the list.

One younger man, who said his name was Lewis from south-central Los Angeles, was quiet throughout the discussion. Toward the end of the hour, out of the blue, he began telling a story about his father dying. "He was a big man, always hard on me, mean you might say." Lewis's voice was so soft I had to lean forward, straining to hear him. "I was sitting by him and he grabbed my hand. He held it so tight, fingers digging in. He was scared. He didn't want to die. My hand was bleeding he was holding so tight all the way up to the end." He paused. No one else spoke. "I knew right then, I needed to figure this shit out. I do not want to go down that same road. I'll do anything not to be scared like that when the time comes."

I was holding my breath, listening intently to Lewis. All I could think of was Eric dying, young and strong, with so much more life to live. "Thank you, Lewis," I said, and smiled. It was time to end the meeting.

All the way home I tried to breathe in all the suffering of the last two days and breathe out the only release I could imagine for these two young men, one in prison and one dead: a clear mind and a fearless heart.

As soon as I walked in the house, I called Nick. The last few times we had spoken, he was distracted, uninterested. I had stopped calling him, too hurt to reach out. "What's up, Mom?" he said when he answered the phone.

"It's been too long, sweetheart," I said. "I just wanted to hear your voice." I was trying to keep it together. "I just wanted to tell you I love you."

"What's happening, Mom; are you okay?" The concern in his voice was too much for me. I couldn't contain the sorrow anymore, and I haltingly begin telling him about Eric.

When I finished, there was a long pause. Then Nick said, "That must have been really hard. I love you too, Mom."

When we hung up, I sat for a long while in the old orange recliner in the kitchen. My mind was empty of thoughts. I could feel my body tingling, my heart full and beating. The turquoise stove was gleaming in the last rays of sunlight. In that moment, a feeling of gratitude for being alive washed over me. I wasn't *thinking* I needed to be grateful, I *felt* grateful. It was a feeling I couldn't remember ever having so strongly before.

Visitors

A fierce wind was rattling the window by my desk. There was something familiar and deeply scary about the rhythmic sound of a branch scratching the side of the house. Every nerve in my body was on high alert.

Across the valley, gusts of wind flattened the long grass in waves cresting and crashing. It had been blowing for days. I was alone; Joe was on a trip to visit his mother in Oregon.

Being there alone in the wind, all reference points were blown to smithereens. I held my breath at the sound of one lone car traveling down the highway, listening to it get close, pass by, and disappear. It was unsettling, but there was a certain freedom to solitude, a feeling of oxygenating my blood with fresh air. Alone, I didn't need to close down. I wasn't using my energy resisting Joe or worrying about him. I could just act, think, feel, and do whatever I liked.

That morning I made myself a cup of tea and sat down at my computer to write Berna. Opening my email, I reread her letter from the day before:

Dear Vicki,

I wanted to tell you about my first love, Lindy, a black stallion. He was my best friend, my confidant, my constant companion. Together we explored the fields, forests, and wide-open cattle pastures of Custer County. I was always terrified that he would take up with a renegade band of wild horses. I had a recurring nightmare where I saw him charge into the yard, past the corral, out the gate and across the highway. He had almost disappeared over the hill when I flew out the door and was running beside him, reaching for his flying mane. "I love you, Lindy!" I cried, and in one quick movement lunged forward and grabbed his forelock. He stood motionless for a moment, and then crumbled into a cloud of dust and vanished like a shadow. I have had this dream again and again.

By the way, I am coming to Florence in two weeks for my 50th high school reunion. I would love to come up for a visit. Would that work?

Love, Berna

I wrote back right away.

Dear Berna,

I loved reading your piece. I am in awe that your horse was a stallion and that you roamed the hills on him alone. I wish I had that kind of courage. Last week I dreamed we had just moved into a very large house in a rundown neighborhood surrounded by a brick wall with a giant gate that was open. Rain was racing toward it. I stood there paralyzed, watching him picking up speed, his eyes wild. He was just about to escape when I realized, I CAN CLOSE THE GATE! And I did. Before that all my dreams lately seemed to be about men trying to control me. Here I was the one in control. It felt good.

The wind has been blowing almost constantly, whistling down the valley for days. It's hard on my already frayed nerves. It feels like I can either shrivel up, or learn how to fly like a kite, dipping and swaying with each gust. Obviously, flying is a more appealing option, but probably out of my pay grade.

I would love to see you. Let me know what day. I'm not going anywhere.

Love, Vicki

I pressed Send and sat back in my chair. The wind had died down, and the dogs were looking at me with that "what are we doing inside wasting a perfectly good day" look on their faces. The horses were getting restless too, pacing in the corral. I had been too anxious to ride during the spell of windy days. I wasn't quite ready to move yet; I was still pondering what I had written Berna about men and control.

For years, as a younger woman, I had lived a double life. On the surface, I would go along with whatever the man I was with wanted. I developed the ability to keep a calm, detached, even amenable surface, while underneath, a cesspool of resentments and judgments, of little resistances and escape plans stewed, until one day it would boil over and I would up and leave.

Sometimes when it got to be too much, I would throw something, usually at a wall. One time, I hurled a kitchen chair through the picture window in our living room after my boyfriend made fun of my first attempt, using a copper bowl that had barely cracked the glass. The chair shattered the window with a satisfying loud crack and landed on all four legs in the snow.

Over the years, I had become less explosive, but I would still, in the face of what I perceived as control, shut down, going dead inside for as long as I could. For most of my life, I had held my breath out for long stretches of time, not breathing back in. It was only when I began riding that I became aware of my habit of keeping my throat closed, sealing off my head from my body. Every time I rode, I would remind myself to breathe past the cut-off point and into my belly. It was gradually becoming easier.

Just then, the crunch of tires on the gravel driveway interrupted my meandering thoughts. I looked out the window as a truck door slammed and saw my son, slinging a backpack over his shoulder, heading towards the door. "Mom, are you there?" he called out and I hurried to greet him. "Looks like those horses are ready to get out," Nick said after we hugged. "How about you?"

After spending his first year of college in Montana, Nick had moved to CSU in Ft. Collins, near enough now to be able to show up out of the blue if the spirit moved him. He had spent the summer at a ranch not too far away riding Chaz, the gray Arabian that Art had added to his herd in the spring. It took many patient hours for Nick to turn the high-strung, skittish, barely trained Arabian into a working cow horse.

Chaz and Rain were standing by the gate, waiting. I put on my boots and grabbed my hat and we crossed the yard to the blacksmith shop where the saddles and bridles were stored.

Chaz whinnied when he saw Nick. "Hey, Chaz, my man. You miss me?" Nick scratched him under his forelock and eased the bridle over his head. We saddled up, led the horses out of the corral, and mounted.

The air was crisp, everything sparkling after the days of wind. The sky was a pale, clear blue with just the right amount of warmth, a perfect day for a ride. Rain was eager to go, and I had to take a few deep breaths to settle my fear as I felt him strain against the bit. "Focus on where you are going, not the obstacles," the litany of Janice's instructions began. Nick and Chaz crossed the creek, and Rain and I followed. Breaking into a trot, we headed toward the slope that led to Vernon's property. "Breathe into your body. Relax your shoulders." The tightness in my neck eased a bit, and I sank a little deeper into the saddle. The hill rose in front of us. Without warning, Nick nudged Chaz into a canter. My breath caught in my throat, and I tightened the reins, holding Rain back. The instructions playing in my head became a jumble of words swirling—"Breathe, relax, look up, what the hell." I loosened my grip and let Rain go. He stretched out his neck and loped up the hill in long, fluid strides. Nick looked over at me as we reached the top, the look on his face that of a child just about to do something he knew wasn't allowed but was too fun to resist. He squeezed his knees and took off again across the wide upper meadow. A split second later, Rain and I followed, and soon we were racing side by side, and the instruction manual in my head was just pages torn from the book, blowing over the trees.

I was released. Free of all the dos and don'ts, the hesitation and fear, the struggle to do everything right. There was nothing but the pounding of hooves on the ground, the cool breeze on my cheeks, the warm sun on my back, my body moving in unison with Rain as he stretched out his long legs again and again, flying effortlessly through space.

We reached the end of the meadow and slowed down as we entered the forest and followed the old miner's road that wound through dense growths of spruce and pine and clusters of aspen. The light was low, alternately disappearing in the deep green and flickering through the bare branches, striations of dark and light. The horses walked slowly and deliberately. I could feel my blood pumping, every cell in my body alive. As we moved through the still forest, Nick looked over at me and said, "You're doing good, Mom." It took me by surprise. I didn't know what to say. "You're tough," he added, "in a sissy kind of way," and I laughed. He laughed as well and we rode on for a while, not speaking, until the light began to fade, and then we turned around and headed for home.

"Thank you, sweetheart," I said as Nick stood up to clear the plates off the table after dinner.

"Of course," he said. "You cooked." By cooking he meant opening a jar of spaghetti sauce and boiling water for noodles.

"No, I mean for visiting, for pushing me out of my comfort zone. For the whole day."

He sat down again and said, "It's been too long."

"It is so good to have someone to ride with," I said.

"Yeah, I don't see Dad getting up on a horse anytime soon."

I took a long drink of wine.

"How is Dad doing?" Nick asked.

"He's okay," I quickly answered. Then added, "I think he's having a hard time adjusting now that he's done everything he can around here. You know Dad; he needs a project."

"Is he ready to move to Yuma?" Nick said, laughing.

I pushed my chair away from the table and stood up. "I'm going out for a cigarette. You want to come?" I asked. We went out and sat out on the glider for a while, smoking and staring up at the stars in the vast night sky. A perfect night to end a perfect day.

Two weeks later, Berna came for her visit. I had made soup, and Joe joined us for lunch. Berna brought with her a copy of her mother, Angelica's, memoir, a self-published book of recollections and old photographs and recipes from her Tyrolean ancestors. "Did you all really make dandelion wine?" Joe asked, thumbing through and finding a recipe for it.

"My grandmother did. Every year. The whole yard was a field of gold each spring."

"Still is." Joe smiled. "Sounds like something I could get into."

After he went back to his editing room, Berna and I settled in for the afternoon. "They were Tyrolean?" I asked.

"A lot of the people who settled here were Tyrolean miners," Berna said. "This was the Brassae ranch when my mother got here." Angelica had been hired as the local schoolteacher at the age of sixteen and was offered room and board at the ranch where Nello Brassae, who was to become her husband, lived with his family.

"The first time she met my father he was trapped in the barn with an angry stallion," Berna said. "She heard a deep man's voice saying, 'Dammit, Bob, when I get out of here I am getting even with you.' He had a beautiful voice, my father. My mother peered in the barn and saw this big, tall, handsome man squeezed up in the corner of the stall trying to talk his way out."

"I guess it worked," I said.

"Yep, they were married a year or two later," Berna continued. "My favorite story in the book is of their honeymoon, in the middle of winter in a little cabin up the hill."

"Where was the cabin?" I asked. Berna drew a map of a hill and a trail on a paper napkin. It looked like it was somewhere above Eustace's place.

"It fell down years ago, I imagine," Berna said, looking a little sad.

"Maybe you could read me that part," I said.

"I would love that," she answered, opening the book.

We started our married life in a one- room cabin furnished with a stove, bed, kitchen cabinet, and eleven dollars' worth of groceries. The snowdrifts in some places were twelve feet deep, and the trail to the cabin was barely wide enough for one horse. We put our groceries and personal possessions on a homemade sled drawn by Bob and started up the trail. It was so cold I stayed under the tarpaulin most of the way. About halfway up, the entire contents went over the bank into an eight-foot snowdrift. When Nello picked up the twenty-five pound sack of sugar, he sank in over his head! We had a sweet, hilarious time filled with laughter before we recovered our belongings.

We sat in silence for a moment. I was transfixed by the images of a young couple starting out their life together in the same place where Joe and I were now living, twenty-three years into our married life.

It was time for Berna to leave, and this time we hugged goodbye. "Thank you for coming. I can't wait to read your mother's book."

"I think you will love it," she said and got into her car.

That night I opened the thin volume, with a black and white sketch of the ranch and the words "My Life as a Mountain Pioneer. Written by Angelica L. Klimpton" on the cover. From the opening paragraph I was hooked:

> *For the benefit of posterity, I have decided to relate the story of my life. Many things have transpired in eighty-five years of living. I will write it as I remember all the events, the good and the bad; that is how they came and that is how we have to take them.*

I felt I had met another mentor, another guide, to living in my new home.

Exposed

"Anyone looking for an easy, painless way through life should burn this book immediately." I grabbed the pieces of paper where I had written that quote and others from Bo Lozoff's book, *We're All Doing Time*, about finding a spiritual path in prison. It was Wednesday, my day to be at the federal penitentiary. Throwing my boots and hat and jeans in the back seat, I climbed in the front. My plan was to go over to Rancho Loco, Rain's new winter home across the highway from the prison, after the meditation group. It was a gorgeous fall day, crisp and Colorado clear. I turned on the country-western station and sang along in full voice to "I Got Friends in Low Places" as I cruised down the hill.

Taking Rain to Rancho Loco had been a real feat—my first time hitching up the trailer to the Explorer by myself, loading

Rain up, and hauling him twenty-five miles down to Florence. He was a perfect gentleman the whole trip, but my heart was in my throat the entire time. Pulling up in front of the stables, I was met by the owners. Ron was the epitome of "road hard and put up wet," his face lined with deep creases around his eyes from years of squinting in the harsh sun, his legs bowlegged from years in the saddle. Laura was younger, closer to my age, with a wide-open face and a sturdy body held in snug jeans, wearing scuffed cowboy boots. Mike, the young horse trainer, was in the pen working with a skittish palomino. I opened the back of the trailer and climbed in. Rain, ever the showman, backed up effortlessly and stood calmly by the corral. I had brushed him before we left, and he was gleaming, his mane long and shiny. Everyone gathered around and oohed and aahed. He was a magnificent creature, and I was the proud owner.

"Looking forward to getting up on that big boy," Mike said when he sauntered over. "Is he a team penner?"

I had no idea what a team penner was. "I'm sure he could do it," I said confidently. "I've only had him a little over a year."

"If you're game, we'll give it a try," Mike said. "We team pen here most Saturdays," he added as he turned back to the palomino who was pawing the ground in the corner of the corral.

I felt I had passed a test—horse owner, trailer puller, rancher, team penner in training. Some combination had come together and was somehow believable to the people at Rancho Loco. After the prison visit, I was planning on riding Rain in the arena for the first time.

Arriving at the prison gates, I went through the entry procedure, a now familiar routine, and checked in with the chaplain. She ushered me into the meeting room where the group was already assembled, handed me the buzzer, and left the room.

I sat down on a chair in front of the men, the buzzer in my pocket. It was a full house, around thirty men. Some were sitting cross-legged on the cushions, some along the edges in folding chairs. I began by greeting them and some greeted me back, most addressing me as ma'am. I asked if any of them had read *We're All Doing Time*. I knew Bo Lozoff's organization had sent copies to prisons all over the country. Two of the men raised their hands.

"What we are talking about today . . . what we began last week," I stumbled into the talk, "is what it means to change our view of things in our lives. Believe it or not, that's what being on the spiritual path is about," I said, and then I asked, "Does that make sense? Do you think of yourselves as spiritual people?"

"I gave up going to church when I was seven. Made no sense, even then," one man answered.

"I guarantee the spiritual path didn't lead none of us here," another added, and the men laughed.

They continued bantering back and forth until one, a tall, elegant Cuban man, said, "I don't believe, just 'cause we're sinners, we can't find our way to being spiritual." A few men nodded. "Where I come from, you don't need a church to pray," he added.

I noticed that Lewis had moved up to the front row. He was sitting cross-legged on a cushion right in front of me, no longer hiding in the back. He was very still; I couldn't tell if he was listening or if he was completely checked out.

"I think Bo Lozoff might agree with Juan," I said. Pulling out the pages I had stashed in my pocket, I continued, "I'd like to read something he wrote, which I really like: 'You may study with the highest teachers, but you will find no one but yourself teaching you. You may travel the world over, yet find nothing but yourself, reflected the world over. So, if you now find yourself in a prison cell, take heart that out of all the teachers in the world, out of all the places in the world, you still have with you the only ultimate ingredient of your journey: yourself." Let's take ten minutes to meditate and then we can talk about this idea that we are all we need to be on a spiritual path." I stood up and Ron jumped up and moved my chair to the side and dragged a cushion over. I thanked him and sat down. There was a small gong on one side of me, and I placed the buzzer on the ground on the other.

I began the meditation with a four-line prayer I had introduced the week before; it felt too naked just jumping in without making any connection to those who had traveled the path before us. "Grant your blessings so that my mind may be one with the dharma," I began the first line. Some of the men chanted after me. "Grant your blessings so that dharma may progress along the path." I had explained that *dharma* meant the truth, reality, things as they really are. "Grant your blessings so that the path may clarify confusion" had needed no explanation. "Grant your blessings so that confusion may dawn as wisdom."

I settled myself on my cushion and struck the gong. The sound reverberated, waves spreading through the room. I took a breath and lowered my eyes to the floor in front of me.

At this point, my memory of the next few minutes breaks into pieces like a mirror shattered into a thousand reflections, vivid images flashing one after another: Lewis, sitting in perfect meditation posture, his eyes closed, shifting slightly to reveal a long tear in the crotch of his tan prison pants. Directly in my line of vision. A view of dark testicles. I froze, my breath held out for a split second. *No, no, not Lewis, please,* was my first thought. Then, *Was it a mistake, just a rip?* I looked one more time. It was a long, clean tear. Unmistakable. Lewis was looking straight at me, with what seemed a hint of challenge mixed with sorrow in his eyes. I lowered my gaze and a succession of images appeared in my mind—the closed door of the meeting room, the clock showing 2:20, Roy lounging on his chair, the buzzer by my side, my hands rigid on my knees.

A wave of sadness engulfed me. This was Lewis, the vulnerable young man who wanted to escape his father's fear of death, now sitting in front of me with his pants torn wide open, exposing himself to me. A strange calm enveloped me. Thoughts began appearing in my mind, a storyline unfolding one instruction after another. *Lewis is one of only two Black men in the room. If you ring the buzzer to alert the guards, Ron and the others will know something's up, and they might kill him before anyone gets here. Keep your gaze soft. Don't stare. Only eight more minutes, then you can ring the gong for the end of meditation, then you can take a break. Then you can deal with the situation.* There was nothing to do but breathe and wait.

Five minutes elapsed in this strange, vivid, slow-motion scenario. Then six. Almost there. Suddenly, the PA crackled, a loud alarm sounded, and the voice of the guard filled the room. "All inmates return to your cells for a full count."

Immediately, all the men rose up and began to make their way toward the door. As if by magic, it opened and the chaplain appeared, holding the door as the men began to stream out. I was on the far side of the room. I saw Lewis slip through the crowd and disappear out the door. I couldn't reach him. He was gone.

From that moment on, the whole situation intensified. First, I told the story to the chaplain. We were standing face-to-face in the doorway, after the men had left. "I was just about to come look for you," I started off, my voice sounding like it was coming from far away.

"Was there a problem?"

"One of the men exposed himself to me." Putting it into words like that, stark and unequivocal, shattered the dreamlike quality of the previous few minutes. I began to shake.

"Come with me," she said, taking my arm and guiding me to her office.

She ushered me in and pulled out a chair in front of her desk. "Sit here. I'll bring someone to talk to you." I sat down. There were no windows in the room, so I stared at the degrees framed on the wall. Some time passed and the door opened. The chaplain had returned, and she had brought a guard, a burly older man. He leaned back against her desk facing me.

"Can you tell me what happened, ma'am?"

I began to describe the events. "He's a young man, his name is Lewis, he's from Los Angeles. He'll be on the list."

"What list would that be?"

"The sign-up sheet! Whatever the men sign when they come to the group." I looked around. There had to be a sheet somewhere. The chaplain who had been standing by the door slowly made her way to her desk. She was shaking her head.

"There is no sign-up sheet," she said, sitting down.

No one spoke for a moment. I could feel my panic rising, "How do you know who is in there with me?" I finally said.

"We don't. The men are free to come to any group they like." She was having difficulty looking at me.

The guard stood up and took charge. "You need to come with me, ma'am." He walked toward the door, opened it, and stood there waiting for me. I felt like a puppet on a string, my movements jerky, not in control of anything. I stood up and we left the chapel area and walked down the long hall toward his office.

Over the next two hours, the guard and I sat in a small, dark room with a computer and a large book on the table. First, he opened the computer and scrolled through the names of every man in the medium-security facility. There was no one with the name Lewis—first, middle, or last, from Los Angeles—in the facility.

Then he opened a large book. "This here has pictures of all the sexual predators in this facility," he said almost proudly, pushing the open book toward me. He began to turn the pages, page after page of men staring blankly out at me. After a while, I turned to him and said, "I don't think we're going to find Lewis, or whatever his name is, in this book. I don't think this young man is a sexual predator."

"How could that be?" the guard said, his tone sarcastic.

"I think he was just sad," I said. The guard shook his head and went back to the book; by then I could tell he was getting fed up with me.

After what seemed like forever, it was over and I was free to go home. The guard said someone would be in touch, but he added that it was unlikely I would be allowed back in the facility.

The sun was dropping behind the mountain as I walked out to the parking lot, the weather had turned gray and cold. I started the car and a loud twangy guitar jolted me back to earth. I turned off the radio and turned up the heat and headed home, my plans for visiting Rain completely forgotten.

Lulled by the warmth and the movement of the car through the now familiar landscape of tumbleweed and the golden stubble left from the last cutting of hay, changing to scrub oak and cottonwoods as the road began to rise, then massive boulders dotted with evergreens, and finally the sheer rock of the canyon walls, images began to appear in my mind. Lewis's face, his eyes empty of all feeling, the dark opening in the tan pants. My hands frozen on my knees. Dream-like images. It took me a moment to realize that other images had joined the slide show: a burnt orange cloth hanging like a curtain across a wide door, a window filled with pale gray moonlight, the silhouette of a leafy branch swaying, a narrow bed, white sheets, the sound of a branch scraping against the window.

I felt my body shut down completely as the images appeared, one after another, playing over and over in my head, uninvited.

I was almost at the ranch, guided now by my headlights on the dark road. I just wanted to get home, to find comfort, to talk to someone, to be safe.

The lights were on in the kitchen. Bone weary, I climbed the porch steps and opened the door. Joe was sitting in the recliner, a copy of the *Wet Mountain Tribune* on his lap, a wineglass and a bottle of tawny-colored liquid next to him. He looked up at me and poured more into his glass. "You were gone a long time," he said, not slurring, but with that very precise diction he had when he drank too much. My stomach sank.

"Something came up," I said curtly. "What on earth is that you're drinking?"

He held his glass up to the light. "Port. You want some?"

"Why the hell would I? It's six o'clock. Port is what men drink after dinner when the ladies leave the room." I dumped my bag by the door.

"Do you know how hard it is?" Joe said, his voice rising. "How hard it is for me? The way you treat me?"

"Jesus," I yelled back, "why does everything always have to be about you?" We glared at each other for a long time, and then I said, "I'm going to take a shower" and left the room. At the door, I turned around. "Not that you give a shit," I said, spitting out each word like a bullet, "but I was just in a room alone with thirty men—criminals—and one of them exposed his balls to me while sitting in meditation in front of me."

Dropping my clothes on the bathroom floor, I stepped into the shower and turned on the water. Hot water began pounding my shoulders, my arms, my back, rivers of hot water snaking down my legs, my body slowly unfreezing. I began to shake, buffeted by fear and shame and sorrow. Images from long ago, trapped somewhere deep in my being, were rising to the surface. I wanted to push them back down, to go back to my hiding place, but it was too late. A door had been opened that I knew I had to walk through. I had no idea how or where it would lead me. All I knew was it was too late to turn back.

Marriage Counseling

I woke up with a jumble of words forming and reforming in my mind. *Menopause, man o' war, men, pause, man, war.* A strange collage forming and reforming in my head. I opened my eyes and sat up. I was alone in our large bed. Joe had slept in the guest room. It was still early, the sky was overcast, the room chilly. *So weird*, I thought, *that the word menopause has men and pause in it. Who came up with that?*

I was not quite in full menopause yet. I was in the in-between state of perimenopause, where I had the joys of menopausal mood swings, and I still got to menstruate. It had started a few years before with my feeling edgier, more agitated; then one day it erupted, and I found myself tearing the cordless phone to pieces with my bare hands, going from a state of minor irritation looking for it, to blind rage when I found it dead, buried in the couch. I shredded it like a coyote tearing a rabbit into bite-size pieces.

The door cracked open and Joe, hungover and contrite, came in bringing me a cup of tea. The dogs followed and jumped up on the bed, wiggling with joy. Joe sat down on the end of the bed. "Maybe you should stop going," he said, "to the prison." I felt myself steeling up. "Maybe it's too dangerous." His eyes were squinting in the way they did when he was out of his comfort zone. *Do something different*, I reminded myself.

"I don't know," I said. "Let's see what happens." I could sense his relief.

He stood up. "Sounds good," he said and left the room.

I drank my tea, not wanting to get out of bed, to start another day, to keep trying. I could feel anxiety lapping at my heels.

Ten years before moving to Lookout Valley, Joe and I had gone to see a marriage counselor. I had talked my mother into paying for an introductory hour with a highly respected and very expensive marriage and family therapist. We arrived at his office in an old house in downtown Boulder and were ushered into his room. I liked him right away. He had a frank, open face, and a relaxed, lanky body. He was attractive in that way that men who don't apologize for being men can be. The three of us sat in armchairs in a triangle in the middle of the room. After some opening chitchat, Dr. R. asked us why we were there, and Joe launched into the story of his emotionally strangled childhood, his failure at relationships, his inability to express the feelings he had for me. I half listened, spending the time formulating what I would say when he was done. After a while, Doctor R. leaned toward me and asked in a conversational tone of voice, "So, how have you been dealing with this? Fucking around?"

I looked him in the eye and said, "Yes." Joe kept right on talking.

The fifty minutes stretched into an hour, then an hour and a half—that moment of raw intimacy hanging like a cloud in the air above us—and then, we were done. I had spoken only briefly. We sat waiting in anticipation for Dr. R. to give us the verdict. "It's pretty clear to me what's going on here," he said. "And I think you would be wasting your money coming to see me. It's all working very well for you both right now." He paused, maybe waiting to see if we had anything to say. I was too stunned by the truth of it to say anything. He went on, "It's like, you want to go to Denver, but you don't have any gas. One or both of you is going to have to be in a lot more pain before it would be worth the time and money to shake it up."

Then he looked directly at Joe and added, "I do have one piece of advice. You might try taking the sock out. Next time you feel like telling Vicki how you feel, do it." With that, he stood up, signaling the end of our time there. We gathered our coats, mumbled goodbye, and shuffled out the door.

"What just happened? I liked him. I was ready to do it," Joe said as we settled into a booth at Tom's Tavern.

I looked up from the menu. "It's not going to happen," I said. "We just flunked marriage counseling." And just like that, it became a story, a movie we had just seen and could now critique and tell our friends about. We didn't touch the moment of raw truth that took place between me and Dr. R. We left it unexplored and went back to the life that had been working so well for us for years.

There was no blame in the unspoken pact Joe and I had entered to stay numb, to not reveal our pain to each other, to let each other hide for all those years of marriage. Neither of us was ready to reveal our pain, not even to ourselves. We both needed to stay in our comfort zones.

For a while after we married, I was caught up in the fantasy of being a good wife and mother. After years of indiscriminate sex, I wanted to be faithful. I enjoyed the role. But it fell apart when I discovered Joe had been sleeping around. I threw him out of the house. He vowed never to do it again, and I let him come back. Two months later, I began an affair that lasted three years. Living in parallel worlds kept some fantasy of intimacy alive in me and kept Joe at arm's length and in the dark, a state that suited us both.

I contemplated leaving Joe. But I never did for the simple reason that I loved our family, and that family included him.

A few years before, I had joined all my friends who were avidly reading Melody Beattie's *Codependent No More*. The definition Beattie used for a codependent person was one who has let another person's behavior affect him or her, and who is obsessed with controlling that person's behavior. I had no problem recognizing myself and our marriage on every page. I wanted Joe to be different. Period. But eventually I was worn out keeping track of his every fault and trying to change him.

We were only three months into the nine months we had given ourselves to work on our relationship or give up on it, and our commitment to the morning briefings was already flagging. So many years of keeping our feelings at bay, the inertia was proving too much to overcome. We were both in pain, and neither of us could figure out how to take the first step toward each other. It was easier to fall back into our old grooves. As winter set in, Joe began drinking more, working more, and becoming increasingly isolated. I was spending more time at the stables, at my yoga class, going to the store in Westcliffe, anywhere but home. Had we reached the point Dr. R. had foreseen all those years ago?

It was impossible to deny that we were both in pain. But old habits die hard. Neither of us was able to just stop, look each other in the eye, and say the simple truth I had blurted out to Pema Chödrön at the retreat: "I just want to be loved."

Settling In

I had settled into a daily routine: each morning I would climb the wooden stairs to the attic bedroom I had turned into a meditation space and spend a half hour or so meditating. Mostly that meant gazing out the window next to the shrine that framed a view of the peak standing guard at the end of the valley. I would sit and let my mind wander.

Every day of living at the ranch, I was becoming more and more familiar with the line of the horizon that circled the valley. I knew the shape of each dip and craggy peak outlined against the sky. I felt the horizon was holding me. I was becoming aware of how the late afternoon light gleamed on the dry grass, turning it into a sea of gold; how the round moon rested in the curve of the hill centered in the dark blue evening sky. I could listen to the sound of an owl's wings flapping, becoming fainter and fainter until it disappeared. Paying attention was creating a sense of belonging.

I was also deep into Angelica's book, reading about her life in the twenties and thirties with Nello at the ranch when neighbors would come over to listen to baseball games on the radio or gather for sleigh rides in the winter. In my next letter to Berna, I told her how much I was loving the book. She wrote back right away.

Dear Vicki,

It was so good to hear from you. I am happy you are enjoying Mother's stories of those years. One of my earliest childhood memories places me in the seat of my father's truck, watching his sharp, angular chin bob up and down as he drove to the Civilian Conservation Camps at 3 a.m. to deliver milk, eggs, and butter. He sang "You Are MY Sunshine" to me as we watched the sun rise on our way home.

In my mythical vision, life was a series of long rides on horseback, searching the woods for arrowheads, splashing in the clear, cold water of Hardscrabble Creek, sledding down logging trails, and ice skating in the back yard.

I know there are other, darker memories that lurk there in the back of my mind, but I'll save those for another time.

Love to you, Berna

I was sensing as I read the book that life was going to get harder as the Depression set in. Berna's email hinted at a darker side to her childhood as well. I wanted to know more, but I didn't want to rush her.

One cold Saturday afternoon, Harold Miller showed up at the door wearing his mushroom hat, his pants held up with bailing twine. I offered him coffee and a slice of banana bread. He told me he was trying to lose weight, as an explanation for why his pants were falling off, but he wolfed down half a loaf of banana bread. When I asked him how he was doing, he answered, "Staying alive." He needed to use our phone to call his wife, who was in Denver dealing with a family matter. It was lonely without her, he told me. "Just the mice and flies and gophers for company."

We sat at the kitchen table, and he told me a rambling story of coming upon a patch of snow behind his house that had been there since the previous winter. "Looking at it, I realized that it had been sixty years since I had contact with anyone I went to school with, so I vowed to myself I would find someone out there who was at Pueblo High School in the thirties." He took a bite of banana bread and continued. "And I did. I found Mary Ellen from my class, but then she died a year later before we could get together for a visit, of a pulmonary embolism, and goddamn it if I didn't have one of those that same year. Only I lived." He stopped, and we sat in silence. There was nothing I could think of to say, and he didn't seem to want anything more than listening from me.

The light was fading as I walked Harold to his truck. Before he climbed in, he took my hand and looked at me with his watery blue eyes. "It's good having you here. I appreciate you being my neighbor."

"And I do too," I answered, aware of how awkward I sounded and how close I was to crying. I watched as his truck coughed and spluttered its way up the hill and disappeared around the curve. In the silence, I could hear an owl hooting on the ridge.

I didn't grow up with the idea of neighbors dropping by for a visit or coming if we needed help. We never stayed in one place long enough when I was a child. It felt good to get to know our neighbors, to feel a sense of belonging in this wild, barely inhabited place.

I was finding another place of connection in my new meditation group at the Camp, the minimum-security facility at the Florence prison. After what had happened at the medium-security facility, I wasn't sure I would be allowed back into the prison, nor did I know if I could handle it. The problem wasn't just that an inmate had exposed himself to me but that the situation had exposed the fact that no one was monitoring who was in the room with us volunteers.

I was about to give up on ever going back when I received a call asking if I could give a talk at the Camp. I said yes, and a week later I showed up and gave an introductory talk on Buddhism and meditation. From that, a small weekly group began to coalesce around four regulars, mostly drug dealers who had been incarcerated for ten or more years. Luis, a tall, dignified Cuban, was the cocaine king of Lincoln, Nebraska. Kenny was an old hippie who dealt pot and a little acid in San Francisco and had probably taken more than his brain could handle. Steve from Ohio, who had a long ponytail and a soft, shy smile, had inexplicably stolen quite a lot of money in some kind of tax fraud. Matt was a sharp-featured, lean, middle-aged man who had been living the good life in the wine country of northern California on the proceeds of a lucrative cocaine business.

At the first meeting, when I introduced the idea of sitting on the red cushions, the tension in the room was thick. Luis sat upright, his arms crossed over his chest, impenetrable. Steve pushed his cushion back to the wall and leaned against it, hugging his knees. Kenny tried to cross his legs and started giggling uncontrollably. No one else laughed. Matt went into full lotus, pretending it was easy, just to irritate everyone. Introducing the actual practice of meditation felt like an insurmountable challenge. I had to get them all to ease up on their attitudes first. Suddenly I remembered something I loved that Trungpa Rinpoche had once said. I grabbed it and ran with it. "So," I said, "none of us in this room knows exactly where this class is going or if anything will make sense, but my Buddhist teacher once used an analogy for embarking on a journey into unknown territory. *We're in a plane, our parachute strapped on our back. Then, we leap, and as we start to fall, we pull the cord and the parachute doesn't open. We're just plummeting through space. But the good news is . . . you want to hear the good news?"* I looked around and could see I had their attention, "*The good news is, there's no ground.*" I finished and waited.

After what seemed like forever, Kenny said, chuckling, "That's some crazy shit. What's the bad news?" They all began to laugh. Whether it was relief or just nerves, it didn't matter; they had relaxed.

When I came back the following week, the four men filed into the room and sat down on their cushions in a circle, ready to start. Now we were in week three, and the group was getting into a groove.

"I got about five steps across the yard before I was lost. I don't know where the hell I was," Matt said, reporting on the exercise I had given them the week before to see how far they could get walking from their cell to the lunchroom without their minds wandering off.

"Shit, man," Kenny said. "I didn't get one step out the door before I was drinking coffee in North Beach." As we all laughed together, I realized I was growing more at ease with these men. I looked forward to our meeting each week.

Meanwhile, the weather was cold and clear, the first snow waiting in the wings. Berna and I were sending regular emails back and forth about daily life at the ranch. In my next email, I described the arrival of winter:

Yesterday, sitting in the kitchen looking out the window, I felt myself settle in and let the gray brown permeate the whole of my being. The weathered wood of the outhouse was the same color as the rocks. The bare aspen trunks and the dead grass were the same shade of gray. Even the dogs are gray and brown. A blue jay landing on the bird feeder, pierced the drab palette like a drop of fresh paint.

Then, in the middle of the night, the snow began to fall, blanketing the world in pure white. And, as the sun rose this morning, it was all new, a clean slate under a frosty sky. We're snowed in, and things are very still. The house hums, the dogs sigh in their sleep, the fire in the woodstove sputters. Quiet has descended. It's a good time to drink tea and watch huge white flakes swirling silently outside. The anxiety of waiting for the storm to hit is gone. Now, all my plans to do this or that can just be left hanging, without guilt. It's time to just relax and let it all be as it is, silent and safe.

Berna wrote me back with an outpouring of memories from snowy days in the 1930s.

> The first snow back then signaled the beginning of a season when farm chores slowed to a walking pace and long evenings were spent by the woodstove listening to Daddy tell stories. "Tell us how you got lost in the woods," I would beg until Daddy wove his tale about following a bear's tracks home through the forest.
>
> For my parents, winter was also a battle with hammering storms that killed newborn calves and buffeted the house with icy winds, but for us kids, life held no more pressing demand than to climb up the hill behind our house and swoop down the logging trails on my Red Flyer and watch the snow from the window of my upstairs bedroom, which was always comforting.

I sat for a while reflecting on how similar our descriptions were of being held in the snowy valley, cut off from the world. It was peaceful. And magical. Everything glistened. The sound of boots stomping on the porch interrupted my contemplation. The door burst open, and Joe came in, waving some papers in his hand. "I made the reservations," he said as he pulled off his hat.

"For what?"

"The Piedra Blanca."

"But when?" I said, confused.

"For Christmas. I made them for three weeks. For all of us."

"Three weeks? What about my mother coming here for Christmas?" My mind was reeling. *Had we discussed this?*

For all the years the kids were growing up, we had spent Christmas in Mexico, most of those years at the Piedra Blanca Hotel in a small town an hour north of Puerto Vallarta. When we started the tradition, there was only one phone in the whole town. Those few weeks each year, letting the days unfold with no agenda and no responsibilities were what kept our family together, what gave us all a shared experience of just being. But our lives had changed. The thought of being in our old familiar haunt at the Piedra Blanca seemed somehow incongruous with the lives we were now living. The kids were both in college; they had moved on. I couldn't imagine leaving my new life for that long. Our time in Mexico seemed like an illusion, impossible to recapture.

I could see Joe crumbling, his fantasy of the family reunion disintegrating. "Maybe for ten days?" I offered. "After Mother comes here for Christmas. We can do both." For a moment we looked at each other, neither of us saying a word.

Then Joe walked to the refrigerator and opened it. "All right," he said with his back to me. "If that's what you want." He popped open a can of beer and went to watch the news. I stayed sitting in my office, filled with a sinking feeling of remorse and exasperation.

Christmas 1998

"Oh my God, it's Johnny Mathis," Joe called out from the living room where the Christmas music station was playing on the television and he was laboriously making wreaths from the fir and pine branches we had gathered that morning on the hillside, trudging through knee-deep snow to haul them back to the house. He had already strung flickering lights over all the outbuildings and stuffed a red ornament in the snout of the deer skull hanging on the wall of the blacksmith shop. I was cybershopping for presents for his mom, alternating between sheer revulsion at how unbearably corny it all was and getting a catch in my throat when the song with the line "fall on your knees" came on.

Growing up, Christmas had been hell. In all the years of my childhood, no one could ever remember whether we "traditionally" opened our presents on Christmas Eve or Christmas morning. I tried with a child's instinct for happiness to hold out, but I gave up at the age of six, after seeing my father eating Santa's cookies on Christmas Eve. As an only child, I was easily tainted by my parents' disdain for the whole thing. In my sixteenth year, I remember the three of us on Christmas Eve lolling on the couch in our basketball-court-sized diplomatic living room in Calcutta, wasted. I sat between my parents, a fragile border to their escalating hostilities, and closed my eyes as they bickered about when we should open presents. "Let's just open the fucking things now and get the whole farce over with," I exploded, staggering over to the tree and hurling packages across the room. Christmas was never my favorite holiday.

That first Christmas at the ranch, our friends sent us cards of farmhouses nestled in snow-covered landscapes with little notes inside saying, "Isn't this yours?" I even made one of our own: "Greetings from Lookout Valley Ranch" in Old Western font across a black-and-white family picture of the four of us leaning against the corral.

In the days leading up to Christmas, a snowstorm blanketed the hillside, and the valley became a proverbial winter wonderland, the fresh snow dazzling white. Then, by the end of the day, animal tracks crisscrossed the hillside, like the wavering lines of county roads on a road map. The next morning we woke to frozen fog coating the trees like sugar frosting. The naked branches of aspen on the hill gleamed silver and ethereal, backlit as the sky lightened in the east.

It was all so beautiful, and so unreal. When my mother and the kids arrived, we went through the motions of present opening, lighting the candles on the long dining room table, serving an elaborate roast beef dinner, the tree lights flickering in the corner. We ate and drank too much and rustled up just enough Christmas cheer to make it seem festive, but it felt as though we were holding our breath waiting for it to be over. The ten days in our old rooms at the Piedra Blanca, going through the motions of morning meditation on the balcony, beers and *camarones al ajo* under the palapa, even seeing how relaxed and happy Joe was, felt heartbreaking. Did I somehow know it was to be the last time we were all together in La Cruz?

"Not much changed here," Joe said grouchily, surveying the snow-covered driveway the afternoon after our flight home.

"It's winter; what did you expect?" I snapped back. We parked in front of the house and began unloading the car, neither of us speaking. I threw the sandy suits and damp towels into the basement laundry room while Joe got a fire going in the stove. The house was frigid. Only the dogs were excited to be back from their Christmas in the kennel.

When I came inside after starting a load of laundry, I found Joe wrestling with the Christmas tree, the ornaments thrown haphazardly into a paper bag, the floor covered in dry needles. I watched as he hauled it toward the door, grunting, hating the tree, hating me for wanting Christmas at the ranch, hating his life, and unable to say a word about what he was feeling. I was numb, unable to comfort or even get angry with him. We had spent our entire marriage terrified of what would happen if we said what we really felt, if we let ourselves get into a real, air-clearing argument. We didn't know how to fight. As an only child living in a cold-war zone, I had never seen a relation-ship where people fought and made up. I had only witnessed relationships where each person silently blamed the other for their lives not working out. Joe's father was a harsh man who spent months away serving in the Coast Guard, leaving Joe alone with his mother, scaring him when he came home. In neither of our families were feelings a topic of discussion.

As winter settled in, the cold outside seemed to reflect the coldness between us. It felt lonely being there together, each of us in our own frozen spaces.

Everything I was reading in Angelica's book was giving me a taste of how cold and lonely it could get, snowed in at the ranch. It wasn't a reassuring picture.

We were snowed in for months at a time. That began to worry me. All we could think of was our first child we were expecting any day. The winter that year was bad, our house was cold, and I was not able to nurse Berna Jean. We had to keep a fire going all night. I was always afraid someone would get sick or have an accident and we could not get help. Nello would comfort me by saying, "No one dies here, we don't have a cemetery."

That week, the winds were gusting so bad they knocked a tree over onto a power line and started a forest fire just up the road. The wind whistled and whined and howled and hissed for two days, working my nerves to the bone. Being without power gave me a taste of what it was like for Angelica and Nello, trapped inside with a newborn baby, a winter storm raging outside, with no heat and no one nearby for miles. I missed the friendly red lights on the power surge boxes and the answering machine, the soothing sounds of easy listening on the Weather Channel, the rumble of the forced air heat, even the whirr of the refrigerator. It felt even lonelier being there without power.

By the end of the second day of fierce wind, our nerves were shot. At dinner, all Joe could talk about was the bad news we kept getting: refinancing that wasn't approved, appraisals that came in lower than what we had paid for the ranch, royalty income plummeting through business circumstances out of our control. It wasn't hard to see how being so far from anything familiar was sinking Joe further into despair and hardening his will to escape. I had no reassuring answers for him.

Then, later that night, I wrapped myself in a blanket and went out to sit on the porch under a vast canopy of stars. Looking up, I saw one star shoot across the sky and my mind stopped. In that moment, I knew in my heart that I didn't want to give in. I knew I didn't want to sink into despair. I knew there was another way to be.

Reaching the Edge

"This whole thing has been a big mistake," were the first words out of Joe's mouth when I arrived back at the ranch after a grueling eight-day trip driving my mother around to visit old friends in Florida. After eight days of carrying suitcases in and out of motels and driving an economy rental car in Miami where half the population is over eighty and couldn't seem to recognize turn signals or stoplights, I was not in the mood to listen to Joe's troubles.

"What are you talking about?" I responded, even though looking at his haggard face, I had a good idea where this conversation was going.

"I can't live here. I just can't do it. It's too lonely. I need people," he said, and then just stood there, staring at me. I didn't know what to say. I took off my coat.

"What do you have in mind?" I finally asked.

"Maybe we could travel, visit people, spend part of the year somewhere else."

I looked at him, speechless. He had followed his dream and dragged me here to the middle of nowhere, and now he wanted to travel?

I was happy to be home. It was late in February. The weather had softened just in the time I'd been gone—tiny green shoots were pushing through the brown under royal blue skies. The sun was warming everthing. It was impossible for me to imagine leaving.

But for Joe everything was wrong, including me. The way I scrambled eggs, dried the sheets, handled the editing equipment. "You don't press play before you finish loading the tape in the machine," he grumbled, not bothering to check whether I was doing what he was criticizing.

I was no saint either. "Honestly, are you listening? I'm only going through this one more time," I hissed at him the third time I tried to explain how to send email on our new AOL account. Every word between us was a poisoned arrow. The claustrophobia I felt trapped in the house smothered in his depression was too much to bear. I wanted to scream, to jump up and down, to throw things. Instead, I picked up the car keys, grabbed my boots, and left the house for the stables.

Sailing down the canyon, I lit a cigarette, put in a cassette, and sang along with Bonnie Raitt tunes blasting out of the speakers until I pulled into the driveway of Rancho Loco, my new home away from home, where each day was another episode of *As the World Turns* with horses.

Mike's training venture at the stables had failed after six months, and there were no more horses coming his way. They had repossessed his fancy new trailer. "His heart wasn't in it," Dee, who worked for him and was a kind person, said. He was way more invested in the fantasy of looking good as a horse trainer than the reality of working, was how I saw it. Thankfully, Dee, who had all the energy in the world, took over the business and began working with the horses.

Rumor had it that the Rancho Loco owners Laura and Ron's marriage was on the rocks. Ron was cheating on Laura with a female guard, and he had lost his job at the prison. Laura threw him out and was spending her evenings drinking beer and fuming. Before she changed all the locks on the doors, Ron sneaked back into the place and took a horse, a trailer, and a couple of saddles, probably to sell.

Everyone at the stables knew everyone's business. Everyone had an opinion about everything, and everyone was right. The guys were the worst.

"I feel like a goddamn kindergarten cop with all the 'he said, he said' going on," Laura snorted as she, Dee, and I sat by the barn drinking beer.

"The craziest was when Max said Mike was a gang member, you remember?" Dee added.

"I've never seen a gang member who wore their jeans that tight," I said, and we all cracked up.

Nobody believed anyone else had any business calling themselves a horse trainer, or, for that matter, having a horse at all, and especially the horse they had, which was for sure all wrong for them. "For some reason," Dee piped up, "nobody ever says anything bad about you."

"I guess I'm too old and ridiculous—not worth complaining about." I shrugged and took a swig of beer. I loved those afternoons hanging out at the stables.

That day, as I was leaving the barn, Lee, whose job was cleaning and feeding and pushing endless wheelbarrows of horse shit out to the pasture, gave me two packets of frozen emu patties. Emu raising was another get-rich scheme that had come and was now going, leaving people with pens full of feathers and freezers full of emu burgers. Emu hamburger, Lee told me, had no fat and was low in cholesterol. "How does it taste?" I asked him.

"Gamey," he said. "It tastes better if you mix it with beef. Put some fat into it."

I giggled all the way up the canyon, my two frozen patties of emu meat on the seat next to me. I couldn't wait to share that story of living on the edge in Custer County with Berna in my next email. I ended it bringing the subject closer to home:

> We aren't immune to the hard times financially either. As soon as we moved down here, our income dropped by half. It's still way above the $19,000-a-year median income of Custer County, but if it doesn't get better, we too might have to call it quits and put the place up for sale.

I am reading about some of the troubles your mother describes during the depression, hailstorms destroying the crops and people being forced to sell the cattle for next to nothing just to survive. Do you remember those times?

It seems like trouble never ends when you are living so close to the edge. Divorce, ruin, death, sadness, rage, and confusion are the stew we all simmer in here. And there's no hiding out.

With love, Vicki

There was a response the next morning:

Dear Vicki,

I couldn't see the hard times at that age. What I remember is Mother moving easily from milking to baking, from haying to hugging, from scrubbing clothes on a washboard to riding herd on the range. When I look at pictures of her harrowing the field and pitching hay and Daddy stretching pelts on the barnyard gate, I see a couple so content and so close to the land it is hard to separate them from it. But it wasn't long before those years came to an abrupt end. I remember the day my father gave me a last kiss right there in front of that sunny window in the kitchen. Then he left for the hospital and never came back.

I will write more about that later. Have you gotten to that part of my mother's book yet?

Much love, Berna

I had just arrived at the chapter in Angelica's book about how life fell apart for them all in the spring of 1936. I had been putting off reading it. It felt like adding one more sorrow, even one that happened sixty years before, was too much to bear. That afternoon, I decided it was never going to get any easier, so I made a cup of tea, settled into the armchair in the kitchen, and opened the book where I had left off.

On March 1, 1938, Nello had a cold sore on his lower lip that would not heal no matter how we doctored it. Later he had a small sore on his chest the size of a dime. It also would not heal. The doctors tried different medicines, but nothing seemed to help. New sores that resembled a severe burn and blisters continued to appear on his entire body. One day, our family physician called and wanted to see me. He told me that, to the best of his knowledge, Nello had a rare skin disease called Pemphigus. There were only two such cases in the United States at that time. He advised me to take Nello to Colorado General Hospital in Denver, where he would have better medical treatment. I was there with him every day. He wanted to see the girls but could only view them from the window. By this time, he knew he would never be with them again. I cannot explain the suffering he experienced when over half his body was covered with blisters. The last few days they placed him in a water bath to relieve the pain. After three days in the bath, he went into a coma, and after twenty days of agony, he passed away at 2:30 a.m. on April 23, 1938.

I remember Nello's last words to me, "Don't stay on the farm; it will be too strenuous for you." But at the time,

I could see no other way but to go back home. I always had a fear of staying alone, but after Nello was gone, that fear left me. I knew I had to face it, the new life I was forced to make.

I put the book down and stared out the window, the same kitchen window where Nello had kissed Berna for the last time. My mind was filled with images of this family I had never met but with whom I had become so close. How could this happen to such loving people? Why were they the ones to have their life shattered by such a devastating loss? My preoccupation with my disappointing marriage seemed trivial in comparison.

I needed to get outside, to feel the air and sun. My heart was full, and I was terrified of all that would pour out if it burst. I grabbed my coat and put on my boots and rushed out the door.

The dogs joined me, and we walked slowly along the creek. Every now and then, Bronco would jump into the water and bite the riffles as the creek flowed over rocks. The grass was a pale gold with green shoots peeping through. It was all so beautiful and so ephemeral.

I had heard once that the word for life in Tibetan translates as "that which arises and dissolves in the same moment." That afternoon, I could feel in my bones how from one moment to the next there is no way to know how the wind will blow or in what direction it will take us. Each moment could be an opportunity, or it could be our last.

By the time the dogs and I got back to the house, it was starting to snow in messy, dandruff flakes, the sun now glaring out from behind a steel gray sky. The phone was ringing as I walked in the house. It was Bill Donley, our neighbor down the back road to Wetmore. He started right in, "You remember I was telling you about Treva and how she wanted her ashes up there at your place when she died? Well, I just picked 'em up." We arranged for him to bring them as soon as the snow melted. "I haven't read the note yet," Donley said before we hung up. "I hope to hell she doesn't want me to scatter the ashes or some damn crazy thing. Digging a hole is more my speed."

I had heard stories about Glenn and Treva Jones, who had lived at the ranch from just before World War II until selling it to the couple who sold it to us. Glenn had gone off to war and never fully came back. His body made it through, but his mind was gone; *shell shock* they called it then. He lived out his life at Fort Logan Mental Hospital. Treva lived the next forty years alone at the ranch. She was a pistol. The story of her fighting off the mountain lion with a broom was a legend, one of many.

What is it about this place, I mused as I started preparing dinner that night. *There seems to be a pattern of women being left here alone, abandoned by death or insanity, living on for years without a mate. Is there something here that drives men away?*

Joe was becoming more and more desperate to leave, to spend time somewhere else, anywhere but the ranch. For me, the secret to moving beyond my fear lay in staying, not running away. I was not about to leave. Were we about to become another story of a man leaving and a woman staying?

I pulled out a chicken from the refrigerator and started a fire in the woodstove to roast it. Then I sat down in the recliner and picked up Angelica's book.

Out of the blue, something Pema Chödrön had said at the "When Things Fall Apart" retreat came back to me. "If we commit ourselves to staying right where we are, then our experience becomes very vivid. Things become very clear when there is nowhere to go." Things were definitely becoming clearer. I could feel deep in my bones that there was no place for me to go. Whatever Joe decided he needed to do, and as scared as I was at the thought of becoming another woman living alone on the ranch, I knew I couldn't run away. I knew that the only way through my fear was to stay there, to become intimate with all my lifelong fears of abandonment, of not having any control, of being a stranger in a strange land, of being alone.

I could smell the buttery garlic of the chicken roasting. There was still a way to go before it would be finished. I opened Angelica's book and began reading the next chapter.

Drive All Blames

"So, what do you think? Who's to blame?" I asked. I was with the meditation group at the prison, the five of us sitting in a circle on the floor in the small, windowless room we gathered in each week. I had just finished regaling them with some of the "he said, he said" stories from Rancho Loco, but now it was time to get down to business. We were reading a book of Atisha's slogans—fifty-nine sayings the purpose of which were to help train our minds to work with challenges and difficulties in ways that didn't keep opening the same wound, didn't keep escalating situations until someone got hurt. Or, as in this case, incarcerated.

I had begun by saying, "The practice of mind training teaches us to reverse our usual me-first logic and offer the good stuff, the larger portion of cake, the best seat in the house, to others." Some of the slogans were a little too Buddhist for the group, but some, like "Don't wait in ambush" and "Don't bring things to a painful point" provoked some heated discussions.

"Your painful point may not be the same as my painful point," Luis insisted. It was difficult to argue with him on that one.

This week, the slogan was "Drive all blames into oneself," which is at the heart of mind training and the hardest thing in the world to do. I had been describing one of the exchanges between Max and Mike, renamed X and Y, in which they were accusing each other of not getting the tires on the trailer fixed, leaving them with no way to get the horses to the team penning on Saturday. They had come to blows over that one. I had described each of the two men's arguments, and the guys in the group had all gotten into which one was obviously right, when I posed the question, "What would have happened if one of them had just taken the blame?"

No one spoke. I could tell the idea that we don't always have to be right was not going over well. Nobody wants to give up being right. It goes against everything we have ever learned.

"I can see how you could save yourself a lot of trouble; just end the whole shit show right there," Matt finally said, and all the men relaxed a bit and we let that be the final word on "Drive all blames into oneself."

After class, Matt came up to help me stuff the cushions in the black garbage bag to store in the chaplain's office. "You know, I thought this class was going to be just a way to relax, but this shit is hard," he said to me. "It's not easy to look at your own shit. But I like it. I've never run from a challenge."

I smiled. "Good to hear," I said.

"It's not easy to look at your own shit." All the way home, his words reverberated in my head, alternating with the phrase,

"Would you rather be right, or would you rather be free?" I couldn't bring myself to float that idea out into the prison group. I was only just beginning to consider it myself, and I wasn't a hundred percent sure I was ready to decide.

"I love the guys in my group," I said as I walked through the front door into the kitchen. Joe was in the alcove off the living room where we had set up the TV. He was hunched over, his eyes glued to the screen. I could see him, but not the screen. I could hear the muffled sound of a news commentator. Joe didn't say anything. I kept talking. "They get so much of the teachings, and they have such a great way of putting it into their own words." Still nothing. "What are you doing?" I said as I walked into the living room.

"Do you know about this?" he answered, pointing at the screen. I looked over at a shot of children, teenagers, hands behind their heads, being hurried in a line around the corner of a school building. They were in a panic, stumbling. The police surrounded them, shouting orders. The sky was filled with the whirring of helicopters and crackling of police scanners.

"What is it?" I asked, panic rising in my throat. I could tell it was bad.

"A school up somewhere in Denver. Littleton, I think," Joe said. "A shooting." I sat down next to him on the couch and watched the story unfold, the images repeating again and again.

The next day, we woke up to mist filling the valley, needles of icy snow that stung my face as I walked up the road. I couldn't stop seeing the desks in the library splattered with blood, the indescribable pain of parents with no one to hold in trembling relief. The sounds of pleading and crying, explosions, and crazy laughter played over and over in my head.

That morning, I had written Berna. It was too much to hold inside. Joe had shut himself up in the blacksmith shop and was sawing something for some project.

Dear Berna,
    Columbine has filled our world with fear and grief. It may be more intense here in Colorado, but I know you are feeling it as well. The fear and grief live in my heart now as well. I breathe it in and wish I could somehow empty the world of this stench, this dark sorrow and evil, this vast, hopeless, never-ending pain.
    Today we woke up to snow falling endlessly. This cold white veil that has descended on the valley, cutting us off from the world, is very welcome. I feel as though I could stay cut off here forever, like an iceberg set adrift in a freezing sea. I had been planning to write today to say I just read the chapter about your father's death and how incredibly sad it was to learn what happened. Everything today seems unbearably sad, the past and the present, and there is no way of knowing what the future holds.
    Sending love your way.
    Vicki

I just managed to hit Send before the power suddenly went out. Everything became still and completely silent.

I was crying as I walked up the valley, the tears freezing on my cheeks. The icy creek cut through the snow-covered valley like a long, ragged wound in the land. The trees held their breath. I dreaded the return of spring: the cheer of sunny skies and lush green grass, the promise of warmth and light. I wanted to be cut off in that bitter cold forever.

Two days later, I left the valley swirling with mist and headed down to Wetmore to load up hay at Chum Hayne's ranch and take it to the stables. Driving down the canyon through hard frozen snow-covered trees was like being in a sparkling Christmas card.

At Chum's place, I met up with Jasmine and her husband, John, who were helping me haul the bails over to Rancho Loco. I had met Jasmine at the stables when she came to team pen. She had tried team penning on Rain, but it turned out he was more interested in running the yearlings into the fence than herding them into the pen. Jasmine was in her early thirties, a fearless rider who had grown up in Berlin. I pictured her skinny and pale, smoking cigarettes in an urban, gray winter landscape. Growing up, she had always wanted to be a cowgirl. As a teenager, she had found a way to ride around bareback on a paint horse on the outskirts of the city. From there, she married a U.S. Army man and got as far as Kansas. When he made her choose between him and her horse, she left with the horse. And a four-year-old daughter. A year later, she was remarried, living in a cabin in the mountains outside of Florence, team penning on Saturday nights in tight jeans.

It took a while, slogging through knee-deep mud, but we finally got the hay loaded into the back of their pickup and we climbed into the cab, the three of us in a row. On the drive to the stables, we started talking about the Columbine shooting, and that brought up gun control, a loaded topic in Custer County where everyone had gun racks with guns in their truck, and the right to bear arms was almost a religion. After John brought in Thomas Jefferson and the need to protect oneself as a God-given right, I sat for a moment before jumping in. Jasmine was watching me, a little nervous.

"Here's the thing: I hear you," I said, "but don't you think life is a lot more stressful and confusing now than it was then, even harder to handle emotionally for some people, and then if you add a gun to that mix, and teenagers, don't you think it can be dangerous?"

John reached into his shirt pocket for his Copenhagen and stuck a wad in his lower lip. "You got a point there." He nodded. "Yeah, you got that right."

The longer I lived at the ranch, the more I understood the Dalai Lama's instructions about joining fantasy and reality. The Dalai Lama had been answering a question about intimate relationships, but he went on to say that the act of joining fantasy and reality is our life's work. I was beginning to understand that we are always balancing fantasy and reality. Nothing is the way we think it is. If we let it, life is always surprising us.

When I first got to the ranch, the thought of living there petrified me. Everything was foreign and scary. But then, after a few months, I found that living there was nothing like my fantasies. There were no huge bears lurking behind every tree or armed NRA members out to get me in every truck that went by. The first time I saw a bear, I was chopping vegetables in the kitchen. I looked out the window and saw a bear crossing the valley. Not the giant bear from my wild imaginings, but a small bear galumphing along at a leisurely pace looking exactly like a Disney cartoon bear. From then on, while I never lost a healthy respect for bears, I wasn't scared to death at the thought of them.

The gun-toting crazies were next. Both fantasies had blurred, and reality had begun seeping through. It had taken some work. I had needed to detach myself from the fantasy, not allow it to color the reality that was right in front of me, constantly surprising me.

After a long, hard day of hauling and stacking hay, I drove home. It was snowing in messy wet flakes. I pulled in and parked by the house. I was exhausted and covered in mud. Wet snow was dripping from the eaves, the wind was blowing clouds of old snow from the trees; the world was in black and white, and it was almost May. If I had been lost in a fantasy of lush pastures with horses grazing contentedly, sitting on the porch with a handsome cowboy at my side, I would have had a hard time with the present reality, but at that moment, I was okay with it all. I didn't need it to be different. All I needed was a warm bath and some food.

As I turned off the engine, I saw Joe come out from his studio in the barn. He wasn't wearing a hat or jacket. Hunching his shoulders against the snow, he trundled across the slushy lawn to the house. My heart hurt watching him. He had put everything he had into this place, into the idea that this place would heal all his wounds. He was still trying to hang on to that fantasy, but it was fast slipping through his fingers.

"Awful weather," I said as I pulled off my muddy boots in the kitchen. Joe yanked the cork out of a bottle of wine and poured himself a glass. I kept going. "I'm going to take a bath. Do you want to join me?"

He looked up, as though he had heard a sound from very far away, and said, "I don't think so," and sat down. I could feel all the goodwill, all the sweetness I had felt minutes before, drain out of my body.

"Fuck it," I muttered under my breath, "be that way," and left the kitchen.

I drew a bath in the long claw-foot tub and sunk deep into the warm water. As I lay there staring out the window, the sun peeked through the late- day clouds and hit the top of the mountain covered in snow, turning it gold. "Would it really be so bad to be left here alone?" I wondered, shutting my eyes and letting myself sink deeper into the bath.

The next few days an air of sadness hovered over the house. The whole world seemed to be drifting; my mind flitted here and there, never finding a safe place to land. Joe was trying to cheer up, but his heart wasn't in it. I was avoiding him, not wanting to be infected by his depression. I hadn't heard back from Berna after my last email. She was usually prompt; it was adding to my uneasiness. Finally, a message landed in my inbox:

Dear Vicki,

I apologize for taking so long to respond. April has always been a difficult month for me. April is the month my father died. After kissing me goodbye there in the kitchen in front of the window, he left for the hospital and never came back. When he waved to me from his hospital bed in April 1938, he knew that he was going. The disease that was quickly destroying his body would soon take him.

It is impossible to capture in words the joy of walking along the stream with my father to inspect beaver dams or search for tracks where deer came to drink. He knew where porcupines and weasels and lions made their homes and could find their marks in the grass or under leaves. In the dark of night, we would quit the house to watch stars waltz on the water. My father taught me the language of the trees and the harmony of the landscape. I can only imagine the tales he did not live long enough to tell.

I will write more later. Take care of yourself. Spring is on its way.

Love, Berna

That year, winter saved its most ferocious attacks for April and May; it seemed as though spring would never come. My body was still steeled against the cold as I left the house and marched down the dirt road that led to Eustace's place. It took me a few minutes to realize that something had changed since I was last outside the house. The creek, frozen all winter, had thawed and was overflowing with melted snow. Soon it would be time to bring the horses up for the summer.

I felt like a convalescent, recovering from a long illness, finally allowed outside. I climbed the small ridge and zig-zagged my way down the other side through a grove of aspen trees whose trunks, silver all winter, were now a pale gold. As I climbed down, I realized that I had arrived at the spot where the tree with my initials carved on its trunk stood. I sat down on a log and let the quiet of the forest envelop me as I con-templated the V.H., perfectly etched in the bark, as large as my hand. *How did I end up in this place, on this ranch, on this trail, sitting next to a tree with my initials on it?* None of it made any sense, but in the depths of my body, I could feel the truth of it. I knew this was where I needed to be. I had resisted moving to the ranch every step of the way, but the place had other plans for me. It was time for me to stay still and listen.

The Moment I Knew

It took becoming a mother for me to realize that my childhood was truly painful. I began to see how as a child I understood the message that if I wanted to survive, I was going to have to become skilled at adapting to all the changing realities life threw my way as a foreign service offspring. The primary skill I learned was to pretend not to care that my needs were way down on the list of things important to my parents, down below the protocols of setting a proper table and the correct length of skirt for the country we were in.

A moment when Nicholas was three woke me up to the damage my childhood had done. I was alone with him in the house, sitting on the floor outside the closed door of his room, listening to him crying his heart out on the other side. I could hear his panic rise and his cries escalate when no one came. I sat, unmoving, for a very long time until he finally wore himself out and spluttered to a stop. I felt nothing for him, just mildly irritated and a little curious as to how long it would take for him to give up. I was totally numb. If I could put words to what I was feeling, it would have been, "You're going to have to figure this out, kid. You're old enough now to take care of yourself. It's time to toughen up." It took me a while to make the connection. My son was almost the age I was when I began my life as a diplomat's daughter in London. At that moment, I lost touch with my parents and discovered it was up to me to figure out the challenges of living. No one was going to help me.

During those days of early spring, I could feel Joe silently crying out for help. Every gesture, every word was a plea for a way out of the pain he was in. "How about teaching?" I would say "There is a need for people with skills in some field to teach middle school, a midlife career change. You could do that—you have a PhD in biology. You're perfect." He would just shrug. Nothing was getting through. I felt myself becoming increasingly irritated. Finally, I shut down as tightly as I had with Nick and watched Joe flail about, adrift in a stormy sea. In my son's case, he had brought me to my senses before it was too late. When he turned seven, he had had enough. He was no longer Nicholas, my sweet, compliant little boy. He was tall and strong, and his name was Nick, and he was angry. When he began lashing out at me, I made an appointment with a therapist. After two sessions with the two of us, I realized I had been following in my parents' footsteps, and I knew I had to change. Luckily, I was able to slowly shift course and I began to spend more time with both my kids and less time going to meditation programs and pursuing a career in Hollywood, where after a number of meetings to pitch script ideas, nothing was happening. It was not hard to give that fantasy up for the reality of spending more time with my children. It was different with Joe. I was sick of trying to help. I didn't care anymore.

That month, Nick was graduating from Colorado State University. Julia was coming from Los Angeles, and Joe's mom was flying in from Portland for the event. The plan was for us all to stay in a motel in Ft. Collins. My parents, who had retired to Boulder and almost immediately got divorced, were coming just for the day, my mother alone and my father with his new wife.

"Where are we staying?" I asked Joe, who was always the one in charge of travel arrangements, as I packed my graduation outfit in an overnight bag. The weather was going to be warm. I was looking forward to the change. "Where are we headed?" I asked again, this time looking over at Joe. He was standing in the doorway, not answering. Without a word, he turned around and headed for the phone. "Shit," I said. "You're kidding?" I followed him into the kitchen. "Do you know how many people will be needing a room in Ft. Collins this weekend?"

Two hours later, he had reached a dead end in Ft. Collins and had booked us two rooms in the neighboring town of Loveland, a half hour away. I gave him the cold shoulder all the way to the Denver airport, where we picked up Grandma Frances and Julia. Once they were in the car, we all made small talk the rest of the way.

Seeing the sign "Welcome to Loveland, nationally famous sweetheart town," I felt my spirits lift, the excitement of witnessing the first college graduation of one of our children bubbling up in me.

When we arrived at the old Kings Court Motel, Joe went into the office and checked us into the two rooms he had reserved. Grandma Frances, Julia, and I stood in the parking lot, surveying the chain link fence around the bathtub-size pool and the row of large trucks parked in front of each room. When Joe came out with the keys, he handed one to me and then grabbed his overnight bag and his mom's suitcase out of the trunk and headed toward a room, leaving me and Julia by the car. I looked at the key. "I guess it's you and me in Room 12. Let's hope there are two beds."

It was a beautiful sunny morning the next day when Julia and I rolled out of our queen bed and poured cups of weak coffee down our throats. The graduation ceremony was scheduled for ten a.m. in the indoor arena at the Equine Center. Julia and I were ready and waiting when Grandma Frances came out of their room, with Joe dragging the suitcases behind her. It took a moment for me to register what he was wearing. He was dressed for his son's college graduation in his most ragged jeans, the legs rolled up at the bottom, faded in the knees, and an old flannel shirt he had rescued from a dumpster.

At that moment, everything became vivid and very clear; a thought penetrated the familiar fog of helplessness and frustration and formed a sentence in my mind: I CAN'T DO THIS ANYMORE. That moment, standing in the parking lot of the Kings Court Motel in Loveland, it became so obvious, so simple, so irreversible that I burst out laughing.

Then I heard from across the parking lot Julia, never one to mince words, say, "Dad . . . what the fuck are you wearing?"

Right then I knew, in the way you know without looking at the color of the little stick that you are pregnant and your life has just taken a whole other road, that there was no turning back. There would be no second-guessing, no accommodating, no allowances, no walking it back. Our marriage was over.

The rest of the day rolled out in a strange haze. Watching Nick cross the stage in his too-short gold gown, wrinkled from having been stored on the floor of his truck all night, had the disjointed quality of a dream. The mimosa, bagel, and cream cheese brunch was like a scene out of an American family sitcom. At the end we gathered for a photograph—Joe, me, Nick, and Julia standing with arms around each other squinting at the sun. It was the last family picture we ever took.

The next morning I broke the news to Joe. We had spent the night of graduation in Denver, and the two of us were having breakfast at Zaidy's Deli, one of our favorite breakfast places. We sat across from each other in a booth and ordered the corned beef hash. Then the words "I can't do this anymore" tumbled out of my mouth. I could have been talking about any number of things, but Joe knew exactly what I meant. He didn't say anything. "I think you need to figure out what you want for yourself. I can't keep trying to help you figure out your life anymore," I continued.

He nodded slowly. "You're right," he said. "There's a lot I need to figure out." He took a gulp of coffee. The food arrived and we ate our hash, our rock-solid pattern of dissociation firmly intact. There was nothing more to talk about.

After years of feeling trapped, of wanting something more, of talking with friends about leaving Joe, of writing about the pros and cons in journals, of trying out techniques from marriage counseling, exactly nine months after we began our nine-month marital experiment, the results were in. It was undeniable. There was no room or reason for further discussion. The marriage was over.

Joe moved into the guest room, and we began the long process of pulling apart, strand by strand, the lives we had created together.

Shifting Worlds

"Not LA," I said, pleading with Joe. "Anywhere but LA. Let Julia have her own life, please." A week after our conversation at Zaidy's Deli, Joe was deep into planning for his new life.

I could see the lights go on in Joe's mind when he got the idea of moving to Los Angeles, where Julia was finishing her first year of college. It was the most excited he had been in a long time. "Breathe, do something different," I reminded myself as the discussion began to disintegrate into hostility. Putting my cup in the sink, I walked away from the kitchen, got dressed, and left for the prison.

As I drove down the canyon, I contemplated the topic for the day's class. My plan was to talk about *maitri*, a Sanskrit word meaning loving-kindness. For years I had considered the teachings on loving-kindness as second rate, something you had to get through in order to be given the keys to the more advanced Tibetan Buddhist practices, the magical, mysterious, tantric ones. When Pema Chödrön began framing the *maitri* teachings to include loving-kindness for oneself, I found myself tuning out. *Wasn't I on this path to try to change myself? Why would I want to love this confused, obviously flawed human being?*

The phrase that Pema Chödrön used to describe that form of *maitri* was "making friends with yourself," not running away or turning your back on yourself, no matter how gnarly it got, no matter how much you would rather be locked into a relationship with anyone but yourself.

My mind had drifted off the teachings of *maitri*, and I was humming a tune under my breath as I swung the Explorer into a spot in the prison parking lot. I couldn't identify the song, the words hovering just on the edge of my mind as I walked through the gates and into the building. The light bulb didn't go off until I entered the room where the group was already seated on their cushions. I started to laugh. "Okay, pop quiz," I said as I sat down. "Does anybody remember the song with the line "If you can't be with the one—"

Before I could finish the line, Kenny and Matt had yelled out the answer, "Love the One You're With," and they were off and running.

Steve, usually the quiet one, joined in, and soon the three men were in full swing, plucking random verses from a time long gone. Luis watched, an exasperated look on his face.

It turned out to be the perfect introduction to *maitri*. After giving the translation, I asked them, "So who do we spend the most time with in our lives?" They all looked mystified.

"Ourselves," Matt finally said.

"Right," I said. "The wisdom of rock and roll."

"I spent sixty days in the hole back when I was younger and stupider, sixty days where all I could do was beat myself up." Luis shook his head. "Man, after all the stupid shit I've done in my life, it's hard to wrap my mind around loving myself." The rest of the men nodded in agreement.

"It makes no sense," Kenny chipped in. "If you are a fucked-up piece of shit, why would you want to make friends with yourself?"

"What if it was your good friend or your brother who did something stupid?" I asked. "Would you give up on them?"

"It would depend on how bad it was," Matt piped up.

"Really?" I asked. They sat there for a moment, wrestling with their minds.

"Maybe," Kenny finally said. "If it was my brother, I'd have a hard time giving up on him."

"What if we treated ourselves like we treat someone we love?" I asked them. "What if we didn't give up on ourselves. *Maitri* practice starts with treating ourselves like a good friend, even when our darker side shows up."

Luis shook his head. "That is some deep shit."

"Here's what helped me," I confided to the group. "I have a couple of dogs. They can just be lying there, doing nothing, and I'll tell them, 'You are such good girls.'" No one was yawning, so I went on. "One day I thought, *Why aren't I as kind to myself as I am to my dogs?* It was one of those light-bulb moments. So, that's my making-friends-with-myself practice. Talking to myself as sweetly as I talk to my dogs."

"Fake it 'til you make it," Matt, who was in NA, said. "It's like, if you can't *be* the one you love, love the one you are." Kenny started singing, and the men took up the chorus and began riffing on his version, adding their own verses.

"If you can't love the one you are, love the one you wanna be." They started clapping along. It was battle-of-the-bands meditation; I had to rein them in before they started dancing. It may not have been a traditional teaching on *maitri*, but somehow it made sense to all of us freezing together in the overly air-conditioned room. Not for the first time, I had the thought that my time with the meditation group was one of the many reasons why I felt good about being at the ranch.

That first spring in the Wet Mountains, there were days when mist draped itself over the hills and settled in the valleys. Sometimes it poured up South Hardscrabble Canyon as though it were being pumped from a dry ice machine at a rock concert. Then the sun sliced through for a moment before the clouds settled in again, the wind picked up, and the skies opened, splattering rain, then hail, on the sodden ground. Each moment was a different mood. I was connecting more and more with the land, with the changing weather. I was noticing more. I could spot different birds, differentiate a hawk from an eagle. I wasn't just familiar with the contours of the land, I could close my eyes and draw in my mind's eye the bends in the creek that meandered through the valley. During breaks in the rains when I rode Rain on the road that ran along the ridge to Eustace's place, I could see the new leaves on an aspen tree flutter and hear the creek rushing and feel the breeze and my body settling in the saddle, all at the same time. Something deep in my body was waking up. The secret to weathering the weather, I was discovering, was to not take it personally. Sunny and stormy days came and went, and so did joy and despair. It was all a profound lesson in impermanence.

After leaving the prison that day, I drove through three distinct rainstorms. Just as I arrived home, a sliver of sun pierced through the clouds and a rainbow spanned the valley. Rain stood in the corral, under the brilliant arch, his deep bay coat glistening. The exquisiteness of everything was almost more than I could bear.

I was quiet through dinner. Joe had made his signature spaghetti with meat sauce, and we had a bottle of wine. I didn't feel like making small talk. Joe wasn't talkative either. He seemed agitated, not really there. "Are you sad?" I asked out of the blue. I wasn't planning on asking that question; it just spontaneously arouse.

"Sad?" Joe seemed confused by the word.

"Losing all this, all these years, our family. I know it's the right thing," I said, staring out the window at the faint outlines of the hill fading as night fell, "but I do feel sad too." I turned my head and looked at Joe. He was strangely still. A door had slammed shut; his eyes were cold.

"No," he said. "I can't wait to never have to hear about your feelings again."

In that instant, I felt myself disappear. I had no sensation in my body. No breath coming in or going out, no thoughts. Just an overwhelming need to leave the room. I stood up without saying a word. Somehow I got my legs, which were now quivering uncontrollably, to carry me all the way to the bathroom, where I locked the door, tore off my clothes, and stepped into the shower. The water ran hot rivers down my body, pounding on my shoulders, soaking my head. I didn't cry. I stood and let the water wash away the venom, the years of rage and frustration that had been growing inside this man I had been living with for so long, venom he had just spewed all over me.

At that moment, the road forward was crystal clear. I was embarking on a new life, alone, at Lookout Valley Ranch.

Summer in Limbo

At the beginning of June, Joe set off on a reconnaissance trip to LA, leaving me to try out my new persona as a solitary ranch woman, strong and capable, managing 160 acres of grazing cows and horses, a vegetable garden, a cat, and two dogs all on my own. It felt like I had been cast as the lead in a movie already in production, but no one had given me the script. I had to make it up as I went along.

One early morning a week into it, I was standing in the kitchen half asleep waiting for the kettle to boil when I heard a crashing sound. Peering through the back window, I saw dust flying from the rubble of what used to be the root cellar, accompanied by a loud commotion of whinnying and snorting. "Oh shit," I cried and ran out the door. When I rounded the house, I could see Rain's head and one front leg thrust out through the small window frame still intact in the pile of dirt and beams. His eyes were wide and nostrils flaring as he struggled, frantically whinnying. Through what was left of the door, I could see his enormous body, his three other legs still on the ground. "It's okay, boy, hang on," I whispered. Whirling around, I ran back into the house and called Bill Donley.

He answered after one ring. "My horse is trapped; it doesn't look good." I could barely speak. "Please could you come . . . quick."

I hung up, struggling to breathe, not wanting to look out the window. There was no way this was going to end well. My knees were buckling. I held onto the counter and tried to think of some kind of prayer or mantra. I was alone. There was no one to blame, no one to hold my hand, and there was nothing I could do for my horse. After a moment, my heart slowed and I peeked out the window. Rain's head was gone. So was his leg. "No, no, please no," I whispered. I ran back out, rounding the back of the house just in time to see Rain emerge from what was left of the root cellar, trampling the door on his way out. He shook his body, sending dust flying, and then, lowering his head, he began nibbling at the tall grass growing alongside the fence. I stood next to him, stroking his neck, breathing in his familiar musty smell. "You had me scared, big boy," I whispered into his mane.

I heard Donley's truck and turned to see him approaching, carrying a shotgun. He stopped, taking in Rain and the pile of rubble. "Son of a gun, look at that. A regular Houdini," he chuckled. We stood together watching as Rain grazed, all 1,200 pounds of him, safe and sound.

"Let me get Houdini back in the corral," I said, "and I'll make us a cup of coffee."

Sitting in the kitchen, I asked Bill to tell me about the original residents of Stillpoint, his neighbors farther down the back road to Wetmore. I had finally met the owners and heard a bit of the story of how the place started. It was hard to believe that a group of back-to-the-land hippies and Gia-fu Feng, a revered tai chi master from China, could move into a ranching community and be accepted. "What was it like when they arrived?" I asked.

"It took a while," he said. "When they first moved in, I would see this small Asian man going for walks up and down the road at night. He was a skinny fella, dressed all in black. In the pitch dark. One night I pulled over and said to him, 'You're going to get your ass run over some night walking around dressed like that.'" Bill chuckled and went on, "Next time I saw him, he was dressed head to toe in a fluorescent orange getup." We both cracked up. "We got along fine after that."

The next six weeks, I found myself careening between moments of pure enjoyment of being at the ranch and moments of pure panic anticipating the soon-to-be reality of living there, for real, all by myself.

Otis and Johanna and Casey had arrived for the summer and, much to my surprise, Casey showed up one day in his scruffy tennis shoes and baseball hat ready for the riding lessons I had promised him. At first, he just watched me, his face blank, never saying a word. After a few days, progressing from brushing to saddling, he got up on Peanuts and rode around the arena at a walk. I stood and watched. As they came around the second time, I took a step forward. "Okay, now let's see about stopping. Settle back in the saddle, pull, just lightly, on the reins, and say whooah."

"Whooah," Casey said in a firm voice, and Peanuts stopped exactly in front of me. I looked up.

Casey was grinning from ear to ear.

"That was awesome. You are a natural," I said, relishing Casey's newfound confidence.

One morning, when Otis and Johanna came to pick Casey up, Johanna rolled down her window as I walked over. "We just heard that Harold died over the weekend. In his sleep."

"Harold Miller?" I asked, shocked.

Johanna nodded. "Seems like he had a pulmonary embolism. Died in his sleep."

"But he was here not that long ago," I said. "Now I remember, he told me he had one before."

"Ain't that strange," Johanna said. "He was a crazy old coot. But a good one."

I nodded in agreement. "I'll miss him," I said.

Otis leaned over. "You take care now," he said.

As he climbed into the back seat, Casey looked over at me and mumbled, "Thanks for the riding."

"It's a pleasure, Casey," I said, and I meant it.

Life and death, moments of joy and moments of sorrow, constantly arose and dissolved without my being in charge of any of it. Walking back into the house, I was struck by the raw intensity of that truth and the futility of trying to hang on to anything.

Riding Rain had become a perfect way to cut through a lot of mental gyrations and useless worrying and to keep coming back to the simple reality of being in the present. Throughout the winter at Rancho Loco, Dee and I had gotten into the habit of riding together, often following it up with a beer at the Alibi Lounge in Florence. We would sit in the armchair stools at the bar and regale each other with stories of growing up. She told me tales of late nights in Clearwater, California, behind the pens after the rodeo, and of edgy times in cars on back roads. My stories were of getting arrested for having my feet in a fountain alongside other teenagers, Black and white, late on a summer night in Washington, DC, and walking around the streets of Calcutta at night, stoned on acid. It was an eye-opening exchange for both of us.

One warm June afternoon, as we were riding across the meadow, she told me about driving by the ranch with her mother a few years before. "I said to my mom, 'That is a little piece of heaven right there,'" she said.

"Did you write the classified in the *Denver Post*?" I laughed. "Those exact words got us here in the first place."

She shook her head, smiling. "Crazy how shit happens." She nudged Chaz into a canter, and Rain and I followed. Side by side we loped up the hill to the upper meadow sparkling with bright yellow dandelions, then, slowing down, we dropped the reins and let the horses graze. Clouds like whipped cream confections were moving slowly across the pale blue sky.

I turned and looked at Dee. "Did you know Joe and I have separated?" I asked.

"I figured as much," Dee answered. "All I can say is he must be one crazy son of a bitch to walk away from paradise."

"The winter got him. He's in LA as we speak," I said, "looking for his next paradise."

"I still say he's crazy," Dee said, sealing it with a raucous laugh. We picked up our reins and settled into a slow trot across the field of dandelions.

The next morning, I wrote in my email to Berna:

I don't know why people hate dandelions so much. Was that something that took hold in the fifties when we invented suburbs? I grew up in cities, so I missed that transmission. I think they are beautiful.

She wrote back:

I have always loved dandelions too. For my Grandma, the dandelion was a precious thing. She began her watch as soon as the snow started to melt. After digging the first tender leaves to serve as a salad tangy with vinegar and oil, Grandma would watch for the exact moment to gather the blossoms for her wine press. She died when I was seven and sadly the winemaking ritual ended then.

Reading her description, I remembered how dandelion wine making was one of the many fantasies Joe had spun back when he was infatuated with visions of our perfect life on the ranch.

I wrote to Berna before going to bed, ending the email with:

I wish you could hop on a plane and come see this year's crop. Let's plan on next year resurrecting the ritual of dandelion winemaking together.

When the next year rolled around, those words would come back to haunt me.

Alternate Realities

It was hard to imagine leaving the ranch as summer rolled along with its sunny days and afternoon rains and cool nights, but I had begun a video project on gangs and had to start filming. I would be gone a month, driving first to see Nick in Idaho, then on to LA and to Crips and Bloods and Wannabees and OGs and shootings—it was all an unfathomable alternate reality.

"Maybe you could find someone in LA who could take care of your problem with your husband," Matt said as we all sat in a circle in our cramped, over-air-conditioned room in the chapel. In a moment of weakness I had told the group that I was separating from my husband.

"You have someone in mind?" Kenny asked.

"Hell no," Matt chuckled. "I'm from Petaluma!" Everyone cracked up, and the room full of middle-aged dope dealers and tax evaders began throwing down ridiculous gang signs.

"Okay, guys," I raised my voice. "We're going to get fined for excessive celebration." I picked up the book of slogans we were studying. "Who wants to read the next one?"

Luis raised his hand. "Don't ponder others," he read, and looked up. "What the hell does that mean?" he asked.

"It's too deep for you, man," Matt said, grinning. Luis slowly put the book down and glared at him. The air was suddenly thick with tension. It was clear Matt's line had not landed well. I held my breath, waiting to see if I would have to intervene. Then Matt said, "It's all right, man. I don't know what the fuck the word means either." We all let out our collective breath.

"I think it means there's no point talking shit about people," Steve piped up.

"It always comes back and bites you in the ass anyway," Kenny said.

Luis nodded and, with a slight smile, wrapped up the conversation, "Maybe it means we can relax and not get into everyone else's business." And just like that, everyone relaxed and the tension in the room eased. I don't know which slogan we had just witnessed in action, but it worked.

As we wrapped up the meeting, I realized how much I was going to miss my routines of sitting with the prison group, riding with Casey and Dee, and meditating in the mornings in the Adirondack chair by the creek. In the month Joe had been gone, I had found moments of what I could only describe as joy that flickered unexpectedly throughout the days. Hearing the creek first thing in the morning or seeing the late afternoon light falling on the grazing horses would suddenly lift my spirits. Pulling carrots out of the garden, hanging laundry on the line, or sitting on the porch steps with Bronco and Abby at my side brought an unfamiliar feeling of well-being. Moments of connection, greeting other drivers on the back road to Wetmore, with a slight lifting of my hand off the steering wheel, or listening to Julia's excitement on the phone as she told me about her mentoring job in LA, all felt real and true. It felt like my lifelong sense of running on empty, pushing myself too hard, needing more was letting up. Some part deep inside me was beginning to relax.

Some years before, I had heard Pema Chödrön tell a story about a time in her life when she was depressed, when everything seemed bleak and hopeless. One day she started recounting her tale of woe to a friend. She ended with, "I don't know what to do to shake off this sadness." After a while her friend said, "I heard you humming in the shower this morning." When Pema didn't stop her, her friend continued, "And you seem to be enjoying your breakfast." She added a few more moments where things had seemed fine until Pema got it. As she told the story, what she came to understand was that nothing is one solid way; everything unfolds moment by moment, each moment with its own possibility, and when you see a moment of joy arising, don't stop it; let yourself enjoy it.

The Explorer was packed and ready to go, and I was filling time, doing odds and ends, edgy as I waited for Joe to arrive. We were tag teaming the ranch caretaking, and it was his turn for the month of August. I had a list of chores for him to do while I was gone and before he left for good. Broken panes of glass to replace, finishing the loafing shed in the corral, changing the water in the hot tub, fixing the seated lawn mower—the list was long. The thought of losing Joe the handyman was more disturbing at that point than losing Joe the husband.

I was playing solitaire when I heard Joe's old Jeep on the gravel outside my office window. I took a deep breath and went out to greet him.

It was a strange, awkward evening. We drank too much wine. I could feel Joe's excitement and nervousness about his move to LA. "It's pretty amazing how it's all coming together," he started. I had a hard time listening to or even looking at him. I jumped up from the table, grabbed the plates, marched them over to the sink, and turned on the water.

Of all the places in the world, he had to choose LA, where Julia was settling in for her second year at Occidental College. *What a fucking coward you are* was the opening line to a long list of accusations I wanted to let loose. I turned off the water and stood, wiping my hands slowly on the dishtowel, staring at the back of Joe's hard, impenetrable head. I left the kitchen before I said something I would regret.

Shutting the door to the master bedroom, I crawled into bed and turned off the lights. It was not an easy night. Shards of memories pierced the thin veil of sleep. Starting with the limp, rust-colored wedding dress, so many moments of keeping quiet, of keeping my feelings of shame and rage hidden, kept swirling in my head.

Toward dawn I finally fell asleep and entered a dream world of cars skidding backward and abandoned babies lost in basements. It was already nine o'clock when I dragged myself out of bed. There was no sound in the house. Joe was out in his office in the barn. I dressed quickly, grabbed my toothbrush, slipped out to my car, and left without saying goodbye. When it came down to it, I was just as big a coward as Joe.

We had yet to have The Conversation with Julia and Nick. We had alluded in phone calls to a few changes, long winters, Joe needing a break, but that's as far as we had had the courage to go. The phrase *trial separation* became our mantra, and maybe we did actually believe it.

My first stop was Twin Falls, where Nick had begun his post-college working life selling Monsanto cow hormones to dairies in Idaho. Ever since he announced that he had been recruited by Monsanto after college, it had taken all my diplomatic skills to navigate that horrifying development and all my confidence that he, my beloved son, would come to his senses and get back to who he really was. Those first few months he was a born-again corporate guy, driving a brand-new company car, making a ton of money. He was insufferable. On his last visit to the ranch, he had gotten angry when he saw the organic milk in the refrigerator. Thank goodness his infatuation with corporate living lasted only another ten months.

For those few days in Twin Falls, Nick was the perfect host. The first night he took me to dinner at the one Italian restaurant in town and ordered the wine. We spent the next day climbing up to the falls and shopping for plates to go with the beige leather couch and huge TV in his company condo. Everything was beige, even his new company Jeep Cherokee.

Monday morning, Nick went off to work, leaving me alone with his tabby cat, Bill. I cleaned up the breakfast dishes and put away the new plates. Then, thinking I could make myself useful by doing the laundry, I peeked into Nick's room, expecting to see his clothes in piles on the floor where he had always left them. But the room was insanely neat. There wasn't a pair of shorts or a T-shirt to be seen. I decided to check the laundry room, and there on top of the dryer were T-shirts, pants, and boxer shorts all neatly folded in a stack waiting to be put away. His dress shirts were hanging on hangers. At that moment, the enormity of all that had changed in our lives overwhelmed me. I barely made it to the couch before I broke down crying. Bill jumped into my lap and I held him tight, rocking back and forth, buffeted by waves of grief, crying for my son who was now living all on his own, for my daughter who was just starting off in the world, for my marriage that was over. Sitting on the beige leather couch in my son's condo in Twin Falls, I knew deep in my heart that everything I had been holding on to, everything I had tried so hard to keep together, our secure and safe life as a family, was gone and there was no turning back.

The Open Road

At our last breakfast, I opened up to Nick about the separation. "I don't know if we are going to be able to find a way back together," I confessed.

He listened, quietly, sat still for a moment, and then said, "Maybe that's for the best." I didn't press him for more. I just let it be.

Before I got in the car, he leaned over and wrapped his long arms around me. With his voice cracking, he said, "I love you, Mom. Take care of yourself."

"I love you too, sweetheart," I whispered, my heart beating like a drum. "Be good."

"I don't know about that." Nick smiled his wry smile.

"Okay, just try, for your mother," I said, laughing, and pulled myself up into the driver's seat. He picked up Bill and held him as I pulled out of the condo parking lot, holding back the tears, too many to let flow.

Out on the open road, I put in a cassette of Vince Gill and let myself sink into that particular melancholy only country and western music can truly express. Over miles of longing and heartache, wide-open spaces and rushing rivers, I let myself sink deep into the place where sorrow and joy mingle as Vince sang "When Love Finds You."

I had no idea what love was or if it had ever found me. The closest I could come was the heartache I had felt watching Nick recede in the rearview mirror: my child, a grown man, standing alone holding his cat in front of his condo. Out of the blue, a memory grabbed my heart of the moment at Casey Middle School when Nick and a friend, both on the football team, won the award for best cooking, and they stood up on the stage in aprons and waved wooden spoons around in a young-male-whooping-it-up victory cheer, and I couldn't stop smiling or crying, or both at the same time. I'm pretty sure that was love.

I had grown up on the cusp of the late fifties, early sixties. What I knew about love came from the lyrics of the music I listened to. My parents barely tolerated each other, so they were no help in understanding what it meant to love someone.

My education on love spanned the years from the Everly Brothers' "All I Have to Do Is Dream" in the fifties, to Etta James's "At Last" as I entered high school. That's what love was. Like a song. Love was what you wrote about in the diary you locked at night. Love was something you dreamed of as you pored over articles in *Seventeen* magazine about how to get the perfect boyfriend. Love was about getting the right man. That was the bottom line: in the world I grew up in, not having a man in your life equaled failing.

Years later, in 1966, I experienced a more vivid version of the same light-headed, stomach-churning, breathless feeling with Richard, my first real love. It happened early on, before we lived together, at a party in a crowded, smoky room filled with funky furniture near the university in Boulder. It was late and hot, the music was loud, and I was sitting flirting with a man on the couch, trying to get Richard, who was leaning against a wall, to pay attention to me. Suddenly he walked across the room and tore the arm off the record player. Everything went silent. He stood there looking at me for a beat, then said in a low voice that penetrated the still room, "I need you." After another long moment, Richard turned and walked to the door. In my memory, it is all happening in slow motion. He paused in the open door, turned around, looked at me, and said, "Are you coming?" Of course I was. How could I not have gone with him at that moment, loaded with so many fantasies fulfilled. If I hadn't gone I would have betrayed every lyric in every song I had ever heard.

Driving across Nevada, steeped in feelings of loss and anticipation and sorrow, I began singing "Ain't No Mountain High Enough" at the top of my lungs. Old fantasies die hard.

I was beginning to feel nervous about being in LA, Joe's new turf, and about having the conversation with Julia. When

I said something to her on the phone, she responded curtly, "We already had the conversation."

After we hung up I remembered that the evening after our breakfast breakup, Joe had blurted out to Julia, "Your mother and I are separating" at dinner. After he dropped the bomb, I had scrambled to repair the damage by saying we were just taking a break.

"I thought you guys got along," Julia had said. And that was the end of the conversation.

This time the conversation would include how she felt about her father joining her in LA at the beginning of her sophomore year. I had no idea what she would have to say about that, or how I should respond.

Leaving the Central Valley, everything rural began disappearing. I missed seeing trucks pulling horse trailers. I missed long stretches of empty road. When I hit the 110 and began to swoop down toward LA, my palms were clutching the steering wheel and I was sweating, even with the air-conditioning on, my eyes glued to the road.

As it turned out, my LA muscles kicked in quickly. Within a couple days, I was flying down freeways, cruising around with probation officers, and filming gang members in San Fernando. In the evenings, I helped Julia move into her new studio apartment near Occidental. On my last night, she cooked me dinner, and we talked. She was putting a good face on it, but I could tell she was sad, worried that she had lost her family, not sure how she felt about her father moving so close to her. "I mean, I love him and it'll be fun to have him nearby, but does he have any friends here?" Julia asked as we sat in her sweltering apartment.

"You know your dad: he's fine with having conversations with the guy at the oil change place. He doesn't really need close friends," I reassured her. "Are you worried he'll want to hang out with you and your friends?"

"A little," she answered and got up to clear the table.

"It'll be okay; just tell him to fuck off," I called out to her in the kitchen.

My nerves were clearly frayed. Too long away from home. It was time to get back to the ranch. It was time to begin my new life as a single woman.

PART 3

Second Year at the Ranch

Impermanence Rules

The first thing I noticed as I turned down the driveway was Joe's Jeep, parked in front of the house, suitcases strapped to the top with bungee cords, every inch inside crammed with stuff. Clearly, he was ready to get the hell out of the Wet Mountains.

The day was as clear and crisp as the first day we laid eyes on Lookout Valley Ranch, the aspen leaves brushed with gold, the sky a brilliant blue, horses grazing on the hillside. Then, it was all brand new for us both, Joe filled with excitement and I with anxiety. Now, three years later, Joe was leaving the ranch, and I was staying there, alone. There was no denying the truth that impermanence rules everything.

Joe was standing on the porch. "Looks like you're ready to leave," I said as I slid out of the driver's seat and stood facing him.

"I thought I could get as far as Flagstaff, if I left now," he answered. His face was red, and panic was coming out of every pore in his body.

Don't let the door hit you on the way out, popped into my head, but I settled for, "Don't let me stop you," which made just as little sense. I got back in my car and backed up to give him room to pull out. Joe stood on the porch watching me as I dragged my first bag out of the back seat. Bronco and Abby bounded over to greet me and began circling, herding me toward the house.

"Do you need help?" he asked.

"I can manage," I answered.

"Well, I'll be going then." I was standing at the bottom of the porch steps. He gave me a quick peck on the cheek as he went by, then got in the Jeep and backed up the driveway. I watched as he straightened up, turned onto Highway 165, and headed south, never looking back.

I dropped my bag on the porch and sat down on the glider. Bronco and Abby came and lay down at my feet. Rain meandered into the corral and was watching me. It felt like all of us—me, the animals, and the valley—were holding our breath, waiting to see where the wind would blow next. I had a knot in my throat, and my chest felt like it was about to explode.

A memory came to me from September, a year before. I was in Denver, sitting in the Armadillo restaurant with Dana Whitecalf, the young Lakota man who had been in my life since I first interviewed him ten years before for a video on violence. He was holding the menu, not looking at it. After a long moment of silence, he turned to me and said, "You remember how I always have a hard time in the fall?" I nodded. "That's how I feel right now."

"You mean sad?" I said.

"Yes," he whispered and began to cry.

It was right there in my chest. The sadness. Suddenly the dogs began barking. A truck had turned into the driveway. "Oh shit," I said, pulling myself back from the edge. It was Scott, the farrier, coming to put shoes on Rain for the winter. I waved at him and, taking a deep breath, walked over to the corral.

"Hey, boy, long time no see," I murmured to Rain as I haltered him, burying my face in his neck, breathing in his deep musky smell before leading him out of the corral.

Scott had brought out his tools and was setting up the hoof stand, which Rain promptly nudged over onto its side then pretended to examine a fly on the fence. Scott chuckled. "He's a real clown, this one."

"Did you know he's an Appaloosa? Solid bay, but Appaloosa nonetheless," I told him.

"That explains a lot." He smiled.

"Really? What else should I know about Appaloosas?" I asked.

"You need to go talk to the girls; they know all there is to know about Appaloosas. I shoe all their horses up there at Singing Acres." He lifted Rain's right front hoof onto the stand and began filing it down.

Since moving to the ranch, every time I drove by Singing Acres Appaloosa Ranch on my way to and from Westcliffe, I had the urge to stop. "But I'm a city girl," I told Scott. "I'm not used to just dropping in on people."

"You won't have any problem dropping in on Margaret and Clara," he said. "They are just about the kindest people you ever want to meet." He set the right hoof down and stood up straight. "People talk. Say they're that way. But I don't give a damn. Kind is more important to me than any of that nonsense." It was the longest sentence I had ever heard him utter. He reached down for Rain's left hoof. I knew enough not to comment. Rain stood calmly between us, his leg extended with his hoof resting on the iron stand, like a Mafia don getting a manicure.

"I'll make us some coffee," I said and went to the house.

For the rest of the hour, as Scott moved slowly around Rain, filing and banging the shoes into the right shape and pounding the nails into his hooves, I leaned against the corral and we chitchatted about this and that, the price of chuck roast at Jennings Grocery, how many times he had been kicked by one of his clients. There was something soothing about the slow, methodical pace, the sound of the hammer, the nickering of Chaz and Peanuts and Red in the corral, the simple back and forth of conversation. Out of the blue I blurted out, "Joe moved to LA—he just left. I'll be wintering here alone. Kind of like Treva Jones." Scott pounded in the last couple of nails then straightened up and looked at me.

"That can't be all bad," he said.

Right there he cut through any thought I might have had of feeling sorry for myself, and I felt a hint of Angelica's and Treva's brave-woman-alone-in-the-wilderness strength rising up in me. Riding that wave, it took no time at all to unload the car. I put things away, moved furniture around, claiming each room for myself, then cooked myself a hamburger, washed down with a couple of Coors Lights. By nighttime I was wiped out, and reality was beginning to seep in. The house was very empty. There was no one to guilt trip into doing the dishes. Even the dogs were agitated. I was feeling as shaky and raw as a newborn chick. I couldn't imagine how Angelica felt the moment the reality hit her that Nello was gone. She had no TV to turn on, no private line on the telephone, no computer to play endless games of free cell. Just two small children and a lot of sorrow. I opened her book and found the chapter on her first year after Nello's death:

The evenings were lonely without Nello. There could be no healing a bruised heart, and I realized that I either had to flee life or live it on a very busy schedule. I chose the latter. Abandoning the ranch would have left me the same person, with nothing that I felt I was capable of doing. It would have been running away and removing all reminders of my old life. I was not yet ready for that.

I thought it would be some kind of comfort to read from Angelica's book, but it only made me more unsettled. And sadder. There was nothing but ads and car chases on TV. I opened my computer to check email. There was one from Berna. As was becoming more and more frequent in our email exchanges, she was in sync with what I was going through.

Dear Vicki,

I think you must be back at the ranch and now facing the painful reality of your new life there by yourself.

Today, I was reading in the *Boston Globe* about the Kosovar refugee camps in Macedonia and a picture of a child with his mouth wide open, his face contorted with pain, his outstretched hand reaching as he is being pulled away reminded me of the wrenching pain I felt when my father was taken from us. When we came back to the ranch without him, the loss was almost impossible to bear. My mother was determined to assure security for her two daughters in the ranch-home they had painstakingly established. She warded off debtors, cold, and hunger by piecing together a series of business ventures. She bought a sawmill, leased grazing rights for a herd of cattle, worked as an agricultural agent for the county, and taught school in a trailer placed on her property. She held it together alone as a farmer, homemaker, and mother.

I know these next weeks and months will be hard. I will be there in October to visit. Meanwhile, take care and keep writing.

Luv, Berna

As I turned off the computer, I could feel my stomach settling. I was breathing easier, my mind no longer spinning. If Angelica could manage living at the ranch with infinitely more challenges, then so could I.

I left the light on over the kitchen table—I wasn't quite ready for total dark yet—and went to brush my teeth. Bronco and Abby were settled on the king-sized bed when I crawled in, nudging just enough space between them to curl up. Moonlight was shining in a long path across the quilt. Quiet settled over us, the light sound of dogs snoring eased my mind, and I drifted off to sleep.

First Steps

In the days after Joe left, everything felt upside down. I started to cry when I found burnt toast forgotten in the toaster from the day before; I couldn't remember if I had brushed my teeth minutes after doing it. I couldn't focus on anything. I would start to vacuum and find myself outside smoking a cigarette, the vacuum cleaner still running. I could tell that friends in Boulder were worried about me in the middle of nowhere by myself. I was a little worried myself. One weekend my friend Helen came for a visit. "I can't figure out who I am anymore,"

I said to her. It was Saturday afternoon, and Helen was in the kitchen sautéing chunks of chuck steak for beef barley soup. I was lying on the couch, drinking beer and watching the Colorado Buffaloes being pummeled by the Nebraska Cornhuskers, feeling twinges of guilt at not helping. "Right now," Helen answered, standing in the doorway of the kitchen wearing an apron and holding a wooden spoon. "Right now, that's who you are."

"Really?" I asked.

Helen smiled and nodded. "That's right, my friend. And I am being exactly who I am," she added and went back to the kitchen. I lay there for a moment, letting the truth of it sink in, and then the Buffs quarterback threw a touchdown and I started to cheer, and I remembered why I loved watching football. Nothing remained the same; reality could shift on a dime, from winning to losing and back again, over and over.

One morning I was jolted awake from a dream of a man's hand, delicately shaped but firm, reaching out to me in a gesture I couldn't recognize. Just before I opened my eyes, I heard him say, "*It's okay. Take all the time you need. I'm here.*" Sitting up in bed, I felt myself wanting to cry, but all I could manage was dry, gasping tears. I hated my useless, shriveled-up tears. I hated Joe. I hated the faceless man in my dream wanting to help me. I didn't need his fucking help. As I began to calm down, I had an image of my Grandma Vic—a difficult, imperious, unforgiving woman. I had come to pack up her few possessions in the room she lived in at her daughter, my mother's, house and move her to a nursing home while my mother was in long-term rehab after botched brain surgery. Grandma Vic was sitting on the edge of her sleigh bed, too high for her feet to touch the ground, her face set in an expression of angry resignation. I sat down next to her. Touched by a wave of sorrow, I reached out to put my arm around her. Without a moment's hesitation, she pushed my hand away with an abrupt, violent shrug of her shoulder. Her habit of automatically shrugging off any help, any love, any sympathy never wavered her whole life.

Six years later, sitting alone in my bed with Bronco and Abby standing by watching me with worried expressions on their sweet faces, I realized that I carried my grandmother's genes; her blood coursed through my veins. That was my lineage. I too was trapped in habits of minimizing, sending people away, dismissing, and rejecting help. I had even turned down Joe's half-hearted offer to help me unload my car.

As the light began to turn the room an eerie gray, I had no idea what to do next. All I wanted was to crawl back under the covers, to be taken care of, fed hot milk and honey, soothed. All I wanted was to be loved. And all I did was push people away. In that moment, it felt like a lack of generosity—another of the virtues Joe and I had vowed to practice at our wedding— not to allow anyone to help. By then it was fully light outside. The dogs had given up and left the room. The sun was shining through the gauze curtains, making boxes of flickering light patterns on the quilt. I checked the clock. It was almost nine o'clock. "Oh shit," I said out loud. Dee was coming at nine to ride. I jumped out of bed and pulled on my jeans.

"You're perching," Dee commented, riding behind me as we traveled up the trail into the canyon on Eustace's place.

"I'm trying to settle. Really, I am," I said. Dee had been harping at me about perching for months.

"Horses are herd animals," she told me, "always ready to bolt if they don't feel secure."

"You know me," I told her. "Just like a horse, always ready to bolt."

"Stop thinking so much," Dee said as she passed me and took the lead. Gradually, I could feel the silence in the canyon soften my strung-out nerves. An eagle rose out of a tree and flew off. Breathing in the piney, earthy scent, I tried not to think about bears.

The trail widened and we rode side by side. "I'm done too," Dee blurted out.

"Done?" I asked.

"I can't do this relationship thing anymore. I can't stand how he does nothing while I work my ass off. He's a lazy son of a bitch. And disrespectful, too."

"Have you told him?" I asked.

She nodded. "Yep, I told him to move out. I'm paying the mortgage."

"What did he say?"

"He threw a beer bottle at me." Dee laughed her husky laugh. "Lucky for me he has lousy aim. Just like everything else he tries to do. I sure know how to pick 'em." I started laughing, and pretty soon we were both doubled over.

"You've got nothing on me, sweetheart," I said, gulping for air. "One month after I got together with Joe, he took off from Thanksgiving dinner at my place with a woman named Susan. He'd already been married to two Susans. He left his car parked in front of my house for two days. And I still married him."

"Really?" Dee slowed down and dropped the reins for Chaz to nibble on the last of the green grass by the creek. I followed her lead.

"Yep," I answered.

"You're right," she said. "You do take the fucking cake, girl."

We got off the horses and let them graze while we smoked. It felt good just to sit there. No therapeutic agenda. No need to say anything meaningful. "How about we have some fun Saturday night," Dee said, stomping her Marlboro butt into the ground. "Let's go to Pueblo to the State Fair. We could bring along that crazy German girl."

"You mean Jasmine," I said, pronouncing her name in the European way.

"Whatever," Dee snorted. "She's about ready to dump her man too. She wants to go to Montana and be a cowgirl." We mounted up and started back down the trail. As we reached the valley, we saw Chum Haynes' cows spread out across it.

"I don't know why she has to go to Montana; we can be cowgirls right here," I said, looking over at Dee and nodding toward the cows grazing near us.

"Hell yes." She laughed, and we took off at a fast trot toward them, splitting up as we got closer, and in the next instant they were moving away from us, and we were circling around them. Then the whole herd was on the move, and we were hooting and hollering, waving our hats, riding back and forth behind them. We slowed down as we neared the house, and the cows settled and began grazing the pasture on the other side of the barn. "Doesn't get a whole lot better than this," Dee said as we rode back to the corral.

"I am most definitely ready to have some shit-kicking fun with the rest of you cowgirls Saturday night," I said.

The State Fair was everything it was cracked up to be. The three of us were in full cowgirl gear, straw Stetsons on our heads, my jeans not as tight as Dee's and Jasmine's. It was blistering hot. We stopped at the concession stand and bought Bud Lights. Across the way was a tent with a sign advertising a "World Famous Hypnotist Show." We went in. The space was huge, packed with people. A slight, dark-haired man with a seventies mullet had just begun his show. We sat down on folding chairs and watched as he selected a random collection of volunteers and brought them up on the stage. There were eight of them—men and women, middle-aged housewives, lanky cowboys, teenagers wearing Metallica T-shirts. The show began. He seemed to be just talking gently to them, but soon he had all eight of them dancing wildly around, doing Cher imitations, then sweating in 120-degree temperatures, and shaking with cold at forty below. The audience, we three included, were laughing hysterically. The best moment was when he told them they were baby chicks, just hatching. All eight of them started writhing in their chairs, elbows thrusting and necks craning, and then, at his command, they were on their feet doing a chicken dance in a circle around the stage while we all cheered.

After the show, we spoke with a middle-aged woman who we had just seen shaking her rather substantial booty in front of two hundred people. She told us she couldn't remember a thing—it was all like being underwater. She was buying the video of her performance. "I hope there isn't anything too embarrassing on it," she said.

"There is," we assured her, "but it's okay. You were great."

There was something so simple and alive just being there. All the angst, trying to do things right, and all the hoops I had been putting myself through for as long as I could remember, dissolved, and I was there with two friends, all of us escaping fucked-up marriages and having a good time on a Saturday night at the Colorado State Fair.

In and Out of Prison

The sun had not yet risen when I climbed the stairs to my attic meditation room one morning late in September. I lit the candles, placed my tea on the carpet next to me, and settled onto my cushion. Right away, my mind was off and running, following a stream of random thoughts: Perching, *such a strange, unsettling word. A perch is for a bird, always ready to take flight. Trungpa Rinpoche would admonish us to not perch on our cushion, no perching when meditating. Always perching, my whole life, always ready to bolt, bail, hurl myself over the edge. Too dangerous to settle anywhere and be yanked away, forced to leave.*

Okay, enough already, take a deep breath, settle your body on the cushion, bring your mind into your body. It helped sometimes to imagine I was instructing the prison group in a guided meditation. It was Wednesday, and later that morning I would be heading down to see them. It had been three weeks. A lot had happened in my world. I had no idea what had been happening in theirs while I was gone. Maybe no one would turn up. I gulped some tea and started again. "Breathe in and out, gap, in again, and out."

As it turned out, I didn't need to worry. All the men were there—Matt, Kenny, Luis, and Steve. There was even a new guy, Ahmed, a Pakistani American who had just transitioned from medium security to the Camp. He was going up for parole soon and thought the Buddhist group might be a way to become more peaceful. "Not sure about that," Matt told him. "It can get pretty scary here, a lot of demons roaming." We had talked about demons in one of our classes, about how we get riled up and think we have to fight off every demon we encounter—our addictions, our fears, the memories of abuses we endured and the ones we perpetrated. I wasn't sure Ahmed was ready for demons yet, so I suggested Matt read our slogan of the day.

Taking the book from me he read, "Change your attitude and relax as it is." He looked up. "I haven't a clue what that means," he said. No one jumped in, so I gave it a go.

"What is the change we talked about with our demons, our anger and resentments, our addictions?"

"To try to make friends with them, not push them away," Matt answered.

"That's a big attitude change, right?" I said, and he nodded, still not quite with me. "Like not suspending the kid who is making trouble in class, figuring out what he needs instead."

"That was me. I couldn't read so I had to make trouble," Kenny added.

"Right." I nodded.

"Okay, but what about 'relaxing as it is.' What the hell does that mean?" Matt went on.

"Let it be," Steve said. "Don't try too hard."

"That's it," I said, smiling at them all. "Don't make a big deal out of changing your attitude. Just relax with it. Anybody else have something to say?"

After a long moment, Ahmed cleared his throat and started talking quietly, "I was two years in solitary, no windows, no room to turn around, one hour outside, cement walls fifteen feet high. Man, I was seriously pissed for the first year. It was hell. Then one day, it dawned on me something had to change. I wasn't going to make it. And something burst open. My mind cleared. And there were all these memories I thought

I had lost: People, the street I was born on. Smells of my mother's cooking. It was all there. Like a movie. I just needed to change something in me so I could see it." The other men were listening intently, not fidgeting. "It helped somehow." Ahmed stopped, suddenly self-conscious. The room had taken on a pensive, reflective feel.

After a moment, Matt turned to Ahmed and said, "Man, that was a huge attitude change. Fucking huge." The rest of the men were all nodding in agreement.

Ahmed smiled and said, "I couldn't have made it without something changing."

The hour was up, and we ended with a bow, a practice I had introduced to begin and end each of our sessions. The men all filed out of the room, and I followed.

Over the months we had been meeting, something open and supportive had developed in the group. It was hard for me to keep in mind the instructions we were given at the training: "These men are all predators. They just want to mess with you." My experience was that they were just people, people who had messed up, who were struggling with their regrets, their anger, their sorrow. All things I had no trouble relating to. We were all trying to change our attitudes and relax, somehow.

I took the back road from Wetmore up to the ranch. The scrub oak was turning red, the cottonwoods along the side of the road were pale yellow. The aspen leaves had all fallen. The forecast called for snow by the end of the week. I could start worrying about the storm that was on its way or just enjoy the moment I was in, driving up the road, my heart open and relaxed. Out of the blue, I found myself singing the words from Walt Whitman's "Leaves of Grass," that my friend Joe

Vest had, in his last few years, put to music as a requiem for people living and dying with AIDS.

> Afoot and light-hearted I take to the open road,
> Healthy, free, the world before me,
> The long brown path before me leading
>   wherever I choose.

The road curved, following Hardscrabble Creek past the sign saying we were leaving the San Isabel National Forest and entering the ranch land.

> Henceforth I ask not good fortune, I myself am
>   good fortune,
> Henceforth I whimper no more, postpone no more,
>   need nothing,
> Strong and content, I travel the open road.

As I pulled up in front of the house, Bronco and Abby jumped up from their lookout on the porch and ran over to greet me. Rain thrust his head over the corral gate and whinnied. Kitty Boy bounded over the grass and rubbed his body along my leg. I was home.

Berna's Visit

I was plumping up the pillows in the guest room when I heard a car pulling up. Berna was arriving. I went out to the porch to greet her. It had been a year since we first met. She was a stranger then, and now she felt like a sister.

As she climbed out of the car, I was struck by how small she was, even smaller than I remembered. There was a gaunt quality I didn't remember either. "You look great," were the first words out of her mouth, preempting any comment I might make. I had become leaner, and my hair was longer and grayer. I wore it in a ponytail with thick bangs, and more wrinkles had appeared around my mouth.

"It's so great to see you here," I said as I picked up her small bag and led us into the kitchen.

"I always feel a little teary when I see the old cookstove," she said as I settled her down at the kitchen table with a cup of tea. "Have you read the story in my mother's book of how I lost my eye?" she asked. I shook my head. "A live round somehow ended up in the ash bucket, and it went off as I was picking it up to empty it," she said matter-of-factly. "It was after my father died. I must have been eight or so."

"So, that's a real glass eye?" I asked, and she nodded, coughing slightly and taking a sip of tea.

I loved Berna's ability to face whatever she encountered without feeling sorry for herself. I was learning a lot from her. There was so much I could ask her, but I could tell she was tired, so I ushered her into the guest room to rest.

I had made dinner, a simple stew, while Berna rested. "Oh my, this looks delicious," she said as she laid her napkin on her lap and surveyed the meal. I opened a bottle of red wine and poured us each a glass.

"Next summer, we'll wash it down with dandelion wine," I joked. We talked late into the evening, sitting at the table, flickering candlelight reflected in the dark window. As time went on, our conversation got deeper and darker. "You know, there is a phrase in a chant I do every morning that sums up impermanence in a pretty stark, powerful way," I said.

"Can you recite it?" Berna asked.

"It goes: Death is real/ it comes without warning/ this body will be a corpse." I took a sip of wine. I felt a little shaky, holding off an unknown sorrow. Berna was nodding, her mind far away.

"My sister Laverna was so young, she didn't understand why Father wasn't at the table with us that first night we got back from the funeral," she said. "For Mother, her husband's death was all too real. She worked herself to the bone, determined to stay here."

I could feel there was something she was holding inside. There was more to the story than the courageous woman alone with her two daughters battling the elements to make a life on the frontier. I had read in Angelica's book about times when she would get stuck in blizzards in her Model T, and the girls would have to be taken care of by neighbors.

"I remember one story in Angelica's book about you and Laverna being stuck for days at a neighbor's—the Braggs, I think—and you got scared when Charlie had to pull out his rotting tooth with a pair of pliers."

I felt something shift and her face take on a haunted quality. "It was a long time at the Braggs. The tooth pulling wasn't the scariest thing that happened in that time."

I wanted to hear more, but I could tell that she didn't want to travel any further down that road. It was time to lighten things up. "Did I write you about the family of skunks that moved in under the hot tub?" I began.

"No. Tell me," Berna said, happy to change the subject.

"I had no idea what to do, so my neighbor, Otis, came over, and he said just to let Bronco move in with them."

"Really? Did it work?" Berna asked.

I nodded. "Yep. I let Bronco loose and the skunks were gone the next day. Of course, it took three baths in industrial-size cans of tomatoes to get the stink off Bronco." We were both laughing by then.

A moment later, Berna's laughter turned into a coughing fit. I got her a glass of water. I could tell she was tired.

"Time for bed," I said and started to clear the table.

"Let me help," Berna said.

"No, no, no," I stopped her. "You've had a long day." She didn't resist, which was not like her.

The next day we wandered slowly around the land, talking about our writing. "We could put our essays together in a book," I said. "And you could design it, create the binding and everything." I had seen some of the books Berna created, hand bound with exquisite covers of wildflowers and old photographs.

"I'd love that," she said.

The last evening, we talked about our present-day lives. About our marriages and children. No matter what topic we landed on, there was a feeling of what Trungpa Rinpoche had called "a genuine heart of sadness" woven through them. Every story had a tinge of loss to it—the loss of my marriage, the loss of her father, the ranch. We were both touching places in our hearts that were raw and vulnerable.

"Now I feel like I am losing my children. They have their own lives I am not part of anymore," I said.

Berna was silent for a moment, and when I looked over, she was crying. "I am losing my son too." She looked up at me. "Not like that, but to drug addiction. I keep hoping he'll come back. But I don't think that's likely." Her hands were cradled in her lap. I wanted to reach out, but she was looking down, not yet ready for comfort. "I finally really understand how sadness can take over your life," she said, looking up at me again. I held her gaze and she continued, "And it helps to reach out. It helps with the pain." She unclasped her hands, and we reached out at the same time and sat together holding hands, not speaking.

The next afternoon, as she was getting ready to leave, I finally got up the guts to ask about the cough that had been plaguing her the whole time she was there. She had all the kindness and good cheer she had had the last time she visited, but her stamina was nowhere near what it had been. Berna was a marathon runner in her sixties with the stamina of a thirty-year-old. She seemed uncharacteristically tired. "I've had it for a while now," she said when I asked. "I've never been a smoker, so it seems unlikely that it's anything like that." She was avoiding the C-word.

"Maybe just an old case of pneumonia or something you didn't get over," I said, and she nodded.

"They'll do some tests when I get back. I didn't want anything to get in the way of my visit." There was a lot that was unspoken in that last sentence. I stopped the questioning and gave her a big hug. She was quivering slightly, like a sparrow that had fallen out of its nest.

"I am so happy nothing got in the way. I have loved every minute of you being here," I said. We stood back and looked in each other's eyes.

"Until we meet again," she said.

"Don't do anything I wouldn't do," I said, and she smiled broadly.

"Unlikely," she said, and climbed in the car before both of us started crying. At the last minute, she rolled down her window and said, "I'm writing about that time at the Braggs. I've been working on it for a while. I'll send it to you."

I had held off smoking for the three days of Berna's visit. As I watched her drive away, all I could think of was how much I wanted a cigarette. I grabbed my wallet and took off for Westcliffe.

I bought a pack at the Conoco, filled up with gas, and turned back toward home. I lit up and cracked the window open. The sun was low in the sky, its rays stretching across the Wet Mountain Valley. Magic hour.

Swooping down the hill to the turnoff to Highway 165, I was listening to Martina McBride on the radio singing a song about broken wings when I came up behind a school bus downshifting on the steep grade. I slowed down. The back window of the bus was crammed with sports bags piled up around an orange water cooler; the seats were filled with boys with baseball hats turned backward. Out of the blue, the thought came to me that it was the Custer County Bobcats headed to Rye for a Friday evening game, and without warning, I burst into tears. It was fall, high school football season, and I knew I would never again see my son play in a high school football game. In the next moment, I had the thought that Berna's son might die at any moment with a needle in his arm.

Life, as the Buddha discovered 2,500 years ago, is suffering, and the reason is simple: there is nothing in this life that we can hang on to forever. No security, no happy ending, no fantasy. I was beginning to see that the best way to navigate this life of constant change is not by trying to steer the ship where you want it to go, but by trusting your genuine heart of sadness to guide you through the stormy waves. It was a tall order, but I knew I had to try.

Martina was still singing, "And with a broken wing, she still sings. She keeps an eye on the sky." I joined in, and together we sang our hearts out traveling slowly behind the school bus down the road. "With a broken wing, she carries her dreams and you ought to see her fly."

Not for the Faint of Heart

Winter came early that year with a fierce and unrelenting blizzard that blanketed the valley for four days and stacked up four feet of snow against the house. It arrived halfway into September while I was filming in Denver, and I missed it. I had just rented the old cabin to a woman who was planning on spending the winter at Lookout Valley Ranch on a solitary meditation retreat. She was there alone, and the storm was so sudden and so relentless that she had been trapped in the main house for three days.

When I arrived home, the sun had turned the driveway into a river and the corral into a large mud puddle. As I parked my car, I saw the cabin door was open, and the renter was hauling all her belongings out to a friend's truck. She could barely hold still long enough to say "hello" and "I'm leaving."

After the storm, everything settled back into full-on Indian summer. But the storm gods had worked their magic at just the right moment. I had begun questioning whether I wanted to have someone else living on the place full time, someone who might need taking care of. I breathed a huge sigh of relief when I saw the truck with the last candidate pull out of the driveway. I was beginning to feel how much I needed to be alone to understand what I was feeling, to be able to relax, to loosen the vice grip of trying to attend to everyone else. I needed time by myself to unravel. The good news was that living on a ranch in the Wet Mountains, it took some effort to connect with people.

Otis and Johanna were my closest neighbors, and they were only there on weekends. That suited me just fine. By the weekend, I was ready for some company. I loved sitting in their living room amphitheater watching the Broncos and drinking beer. Or if the spirit moved me, I would cook up some pasta and invite them over. We could keep up a free-flowing conversation for hours. Sometimes Otis would tell stories of his years working in the steel mill. Hot, grueling work, thirty-two hours straight, week after week, coming home and sleeping and going back to work, entire childhoods of his son and daughter missed. He had retired on disability five years before and wore a back brace, but I never heard him complain about the toll it had taken on his body. Meanwhile, I saw every bump in the road of my emotions as a major earthquake, daily monitoring my intake of St. John's wort and vitamin B and fish oil to try to keep my system running smoothly. I couldn't imagine living with the level of stress and exhaustion that had been Otis's natural habitat.

The weekend after the big storm, I asked Otis and Johanna over for a dinner of burgers and potato salad. As I dished out the food, Johanna launched into politics, her favorite topic. A lifelong Democrat, she was thrilled to have Bill Clinton take over from George H. W. Bush. "I'd rather have a president like John Kennedy who can't keep it in his pants than a sanctimonious warmonger like Bush," she pronounced. Otis sat, settled, filling up the wooden kitchen chair, beaming at everything she said.

When I told them about the renter bolting, he commented, "Life up here ain't for the faint of heart." I couldn't tell if he was including Joe in that observation, but I felt a tinge of satisfaction at being the one who hadn't bolted.

Looking in any direction, it was impossible to avoid the truth that life in the Wet Mountains was not for the faint of heart. Every story I heard was another confirmation. Dee had started working as a dog catcher in the foothills around Canon City. She told me stories of encampments of survivalist families, with ragged children, no more than four or five, roaming shoeless in the trees and packs of pit bulls chained to stakes around the camp. She would get a haunted look in her eyes as she described the rescue scenes, standoffs with armed crazies ranting as the police handcuffed them while she loaded the horses, goats, dogs, and cats into trailers and drove them to the pound.

One day, Jasmine stopped by with her daughter, Jenny, and her friend, a tiny, wispy blonde girl with legs so skinny I could have circled each one with my hand. I thought she was four, but Jasmine told me she was eight. Her name was Rebecca. "Her mom is not doing well," Jasmine told me. "She needed a break."

"Not doing well how?" I asked. The story was long and convoluted, but the gist of it was that she had fibrous cysts in her uterus and no money for treatment, which she wouldn't have agreed to anyway because she didn't believe in doctors. "God is my doctor and my insurance," she told Jasmine.

Rebecca barely spoke. She flinched when I accidently dropped a cup on the floor. But by the end of the afternoon, she and Jenny were lying on their bellies in the attic drawing pictures of horses on large sheets of paper. When they left, I invited her back, and the next time Jasmine came to ride, Rebecca and Jenny came too. That visit, she curled up next to me on the glider, and we read *Where the Wild Things Are*, a favorite from my kids' childhoods. She told me she had no books at home. Then, a week later, when Jasmine and Jenny came by, she wasn't with them. "Rebecca couldn't come?" I asked.

Jasmine shook her head. "She can't come anymore," she said. "She's not allowed." We were standing out by the corral, watching Jenny feed apples to the horses. "I don't know what got her mom mad," Jasmine continued. "She yelled at me that she didn't want Rebecca to go to the house of a Satanist anymore."

I stared at her. None of it made any sense. "A Satanist? Because of *Where the Wild Things Are*?" I asked.

Jasmine shrugged. "For her, that's anyone she doesn't agree with," she said, and handed me a rolled-up piece of paper. "It's from Rebecca, poor little munchkin."

After they left, I sat down on the glider, unfurled the paper, and read the words scrawled on the top of the page: "The mos fun I am havin tis sumer is wit my fren at miz vici's hose. i luv it here."

The rest of the page was filled with a drawing of a pale yellow house, and standing in front, a tall woman with wild hair wearing jeans and a shirt with many different colored lines, flanked by a big brown horse and two gray-speckled dogs. In the bottom corner, almost falling off the page, was a tiny child with wispy yellow hair, wearing a yellow polka-dot dress.

I put the paper down next to me on the glider, my heart aching. Why did I feel such a strange kinship with this child? I had been a thin, blonde, sad child, but I was never smacked, or deprived of books, and even though my parents may not have been loving, they weren't crazy.

It felt like I was living in an incomprehensible world. A world of opinions I would never understand. A world where it was easy to see how people, pushed to the edge, made bad choices and got trapped in narrow, crazy views.

Then, as if there weren't enough sorrow for one day, that evening an email arrived from Berna. It had been over a week since her visit to the doctor to check on her cough. The message was short. It was just what I had been hoping to high heaven it wouldn't be.

Dear Vicki

Well, the news was not good. I wasn't really expecting it to be. But for someone who has never smoked, it was hard to fathom hearing I have quite advanced lung cancer. I am proceeding with a treatment plan which looks ominous, but with a team of very sensitive and caring physicians, nutritionists, nurses, etc., etc. I feel hopeful and as good physically as I have in the past several months—which today is quite good. I must admit I haven't done much serious writing since all this came up except for a factual journal. But I am still working on the Charlie Bragg piece. Will be in touch.

Luv, Berna

As I crawled under the covers that night, I felt I was carrying a weight of unfathomable sorrow—for Berna, for Rebecca, for the world of confusion and fear in which I was living. It was a long, sleepless night.

The next morning, fog was pouring up the canyon and traveling through the valley like a snake. Then the rain started. Sheets of rain blurred the view from my office window. The wind whistled around the house. I sat in the dim corner of my office, my mind filled with thoughts of Berna. I opened her email and read it again. Her message had that unadorned style I had come to know in her letters. She didn't want to concern me. But her heart shone through, and I could sense her worry. I wrote her a short encouraging note and decided I wanted to follow up with a real card, which meant driving to Westcliffe.

I felt like I was moving in slow motion, an exaggerated pantomime of mindfulness—turning off the computer, straightening the pen next to it, pushing my chair back, standing up. The dogs barking wildly put an end to the strange charade.

A truck had pulled up outside. I could see it was the San Isabel Electric meter reader come for his annual visit, which meant another big bill was about to land on me. The meter reader was an older man, short and lean, wearing a well-worn cowboy hat and boots. He was standing by the pole staring at the meter when I came out. "Howdy, ma'am," he said. I nodded and smiled, steeling myself for the bad news. "Have you been living here this past year, full time?" he asked.

"Yes."

"Well then, the meter must have broken down some time ago. It's telling me you used a lot less power this year than last year."

"What am I supposed to do about it?" I asked. I was working up a head of steam about how it wasn't my fault the meter didn't work, when the man said, "As far as I'm concerned, nobody at the head office needs to know you were living here full time." He smiled and looked me in the eye. "You have a good day, now."

"Thank you," I said, pulling myself together and smiling back. "You just made my day." And I meant it.

All the knots of sorrow for Berna and Rebecca and the righteous indignation at the San Isabel Electric and the rest of the uncaring world evaporated in an instant. The rain had stopped. I grabbed my keys, told the dogs to take care of the place, and took off for Westcliffe.

As I drove slowly down Main Street, it was easy to tell that summer was over. There were parking spots everywhere. At Jennings Market, the woman at the cash register didn't bother asking if I wanted paper or plastic. It felt good that she recognized me as a local and loaded up my few supplies in a plastic bag.

I found a card at the corner store and wrote a short message to Berna. After dropping it at the post office, I couldn't think of anything more to do so I headed home.

Driving out of town, I felt my whole being as wide open as the valley I was driving through. One side of the vast sky was gray, with lightning. The other a brilliant blue. The sadness had washed through me, and there was nothing on my mind. It felt good.

Winding down the canyon, I could see Singing Acres Ranch coming up on my left. An old truck was parked in front of the log house and a short, stocky, middle-aged woman with hair that looked like she had taken pruning shears to it was unloading boxes from the back. Without thinking, I pulled in behind her, got out, and introduced myself. "Come on in," she said in a gruff but not unfriendly manner. "I'm Margaret."

The house was small and dark, the living room filled with old leather armchairs and books and antlers. The place smelled of wood smoke. Margaret dropped the box she was carrying onto the floor and ushered me into the kitchen area. Chunks of raw meat were stacked on a wooden table next to a large meat grinder. "Shot him last week," Margaret said, nodding at the meat. "I'm making ground elk for the winter. Have you ever had an elk burger?"

"I'm afraid not," I said.

"Good and good for you," she said and poured us each a cup of thick black coffee from a percolator sitting on the cookstove. Nodding at a chair next to the table, she told me to have a seat and said she had to keep going, but I was welcome to stay. I sat down.

We talked for an hour or more as Margaret cranked the handle on the grinder churning out ground elk meat. She told me how she and Clara had met working as counselors at a Girl Scout Camp in 1958. "Clara's the real horsewoman—she grew up in a family of Kansas ranchers. I came from Oakland." She laughed. Over the next few years, working as schoolteachers in Kansas, they dreamed up the idea of buying a ranch in Colorado and breeding Appaloosa horses. Listening to Margaret tell the story of how they made this dream happen, two women in 1965 with very little money, made our journey to Lookout Valley seem like a stroll down the Champs-Élysées.

"How did you even come up with the idea, much less make it happen? I bet there were a few men along the way who thought you couldn't do it."

Margaret chuckled and nodded. "We got asked a lot of questions . . . there was a lot of *skepticism*, would be the polite way to say it. People asked why the hell would we do such a thing. And we would always say: 'Because we wanted to.'"

I couldn't stop smiling at the stories, the place, the piles of elk meat, the ease of being with Margaret. There was so much I wanted to know, so many questions about how they made it work, but the light was fading and I didn't want to overstay my welcome. "Come back anytime," Margaret said as she stood in her doorway and waved goodbye. Her last words were, "You're going to do just fine down there." I coasted on those words all the way home.

It had been a couple of long and full days. I needed time alone to let it all sink in. I grabbed a beer and went to the back-yard. Dropping my jeans and shirt on the ground, I climbed into the hot tub and, sinking into the warm bubbling water, I lay back, held by the tree-covered hills surrounding me and the pale gray sky above slowly settling into darkness.

Stillpoint

The nights were getting colder. It was time to begin prepar-ing for winter. Our first year, Joe had cut all the firewood and attached the snowplow to the truck. I remembered him sweat-ing and cursing, kicking the plow until it finally connected. I was getting pretty good at splitting wood, but I had no idea how I was going to manage attaching the plow, much less plowing the uphill driveway. I could feel the anxiety rising at the thought of having to deal with everything by myself. So far, the only jobs I had taken on that had been Joe's terrain were changing the water in the hot tub and cranking up the seated lawn mower and riding it around the yard.

I decided to tackle something easy first, so I pulled out the winter duvet from the closet and lay it on the bed. I was getting ready to lie down when the phone rang.

"It's Leon," a man's voice said when I answered. No "hello" or "hi"; just a pronouncement. I felt a flutter in my chest as I heard his voice. Leon was a Native American man from South Dakota I had met through a film project some years before. I had reconnected with him when I learned he was working with Native American gang members and I was looking for consultants for my gang video. The winter before, he had spent a couple of days with us at the ranch talking with me about the project. He was my age, with a rough complexion, a barrel chest, skinny legs, and a long black ponytail streaked with gray. He was not a handsome man, but he was magnetizing and complicated and passionate about his culture.

"There is a kid I know, names Augie, getting in trouble on the res, and I need to get him out of there. I thought I'd bring him down to your place," Leon said and then went quiet. There was no point in backtracking to add any "hi, how are you" small talk to the conversation.

"When were you thinking?"

"Tomorrow," he answered.

I loved the fluid sense of time I had encountered among the Native Americans I had met over the years on film projects: no dithering, scheduling, looking at calendars, or unnecessary planning.

Leon and I talked a few more minutes. He wanted to know if there was any work he and Augie could do around the place—building or fixing anything. It would be good for the kid to do something physical, he told me. "Too many Cheetos and video games."

"I'll think about it," I said.

I spent the next couple hours getting the cabin ready for Leon and Augie, all the while trying to figure out some project for them to tackle and coming up with nothing. Joe had spent the summer fixing everything around the place. There was nothing left that needed doing, and there was no money to pay them to do something that didn't need doing.

Finished, I sat down on the porch and lit a cigarette. The evening sky was a clear, pale blue with a hint of pink along the ridge. I settled into the space filled with the familiar sounds of the murmuring creek, the horses blowing contentedly in the corral, and, every now and then, the screech of an owl. I loved that moment at the end of the day when I would sit on the glider and smoke my daily American Spirit, dusk gathering around me, everything slowing down. For those few minutes, all would be right with the world.

"I got it," I suddenly burst out as I took my last puff. "Stillpoint. They could work at Stillpoint."

Earlier that week, I had had dinner with Carol and David, the owners of Stillpoint. When we had met a few months before, we discovered we had many things in common. They were both educators and lived most of the time in Boulder. We knew people in common. Over salmon and a bottle of wine, they told me more strange and magical stories of the land and its eccentric founder, Gia-fu Feng, who, as well as being a tai chi master, was a teacher at Esalen, the translator of a popular edition of the *Tao Te Ching*, and a friend of Alan Watts and Fritz Perls. Carol had taken on the daunting task of writing Gia-fu's biography. She told me that the name *Stillpoint* came from a line in T. S. Eliot's "Four Quartets." The evening was winding down, and I was getting ready to leave when, out of the blue, David asked if I knew anyone they could hire to help with their current project of building a new deck on one of the cabins. I said I would give it some thought. At the time I couldn't imagine who it could be.

I stubbed out my cigarette, went in the house, and called David and told him if he still needed helpers, I had just the pair for him.

That night I spent extra time in the shower. I washed my hair, shaved my legs, scrubbed my face, and slathered myself in lotion. It was all so transparent that even as I was doing it, I was shaking my head at how ridiculous I was.

Before turning in for the night, I went searching for my old copy of *The Collected Poems of T. S. Eliot*. Settling into my bed, I opened the book and found the passage:

At the still point of the turning world.
Neither flesh nor fleshless;
Neither from nor towards;
at the still point, there the dance is . . ..

Something was stirring deep inside of me in those early days of being at the ranch by myself, some shift happening in my being I found mirrored by the words of the poem. As I turned off the light, I felt myself sinking into a ground-less space, unattached, dancing at the still point of my own turning world.

After a long and restless night, I woke up breathless from a dream where I was trapped by dervish dancers in rainbow-colored skirts swirling and twirling around me. My head was spinning as I opened my eyes. Something was coming up I didn't want to look at or feel. As I sat up, trying to come back into my body and allow some space into my mind, it dawned on me what was bugging me: Joe. I was furious at Joe.

The first few weeks after he left, he had called with regular updates on his life in LA—the perfect weather, the beach, the neighborhood. Then he began suggesting places we could move to together, as though we weren't separating; he was just scouting the next location. "I think you'd really like Santa Barbara. People have horses there," was one of his suggestions. Then he called to tell me he had seen a psychiatrist and had been diagnosed with severe clinical depression. I could hear a new tone in his voice. He was triumphant. He was vindicated. "I stopped drinking," he added, rubbing it in, "and I'm going to the gym." Everything I had harped on for years—therapy, exercise, antidepressants, cutting down on the booze—was now a fresh and exciting new idea coming from his psychiatrist. I stewed on that for a while, and then he called again. The Prozac had kicked in. "I can't believe how good I feel," he said, brimming with irritating cheer, "and I think you're right. It's better if we don't get back together."

Just like that, he no longer needed me. After years of having me as his unpaid therapist, all he needed was the right drugs. He had moved on, and I was furious. It felt good to finally name it—RAGE—and to feel it, not swallow it, push it down, or numb myself.

Suddenly a memory flooded my mind. It was the day before Thanksgiving seven years before. The day I miscarried. The day that was a turning point in our marriage. If the child had been born, Joe and I would never have been able to separate.

I was forty-three, way beyond the time I thought I could get pregnant. Joe and I were in one of the periods of trying to make our relationship work by leaving our separate bedrooms and buying a king-size bed to share. It had been three years since I had sworn off my extramarital activities, after a friend punctured the bubble of self-justification and denial I had been living in when he looked me in the eye and said, "You know, if you don't stop fucking around, you can kiss any thought of reviving your marriage goodbye. There's only so long you can't water a garden before it dies." Harsh, but true.

Refocusing on the marriage felt good. Then one morning I woke up feeling a telltale tenderness around my breasts and a slight sagging sensation in my belly. I had ignored the missed period, thinking it was the beginnings of menopause. Menopause made sense, more sense than pregnancy. After a few days of trying to ignore my symptoms, I woke up feeling queasy. I bought a pregnancy kit, even though, deep down I knew. The test was just confirmation.

"Oh, yuck," was Julia's response. She was thirteen at the time.

"When he graduates from high school, I will be thirty-five," was Nick's gleeful response.

Joe was excited. He loved babies and small children. I was horrified. I moved into the guest room, shut the curtains, and plummeted into a deep hole. After three days, something began to stir. A hint of excitement, a feeling that this might be just what Joe and I needed to bring us together. It was a new beginning, romantic in a midlife kind of way. But just as I opened my heart to the idea, it was over.

That morning I woke up with blood pooling under me, my belly squeezing, my back cramping, drenched in sweat. Everyone was downstairs, getting ready to leave for school and work. I dragged myself to the bathroom and collapsed onto the toilet. When Joe came upstairs to say he was leaving, I was hunched over, hugging myself, the bloody mess floating in the toilet bowl beneath me. "What's happening?" he asked, standing in the doorway.

"The baby's gone," I said without looking up. He didn't say anything. When I finally peered out, he was still standing in the doorway with a look of sheer panic on his face. "What's the matter?" I asked.

"I'm supposed to be at the sound mix this morning in Denver." I waited to see if there was more.

"Just go, I can deal," I finally spit out and, without looking, I reached back and pressed down the handle.

"You sure?" he said, doing a poor job of concealing his relief. I nodded. I was listening to the sound of the water, flushing the baby away. I crawled into our bed and lay there in the quiet after everyone left the house. I stared for a long time at the large cottonwood tree in the backyard, a few tenacious leaves still clinging to the bare branches. I cried softly off and on, my mind empty, my body empty.

Sometime in the afternoon, I felt myself emerge. I sat up, and at that moment I realized that I needed to get to know my own body—inhabit it, not just use it. I decided that with no new life in my belly to nurture, it was time to nurture myself, my own body, my own feelings, to find a way to connect with myself, not with my mind, but with my bones and muscles and belly and heart.

Seven years later, in my bed at the ranch, the memory of that moment came back to me with excruciating clarity.

As the morning light began filling the room, turning everything gold, it dawned on me that the reason I was living alone in this remote mountain valley was to deepen this connection with myself, to live in my body, to feel the release in my belly as the fear relaxed and I urged Rain into a canter up the hill.

To know sadness and joy from the inside, to turn off the running commentary of my mind. To feel everything. Even the panic I felt when the wind wailed like a banshee around the house and the power went off and the world was pitch black was good; it was alive.

The sun had warmed the room. I was getting hungry. I had been sitting there for a long time. As I threw off the covers, I heard the dogs bark outside as a truck pulled up. I grabbed a sweater and left my room.

"How about some pancakes and bacon?" I said to Leon as I opened the kitchen door to greet them.

"We won't say no to that. We've been driving all night," Leon said, smiling.

"I'll make coffee." I smiled back.

He nodded toward the hefty young man coming up the stairs behind him. "That's Augie." I smiled and greeted him. He was taller than Leon, still carrying some baby fat. He nodded shyly, and they both came in and sat down at the table. I put the kettle on for coffee, laid some strips of bacon in the skillet, and started whipping up a batch of pancakes.

The Eagle's Cry

It had been a long day. I was still stuck at the computer writing yet another request to another school, another detention center, another program for at-risk youth, trying to set up more interviews for the gang film. Bronco and Abby sat nearby, staring at me, willing me to do something more interesting. The day had begun with stepping on a dead mouse Kitty Boy had left in the middle of the kitchen floor, with bare feet. The refrigerator was almost empty. I had forgotten how much two grown men could eat. I was edgy and irritable, and all I wanted was to take a walk down the valley with the dogs and lay in the hot tub soaking up the last rays of sunlight. By the time I finally turned off the computer, the sun had dropped behind a bank of clouds, and it looked like it could rain. I stormed out of the house and stood shivering in the cold.

Leon and Augie were back from work at Stillpoint, and Leon was building a fire in the barbecue pit, splitting the wood into little pieces and calmly stacking them in the blaze. I walked over and stood next to the fire. "I'm too burned out to take the dogs for a walk and too cold to get in the hot tub. I'm getting old," I announced. "I'm just going to smoke cigarettes."

"That's fine," Leon said. "It's all good. That's what we say: it's all good."

I sat down and we both lit up and smoked together in silence. Then, when we finished, I got up and took the dogs down the road and watched with delight as they ran along the tree line, racing an unseen animal hidden in the pines. By the time I got back, the last rays of sun were illuminating the mountain. Leon had cooked pork chops on the grill and baked potatoes in foil in the embers. No one even mentioned vegetables, and it was all good.

After dinner, Leon asked if I wanted to get in the hot tub and I realized that I did and that, cloaked in darkness, I didn't feel shy about going naked. The water was perfect, the sky vast with a half-moon nestled in misty clouds above the ridge. We sat on opposite wood benches submerged in the warm water and talked quietly. I asked Leon about the two raised scars I could just make out on his chest, and he told me how each summer he would go to South Dakota to attend a Sun

Dance, a sacred time of purification and ceremonial dancing for Plains Indians. "After your time on the hill without food and water, you get pierced with a piece of bone. For men, it's here on our chest." He reached out for my hand and held it to his chest. "Then, they attach the bone with a piece of rawhide to the tree in the center of the circle." He went on to describe how the dance would begin at sunrise as a slow shuffle and, as the sun rose in the sky and the heat intensified, the dancing would intensify and the dancers would move farther and farther away from the tree, pulling on the rawhide until the bone broke the flesh and they were released from the tree. What I was feeling on Leon's chest was years of torn skin that had formed two ridges of scar tissue, rough to the touch.

Gradually, our conversation slowed, and the space deepened in long pauses. We sat gazing at the star-studded sky and then I closed my eyes. After a moment, I felt Leon begin massaging my feet. For an instant, my mind tightened. *What is this, and where is it going, and what should I do about it?* Then all thought, all worries, began to unravel, strand by strand, as he moved up my leg, kneading and stroking, moving slowly around my buttocks, cupping them before moving up to my waist and circling my belly. I could barely hear his voice over the rumble of the pulsing water. "You're not getting old," he said and started on the other leg. I reached out and rested my hands on the scars on his chest. I slowly began to lose track of where his hands were moving. My mind was drifting like seaweed on the water's edge. Moving here and there, going nowhere, it was just a body being touched by hands and water, arms and legs entwined as we floated circling in the water, pressing together and easing apart. Everything was pulsing, like being inside my own heart, water and blood moving together. As he entered me, I felt hollow, a vast cave in the ocean. The waves broke and lapped against the rock and swept back and broke again. Nothing was solid; time disappeared. We eased apart and lay back on the wooden bench, listening to the night sounds. After some time, we climbed out and went in the house. I made hot tea and we sat side by side, our arms touching every now and then as we drank it, and I could feel the waves still lapping softly in my belly. Then Leon put his cup down and stood up. Reaching over to lay his hand on my cheek, he said, "Sleep well," and left to join Augie in the cabin.

All night, I lay in my bed naked and alone, still rocked by the waves, awake and asleep, and the sheets were cool and warm against my body as I drifted in and out of consciousness.

It was early when I got up, but Leon had already brewed a pot of coffee and was packing up the cooler with food for work. A blazing fire was radiating from the blue cookstove. I began making French toast for breakfast. As I stood by the stove in my old cotton nightgown, he came up behind me and wrapped his arms around me. My belly softened as I felt him pressing up against me. We heard the sound of Augie's boots on the porch and Leon eased back and sat down. "Morning, Augie," I said. "How'd you sleep?"

"Good," he mumbled, looking like he would like another ten hours of it.

"He sleeps like the dead." Leon chuckled. "Not used to all this physical labor."

"I'd like to build a sweat lodge on that island in the creek," Leon said as we finished breakfast.

"That would be nice," I answered the question that hadn't been asked.

"We'll pick the site and gather some willow branches later," he said to Augie. And just like that, it was settled, and they got up to go to work and I went to get dressed. I was pulling on my jeans when I heard the two of them outside my window whistling—one long whistle, then a pause, then another. I looked out and saw them standing by the truck, looking up. I grabbed a shirt and went outside.

Before I could say anything, Leon pointed up at an eagle circling low above the house. Augie whistled and the eagle circled once more and landed on a nearby pine tree and called back. I had heard that sound before but never known what it was. "Checking us out," Augie said, and we all laughed.

"It's all good," Leon said.

Chaz was standing in the corral watching us. I could see Rain way off at the bottom of the pasture. "Could you do me a big favor?" I said to Leon.

"Depends how big." He smiled back.

"Dee is coming to ride soon, and Rain is way the hell down there," I said, pointing.

"You want me to get him?" I nodded. I had seen Leon ride the year before. He had grown up on a horse on the reservation. "Your wish is my command," he said and grabbed a halter hanging on the corral fence. In one fluid motion, he mounted Chaz, holding his mane, and guided him with almost imperceptible movements of his seat and legs out of the corral and into a smooth canter across the meadow. As I watched I could barely see where he ended and Chaz began. It was magical, and earthy, and very sexy. Coming back leading Rain with the halter, all three were moving seamlessly together, cantering across the valley.

"Look at you," Dee called out later as she cantered up behind me to the top of the hill below Lover's Leap. "I've never seen you sitting so deep in that saddle. No perching. What the hell happened?"

I laughed. "I finally understand what the big deal is about being in a hot tub with a man."

"You didn't?" Dee looked at me incredulous. "You are fucking kidding."

"Perfect choice of words." I smiled back.

She laughed. "Whoa! You are one dark horse. Hell, why didn't I come up with that solution a year ago?"

"I was still married a year ago," I said and urged Rain back into a canter. Dee gave Chaz a nudge, and soon we were racing side by side across the meadow. I knew exactly what she was talking about. I could feel how my body had relaxed completely, my sit bones soft and wide open, deep in the saddle. I wasn't holding back. I was completely out of my comfort zone, and it was exhilarating and terrifying, and I never wanted to go back in.

The Sweat Lodge

"I'm doing a sweat here tomorrow night. There's some people coming," Leon said as he poured a cup of coffee in the kitchen. It was early morning about a week after he and Augie had begun putting up the sweat lodge, a process that was both painstaking and magical.

The first day, Leon had picked the site at the end of the small island in the creek, then the two of them cleared the land. I sat nearby as Leon blessed the site with tobacco offerings and prayers. The pungent smell of peppermint and burning sage and the sound of the creek riffling and Leon singing were intoxicating. Each day they added another element—first harvesting and peeling the willow from along the creek, then building the dome with the bent willow branches around a depression at the center to hold the hot rocks. Finally, Leon sent Augie to the truck to fetch a pile of army blankets to lay over it. Watching Leon create a sweat lodge was mesmerizing. The whole process had felt slow, spacious, and private. Now, suddenly, it was going to be open to the public.

"Who's coming?" I asked, flipping the eggs over.

"Just a friend from Pueblo and her kids. You'll like 'em. She needs some guidance," he answered, adding, "Of course, you're welcome to come." *I'm welcome to come? Really.* I kept quiet as I served breakfast and sat down. I was suddenly sick of serving breakfast each morning, washing up, shopping for dinner. What had seemed sweet for those first couple weeks had become claustrophobic and overly domestic. It was stunning how quickly I flipped from one state of mind to the other. "Are you okay?" Leon asked.

"Did I ever tell you about the sweat we did with Howard Bad Hand?" I said in response. "It was for a friend who was having problems. Joe and I both went. It was down near Taos."

The sweat had begun in the early morning. Joe and I had entered the dark lodge and settled into our places, eight of us in the circle. The hot rocks were brought in on a shovel and, as Howard began to drum and sing, the space grew hotter and hotter, almost unbearable by the time he opened the flap to cool it down. I had been struggling for a while, desperately wanting to escape the heat and the beating of the drum. During the break, I took gulps of cool air and gazed out at a nearby cottonwood tree, wishing I could leave and sit under it. Then Howard closed us back into the dark and began talking. He moved slowly from person to person, delivering whatever message Spirit wanted him to convey to each of us. Some people entered into a dialogue, looking for more information. I don't remember all of what was said to Joe, but I vividly remember Joe talking about his love for old things, antiques, old houses. After a while, Howard turned to me and began, "Spirit is showing me a trunk, an old trunk, filled up. Does that ring any bells?" I shook my head. "Okay, let me see if I can learn anything more . . ."

Suddenly I proclaimed in a loud voice, "I hate other people's old shit," and abruptly pushed myself up and edged my way, crouching, toward the door, frantic to get out.

"It took awhile for my racing heart to slow down. I just sat on a rock under the cottonwood and listened until I could finally relax," I finished telling the story.

"Spirit sure had your number that day," Leon commented enigmatically and got up and cleared the table, leaving me sitting, still rattled from the telling of the story and the dawning of a deeper understanding of what it was about. A lot had happened since that day. Out with a lot of old shit and in with who knew what.

It was a prison day, so after cleaning up the kitchen, I headed off. I needed to stop by Rancho Loco and make sure they were ready for me to bring Rain down for his winter stay. I had secretly been hoping Leon would offer to haul the trailer, dropping hints about how I was a little worried about doing it by myself. "I have faith. You can do it," he had said, not leaving much room for me to ask. I was going to have to bite the bullet soon, before the weather turned.

It was a full house at the prison; all five of the regulars were there. I had been reading sections from Trungpa Rinpoche's seminal book, *Cutting Through Spiritual Materialism*, to the group and at our last meeting had come up with the idea of book reports. "How about if everyone picks a chapter and talks about it—any chapter is fine," I had said and, to my delight, they were excited about the idea. Kenny volunteered to go first, so I gave him the book to keep for the week.

"I couldn't decide what chapter," he began, "so I just opened the book, and sure as shit, I got the one about suffering." I realized I had been holding my breath, waiting to see how this experiment was going to go, but at Kenny's opening line, I knew it was going to be fine. "The deal is," he continued, "life is no picnic, you don't get what you want, and then you get it and you don't want it and the Buddha realized it's all a clusterfuck of sorrow, and that's the truth of it." That took care of the first and a lot of the second Noble Truths: the Truth of Suffering and the Cause of Suffering. It was the third and fourth truths of the Cessation of Suffering and the Path Out of Suffering that provoked the most heated discussion. "There's no easy fix out there," Kenny said, looking around the room at his fellow inmates. "The book says it's all about letting go of wanting the fix. Just being with the wanting."

"Whooah, *man*," Luis said. "That's a head full." I looked around and could see all the men were deep in thought. Part of me wanted to jump in, but I held back.

Then Kenny opened the book and read: "'Ego must wear itself out like an old shoe, journeying from suffering to liberation.' I don't know," he said, closing it, "that made some kind of fucked-up sense to me."

They were quiet for a minute, then Matt said, "It feels like that's what I'm doing when I meditate in my cell: shit comes up and there's nowhere to go . . . over and over." Our time was nearly up, so I stepped in to wrap up the conversation.

"Let's give Kenny a round of applause for an awesome presentation." As the men clapped and Kenny bowed, I felt my heart ache at the beauty and the sorrow of it all held in one ineffable moment.

Matt's mantra—"the shit comes up and there's nowhere to go"—kept chiming in my head as I drove home. Rounding the curve to the ranch, I could see an old RV and a white pickup truck pulled up in front of the house and a group of people standing by the corral. Kids of all sizes were chasing each other around the yard, Abby valiantly trying to herd them into some kind of order. There was a lot happening at Lookout Valley Ranch.

In a moment of clarity, I knew that some kind of allegiance in me had shifted over the last few years from loving chaos to wanting peace, and now I was going to have to find some way to let go of my attachment to my newfound allegiance or I was going to be in a world of sorrow. As I got out of the car, I could make out a largish younger woman with long braids, an older man and woman, and Leon and Augie, all leaning against the corral fence. Chaz was nuzzling Leon. As she leaned toward him, it looked like the younger woman wanted to nuzzle Leon from the other side.

It had been a long day. All I wanted was to open a beer and lie on the couch and watch Thursday Night Football. I didn't care who was playing. I waved half-heartedly at the group who had turned to look at me and headed toward the house. Only Bronco and Abby came bounding over. Leon didn't make any move to follow. Inside, I stood in the middle of the kitchen, every conceivable emotion swirling through my mind and lashing my body: anger, confusion, fear, resentment, jealousy, sorrow. I knew the only way through was to let it go, but there was no way I was ready to follow those instructions. I threw off my coat, stormed into my room, and slammed the door. Shit was coming up, and there was definitely nowhere to go.

The Sweat

"Take any seat," Leon said as he held open the blanket and we all stooped and made our way into the sweat lodge, covered now in a green tarp. There were seven of us. The older couple, Mavis and Jeremy, went in first. Karen, the woman with all the children, wearing what looked like a cross between a towel and a muumuu, crawled in after them. I followed in a long, cotton skirt and T-shirt and sat next to her. A young man with long braids, a narrow face, and a lanky body tended to the lava rocks in a fire pit nearby, Augie helping him.

That morning, after a restless night of little sleep, I had emerged from my room and found Karen cleaning up after what looked like a large breakfast of bacon and eggs. "There's coffee and some food left. I could make you a plate," she said as I looked around at the cups left on the table and the plates teetering in the sink.

"I'm fine," I said, even though, having skipped dinner, I was starving.

"It's always us women, right?" Karen smiled at me as she began to tackle the dishes. Her voice was soft, at odds with her sturdy body. I could tell she was used to being left with a ton of dishes. I picked up the empty cups and brought them to the sink.

"Very true," I said, smiling at her, my snit miraculously gone. The rest of the day, Karen and I worked together, side by side, preparing food for the gathering. She pulled a huge slab of chuck roast out of the refrigerator and began cutting it up into chunks and throwing them into sizzling oil in the Dutch oven on the woodstove. She cruised around the kitchen as though she had been cooking there all her life. While we chopped onions and carrots and celery and sautéed and stirred, we talked about food and kids and life. I could see her children, who ranged in ages from five to twelve, jumping over and over again into the creek, splashing water everywhere, and throwing sticks for the ecstatic dogs. "It's good for them to be out in trees and fields," Karen said. "They don't get out much at the motel." She stirred the stew, liberally dousing it with salt and pepper, and put the lid on.

"I don't know how you do it," I said. "Two was all I could handle."

"I won't say it's easy," Karen said, "but after three, it doesn't seem to make any difference how many more you add." The three oldest, she told me, had the same father, who was in prison in Oklahoma on a manslaughter charge. "He had a bad temper, that man." The last two had two different fathers, both deadbeats. Karen worked two jobs, one behind the cash register at the Loaf and Jug and the other emptying bedpans at the old folks' home. "I guess I don't have the sense I was born with," Karen said. "A sucker for sweet-talking men." She laughed, and I laughed with her, marveling at how she didn't have an ounce of self-pity. My whining about Joe leaving me alone on my own 160-acre ranch would for sure qualify as bourgeois suffering. Luckily, I had the good sense to keep it to myself.

"I told Leon I needed some help, clearing some of the cobwebs in my thinking," Karen said, an edge of sadness in her voice.

"I'm looking forward to some cobweb-clearing myself," I said as I set out loaves of white bread and stacked up bowls and plates on the kitchen table. Karen brought over bottles of Coke, and we surveyed our handiwork. All was ready for the feast after the sweat.

"We're here to help our sister, Karen, whose spirit is low, and she is tired. We are here with her in the womb of the universe, where we can heal together all that is impure. And live fully again." Leon began the ceremony speaking in English. After a pause where everyone nodded and made noises of agreement, he asked the young man, whose name was Rex, to bring in the rocks. After setting them down in the depression, Rex closed the flap and sat down. The space began to heat up quickly, the rocks glowing orange in the center of the lodge. Leon began to pray. "*Tunkashila Wakan Tanka, pilamayaye. Onsimalaye. Wani wachiyelo omakiyaye. Mitakuye Oyasin!*" ("Great Mystery, thank you for my life. I am worthy of Divine Grace. Help me, I want to live. All my relations!") He passed a bowl with herbs to Karen, who was sitting next to him, and she sprinkled it on the fire. Then, he continued singing and drumming, the sound slow and melodic, growing faster and more intense and then easing back again.

It was eerie, and beautiful, and unsettling. I could feel myself resisting and then letting go, over and over, panic rising as the lodge got hotter and then relaxing again as the flap was opened and I could breathe. It went on and on. I knew from years of meditation that impatience and irritation would only make the claustrophobia worse. I breathed in and out, willing my body to relax, and then suddenly it was over. We all crawled out into the evening light, the sky gray-blue with wisps of gold, a fall chill in the air. The smell of the peppermint all around us was overwhelming. My mind was wiped clean. I looked over at Karen. She was radiant, smiling. She went up and shook Leon's hand, holding it for a moment. Together they walked toward the house to bring out the food. Suddenly, I felt lost, like I had landed on another planet and forgotten who I was.

For the rest of the evening, we all sat around the firepit, eating stew and slices of bread and drinking Coke. I kept to myself, a little apart. Every now and then Karen would look over and smile at me, and I would smile back. But my heart wasn't in it. There was a lot of easygoing banter and joking going on. Leon was right at home. I was exhausted; every bone in my body felt like it had turned to jelly. After a while, I slipped away, crawled into bed, and fell into a deep sleep.

When I woke up, it was almost nine, and I could hear voices and truck doors shutting and engines revving. I waited until they were gone and all was quiet before leaving my room. Suddenly I was sad I hadn't said goodbye to Karen, sad everyone was gone, sad for no reason.

Leon's truck was still there, but he and Augie were nowhere to be seen. I felt at loose ends, unsure what to do with myself. I made a cup of tea and sat on the porch. It was a crystal-clear day, the hillside covered in shimmering gold. A steady stream of cars and motorcycles passed slowly by on the road, now designated a Scenic Byway, sightseers catching the last of the autumn leaves. Winter was just around the corner.

I saw Leon coming from the creek, carrying the stack of blankets from the sweat. "Where's Augie?" I called out.

"He left with Rex, went back home."

"Why didn't you tell me?" I asked.

"It just happened; you were in your room." Leon kept walking to his truck and threw the blankets in the back. I went in the house, slamming the door behind me. Every cell in my body was on fire. I was still seething when Leon came in the door. "I am leaving in a couple days," he said, jumping in before I could let loose on him. "There's an indigenous conference happening in South America. And before that, I've been invited to teach at a Quaker school in DC for a couple weeks."

If he thought that laying out his credentials would make him more appealing, he was dead wrong. "What the hell do I care? You have done nothing but ignore me the whole time your friends were here—you don't think I noticed?" Leon walked over and sat down at the kitchen table, leaving me standing in the middle of the room.

"What is it?" he asked.

I sat down. "You were embarrassed, weren't you?" I went on, not ready to give up. "You didn't want anyone knowing you were lolling around with a white woman in her hot tub?" My body was shaking all over. I was way out of my comfort zone. "That just wouldn't fit with your shaman, Indian-rights-advocate, indigenous revolutionary image, would it?" That last line did it. Leon's face was no longer impassive. He was angry. I could feel that I had taken it too far. But something about it felt good.

He pushed his chair back and stood up. "What about you?" he said in a low voice, looking down at me. "Was I just a notch in your belt? You got yourself a real Indian lover?" We glared at each other for what seemed like an eternity. My heart was pounding. I knew I needed to just stay still, not take it any further.

Leon turned and walked away, got in his truck, and drove off. I sat and stared out the window. I felt empty. No longer angry. Just completely emptied out like a fire had burned through me and left nothing in its wake.

I went through the day in that strange state, empty but very aware. Aware of the sound of the wind rustling the dead leaves on the aspen tree next to the porch, aware of my hands holding the reins and my foot in the stirrup as I climbed up on Rain for our daily ride. My senses were alive; it was my thinking mind that had been burned up in the fire.

Fantasy Meets Reality Again

"That should hold," Leon announced, hammering the last nail into the root cellar door. He was still there; he hadn't left for good. All day, he had been fixing odds and ends around the place. I had spent the day in the editing room, cutting the gang video. And listening to the sounds of him moving around outside. I had just come out to stretch my legs and get some air.

"Thanks," I said without looking at him.

He went on, "Only thing I didn't get to was changing the oil in the truck."

I looked out at the now bare aspen grove across the meadow. *What the hell*, I thought. *Do something different.* I looked at Leon and let myself smile. "I guess you'll have to come back then."

He smiled back. "It's all good," he said, and we walked back toward the house together.

I had been pondering, over the two days since our fight, how the initial passion between us and the eruption of anger between us seemed to have the same energy. Time and again, I had heard Pema Chödrön say that the way to move through difficult times is to "drop the storyline and stay with the energy." I had never been very successful at the instruction, but here it was, so obvious, right in my face. Only the story lines changed, the waves of emotions were just that—waves of emotions, pounding. Now both waves had calmed, and everything had come full circle. The drama was over, and we were at ease with each other again.

"You have to show me how you make those pork chops so they aren't tough and tasteless like mine," I said as we came in the kitchen. The secret, it turned out, was a hot oiled skillet, lots of salt and pepper, and searing them until each side was crusty brown.

"Don't mess with them or move them around the skillet. When they're done, take them off the stove and just let them sit for a few minutes. That does it," Leon said as he started to cook us dinner.

We ate pork chops and boiled potatoes with lots of butter and drank a glass of red wine and talked about this and that. "Do you believe things as we know them will end when the century ends?" I asked. "All the computers will crash and everything they are predicting with Y2K?"

"May not be a bad thing," Leon said. "We could do with a reset."

"It's all good," I said, raising my glass and drinking the last of my wine.

"How about a soak?" Leon said.

The moon was full, a deep orange, full harvest moon. A pack of coyotes was calling out from the woods, trying to lure

Bronco and Abby out to play. Kitty Boy was padding across the silver moonlit grass in search of mice. Our bodies felt like sea creatures, tentacles entwined. Everything felt just right. Not transcendent like the first time, but sweet and loving. "I'll be back," Leon said, "by December."

I reached out and took his hand. "That would be good," I said, leaning toward him, letting my body relax onto his. "You better get here before the world ends." I held his hand to my cheek. We sat like that for a while and then we went inside and lay down in my bed, relaxed by the warm water and the vast night sky, and fell asleep right away. I woke up alone. I could see my truck parked in front of the house, the hood up. I went out on the porch and saw Leon pouring the last of the oil into the oil pan. "Does this mean you're not coming back?" I asked.

He tightened the lid. "I didn't want you hauling the trailer without an oil change." He put down the hood, got in, and backed up to the trailer. Together we hitched it to the truck. "All set," Leon said and then, "time to go." And just like that, he loaded his few belongings into his truck and got in. I caught myself before I got wound up and yelled at him, *You're not going to say goodbye*? Why state the obvious?

"Thanks for the oil change," I said instead and reached for his hand through the window. "See you soon."

He leaned over and kissed my knuckles. "Sure thing," he said, turning the key. The truck fired. I stood back and watched him leave.

It was déjà vu all over again, again. Me standing by the corral watching a man drive away. The man was different, the storyline had changed, but the feeling of loss had a similar flavor. A mixture of sorrow, anxiety, and determination not to fall apart, and an inkling of relief. It had only been a little over a month since Joe had left. I had managed in that short time to burn through the fantasy of the perfect man riding in on a horse and sweeping me away, leaving all my problems behind. I was still alone at the ranch facing the arrival of winter.

The Puzzle

"You made it," Dee exclaimed as I swung into the driveway at Rancho Loco in my old Ford pickup and pulled up in front of the barn. Rain hung his head out the window of the trailer and whinnied loudly. "Hey, big boy, welcome back," Dee said, giving him a kiss on the nose.

I gave her a thumbs-up and got down from the cab, stretching the tension out of my lower back. I opened the trailer and climbed in, untied Rain, and nudged him out.

I had driven there using the back road, past Donley's ranch and Stillpoint, taking it slow and easy. At some point I realized it was pure habit that made me feel I needed Leon to haul the trailer. I had done it before. I had fallen for the old idea that a man could do it better. Or should do it. The windows of the truck were open, the air was autumn cool, the country and western station was playing. I was wearing my flannel shirt with the silver buttons, and I felt like a real cowgirl. Up to a point. "There is no way I can back this thing up," I said, handing over the keys to Dee. As she parked it, I walked Rain to his stall, past the outhouses marked Studs and Mares, and the crosses that marked the entrance to the big arena. The year before, this world had seemed as foreign to me as the steaming streets of Calcutta once had, but now it was my world. Everything that day was feeling just right.

Throughout those fall days, I found myself noticing more and more moments where everything felt just right, where a sudden flash of pure joy filled my whole being when I least expected it—driving to town in swirling mist, stroking the horses' necks at dusk in the corral, watching Kitty Boy chase off after the dogs herding the cows away from the fence, glancing up in time to see three deer racing along the ridge, even sweeping the worn wood of the kitchen floor. The ceaseless chatter of evaluating my experience stopped, and happiness was just there, like Boo Radley behind the door at the end of *To Kill a Mockingbird*. Boo had always been there, out of sight, watching over things, making sure no one got hurt.

Happiness, it seemed, was shy like that. It didn't like a lot of fanfare. The trick was not to scare it off by grabbing hold of it and hanging on.

The cottonwoods along the creek had almost all turned yellow. I knew the next time I drove by, they would be bare. I could sense a growing unease in my mind. How was I going to manage being alone at Lookout Valley Ranch for the long winter? Would I be able to find my way home in a blizzard? Could I plow the uphill driveway, crank up the generator when the power was out, not panic when a storm dumped five feet of snow on the valley and I was trapped inside for days and my food supplies were dwindling?

Along with my winter fears was another worry that had been nagging me for a few days. Berna. I had not heard from her in a while, even after the last writing I had sent her about the sweat lodge on the little island in the creek. In the past, that would have tickled her fancy and called forth a story about the creek, her father, something sweet and sad. But there had been no word for days.

After a plate of mashed potatoes with a poached egg nestled in it, one of my go-to comfort foods, I sat down in front of the computer with a cup of chamomile tea and opened my email. Berna had finally written:

Hi Vicki,
    Have finally shaped this piece somewhat, so will send it along. It was hard to go back to that time. It is also a challenging time here with treatments and so on. But it's going well. Anyway, hope all is well with you. I had such a lovely time when I was there with you.
Luv, Berna

The Evil in Eden
I awake to the rhythmic vibrations of a country-western song and breathe a sigh of relief that a new day has begun. The truth is, I am relieved to be rid of the nightmare that crops up, seemingly without provocation at unexpected times.
    In the dream, I am being chased down a long hallway by a bearded man who holds a gun in one hand and a pair of pliers in the other. I hear his clumsy feet hammering at my heels; feel his breath on my neck. I race toward a door at the end of the hall. Sometimes, in my dream, the door is locked, and a hand squeezes my shoulder. At other times, I turn to face my assailant, and his feral eyes bore through me. He points the gun at my head. I always sit up in bed and switch on the lights. Fully awake, I realize it is simply a rerun of the nightmare I have had since childhood.

It is disquieting to think about Charlie Bragg, the shaggy old man who prompted these dark thoughts when he took me on his lap, wrapped one big, hairy arm around me, and tried to unbutton my jeans. I was six years old, snowbound in his house during a three-day blizzard. Wordlessly, his wife, Kathryn, pulled me from Charlie's embrace and kept me at her side for the next two days.

It was one of several experiences that have not only unleashed nightmares, but also sullied my memories of the years I spent in the majestically beautiful mountains and valleys of Custer County. These troublesome recollections do not come easily. They are buried beneath layers of time that have to be pulled away one by one, like the skin of an onion to clean the membranes that hide reality.

I couldn't read anymore. My breath was ragged, and the palms of my hands were sweaty. "Buried beneath layers of time that have to be pulled away one by one, like the skin of an onion." My heart was beating in time with the words "one by one" over and over.

A moment that seemed playful with someone familiar and trustworthy, who seemed to care for you, a moment that in an instant became dirty, scary, shameful, no longer fun—I knew exactly what she was describing.

I was also six when that moment happened in my life. When everything changed in the middle of a game of hide-and-seek, one minute giggling under the covers of a single bed with the young Italian man who lived in our house in London, the next, opening my eyes to something wet and quivering pushing against my laughing mouth, sticky and fishy tasting, a sickening sensation rising up in my throat. My body was instantly electrified and paralyzed at the same time. My mouth clamped shut. I had no way of understanding what was happening. I just knew it was wrong, and I could never speak of it to anyone.

In that unspeakable moment, shame was seared forever into the deepest part of my being, and trust became a thing of the past.

The next morning, the man and his wife, an older woman who cooked for us and had a cross over her single bed on the other side of the room, were gone. They packed up and left in the night. My parents never knew why.

Years later, when I asked, all my mother could remember was how they left suddenly. "There was a young woman from Amsterdam who came after—she was wonderful," she said. I could remember every one of the people hired to take care of me: Ruby the Jamaican, Madge the Irishwoman, the couple from Italy, but I had no recollection of a young woman from Amsterdam.

The sun had set, and the room was completely dark when I opened my eyes. For a second I didn't know where I was. Had I been dreaming? I was still sitting in front of the computer, the screen dark. I touched the keyboard and Berna's email popped up. Suddenly, my mind was filled with an image of a small, skinny child in faded jeans standing in a darkened room. Was it Berna or me? I had so many questions I wanted to ask her. Were you haunted your whole life by those few minutes? Did you tell anyone? Did you feel betrayed? But I couldn't. All I could say in my email response was, "I am so sorry, Berna. I do understand how that must have scared you so badly."

It would be another three years before I was diagnosed with post-traumatic stress disorder. Back in 1999, I only knew of PTSD as something returning Vietnam veterans suffered from, not someone like me. I wasn't pacing along the freeway spewing obscenities at the sky. I had graduated with honors from the London Film School, the only woman in my class. I was fully functional.

I turned off the computer. I couldn't read anymore. The house was cold. I climbed into bed and nestled into my soft flannel sheets. The moon was almost full, framed in the window, floating in the night sky. As I lay there in the dark, Bronco and Abby snoring softly at the foot of the bed, a simple instruction arose in my mind: "Whatever you feed, grows." I had heard it before in relation to my marriage; now I was seeing it closer to home. I had a choice. I could sink into a dark hole, grappling with the sickening story of what had happened to me that night forty years before, nudging it like a sore tooth, trying to make sense of it. Or I could bring my mind back into my body at that moment, into my bed, into the rays of moonlight holding me in the place I loved and let myself be there, safe and alone. I closed my eyes and breathed deeply until I fell asleep.

For the next couple days, I kept busy with easy tasks, nothing challenging. I cleaned out the refrigerator. I filled up the hot tub with fresh water. I didn't turn on the computer. The second evening, I stretched out on the couch and started to read the latest issue of the *Wet Mountain Tribune* cover to cover. I had arrived at the obituaries when I read: "A funeral was held in the backyard of a Walsenburg resident for the death of Brownie, a rabbit, who was nine years old. His cause of death was not given, but it is believed one of his owners pushed him over the edge."

For a split second, I thought it was funny. Then, a second later, I burst into tears. "Pushed over the edge." That's it. I was way over the edge, falling through space; groundless, with no parachute, nothing to hold on to. I was in mourning—for myself, for the life I thought was real, for my role as mother and wife, for my dreams of the future, for my birth into this world and loss of innocence at such an early age, for the death that is the only way out. Everything in my life was breaking apart. I could feel all of it, and I couldn't stop crying. That is what I had wanted when I moved to the ranch, frozen in panic, afraid to feel the sorrow I knew was deep inside me, longing to be touched by something, to feel something, anything. It was becoming clear that in order to unfreeze, I had to embrace sorrow and let my heart break. Now there was no denying that my heart was breaking and there was nothing I could do about it.

Troublesome Recollections

The next morning, I felt strong enough to finish reading Berna's story of Charlie Bragg. I turned on the computer and reopened her email. The first thing that popped up was her dream:

> In the dream, I am being chased down a long dark
> hallway by a bearded man who holds a gun in one
> hand and a pair of pliers in the other . . .

I took a deep breath and scrolled down to the last section:

> In my mythical vision, life was a series of long rides
> on horseback, searching the woods for arrowheads,

splashing in the clear, cold water of Hardscrabble Creek, sledding down logging trails, and ice skating in the back yard. It is tempting to edge out the relentless realities of isolation, loneliness, alcohol, and Mother's endless struggle to make a living farming.

It was all too much. I hated nightmares of large men in dark hallways. I hated facing reality. I couldn't stand my vision of Berna's idyllic childhood shattered. I didn't want to join fantasy and reality. Why couldn't we just keep our fantasies and ignore reality, for Christ's sake?

I stormed out of the house. Dark clouds were hovering over the mountain. A swirling, icy mist was filling the valley. A storm was coming, and I was totally unprepared. For weeks, I had been putting off attaching the snowplow to the truck. I was going to die, buried in snow, all alone. "Fuck," I yelled at the top of my lungs, and suddenly the sky opened wide, letting loose a shower of tiny crystals of snow. "Fuck," I screamed again, stamping my feet. I tried to light a match for the cigarette I clutched in my hand. The match sputtered out again and again. The snow was thickening. The dogs cowered by the door, shivering, wanting in. "Why am I the one trying to figure this shit out?" I yelled into space. "Doing all the work. Endless fucking hours meditating. Why am I the one who is stuck here by myself, dealing with everything, in the freezing ass cold, miles from anywhere? How come Joe is out there boogie boarding, painting, happy as a pig in shit? Clinically depressed, my ass. This was his goddamn fantasy. What is wrong with this picture?"

Suddenly the rant was over. I was shivering uncontrollably, my thin sweater soaked through, snot icicles forming on the tip of my nose. I herded the dogs into the house, got back in bed, and watched the snow falling in flakes as large as dessert plates.

Quiet descended. The aspen tree out my window disappeared under a blanket of snow. The whole world vanished into deep white silence. I never turned on the lights. The dogs settled on the foot of the bed and we drifted out to sea. Unmoored. I contemplated dying, freezing to death, the light failing, movement ceasing, becoming one with the great white void.

Hours went by. Thoughts arose, disconnected and random. *I need to tell Berna that it's more like tearing off a bandage than peeling the layers of an onion.* All those years, Joe and I kept our hearts bandaged so tightly. The hurt places were so deep, the sticky covering too painful to tear off. Living in a cocoon. *I love my cocoon*, I told myself. Or I may have said it out loud to the room.

Every now and then, my mind would send out a message, a banner flying overhead: *Are you hungry? Are you cold?* The questions weren't compelling enough to answer. The thought of eating was interesting in the way that watching a TV show of a lion tearing the flesh off a hyena was interesting. I just couldn't imagine doing it. "All of me, why not take all of me . . . " was playing over and over in my head, drowning out everything else.

Berna called them "troublesome recollections." Such a polite, old-fashioned name for the rough, insistent hand, the whiskey breath, the scratch of whiskers on her six-year-old neck.

I had kept my memories hidden behind more palatable language as well. "We were playing. It was a game. He wasn't trying to hurt me. I'm not really sure what happened. I was too young to remember." But the shame I felt the first time I willingly put a man's penis in my mouth told another story.

A box had opened, and the pieces of a puzzle had scattered everywhere. It would take many more years of searching to find all the pieces, but the border of the puzzle was in place and pieces of the sky were beginning to connect, stars appearing, a faint moon in the corner.

Back in my bed, my mind had become an octopus, long tentacles groping here and there, stinging at each encounter with another old wound. Recoiling at each fragment of memory. At last I fell into a deep sleep. I dreamed I was in Berna's house, and I couldn't open my eyes. *I was feeling my way through the rooms when a man came and told me it was time for him to take me to dinner. I didn't want to go, but I didn't know how to say no. Berna appeared and said, "Never mind, we are staying in and having sandwiches."* In the dream I felt a deep sense of relief.

I slept until the next morning. When I opened my eyes, the room was radiant with brilliant sunlight. Everything had changed. Snow was dripping off the eaves. I got out of bed, put on my slippers, and went to the kitchen to make a cup of tea. By the afternoon, the snow had melted on the driveway and I was determined to hook up the snowplow. After staring at it for a while, I realized I needed help. It was Saturday. Otis and Johanna and Casey would be up from Pueblo for the weekend. I dialed their number.

"Sure thing, girl. Casey and I will be there momentarily." Otis's deep voice sounded like the voice of a benevolent god. "And Johanna is making her famous potato soup, so come on up for a bowl after."

It took a matter of minutes for the three of us to hook up the plow. Otis had me climb up in the truck, and he showed me how to maneuver it from side to side, even testing it out on a pile of snow still lingering on the shady side of the driveway. By the end of the afternoon, I was snowplow ready. I grabbed a bag of cookies from the kitchen, jumped into the Explorer, and followed Otis up the hill.

The History Channel was playing on the big-screen TV, silently flickering grainy black-and-white images into the overheated living room. We carried our bowls to the dining table, sat down, and dug into creamy potato soup glistening with butter. I helped myself to two large hunks of cornbread from the platter on the table. I couldn't remember the last real meal I had eaten.

"I don't know about you," Johanna said as we sat back, our bellies full, "but when I saw Bob Dole of all people on the goddamn television telling me about some drug that was going to give men a hard-on for hours—old men—I'm like, what the hell is happening to this world. Give me Y2K, and let's put an end to this goddamn insanity." Even Johanna couldn't help smiling at her last line. I was laughing so hard my belly hurt.

"Think of the boy, Jo," Otis said, nodding toward Casey. It was hard to tell how much Casey was hearing—his head was buried in a comic book.

"How about some dessert?" I said. I laid out the Pepperidge Farm cookies I'd brought on a plate and carried it into the living room where Johanna and Otis had taken up their positions in side-by-side recliners.

I passed the plate around and sat down in a third large chair.

"Did I tell you I found a place back in the woods where Eustace had moved the fence between our properties? Dug up the old posts and gave himself maybe five feet of my land."

"That son of a bitch," Otis said and reached over for another cookie.

"You think I should call him on it like Harold Miller did?" I asked.

"Pathetic piece of shit." Johanna snorted. "Useless needs another few feet of dirt to feel like a big man. He needs some of that Bob Dole medicine.

"Jo's got it right, don't even bother," Otis said. "Just be thankful it was all he wanted."

With that, it was settled, and we turned our attention to the screen.

The sound was still off. I watched, transfixed, as old images of men scurrying through trenches and flashes of light in the distance played out, when all of a sudden an image of the brown WWI combat boots I trudged around campus in flashed in my brain. A ping of anxiety grabbed my chest. I shook my head and looked away. Otis was watching me, a look of concern on his face. I realized he was speaking. "They used to call it shell shock in those days," he finished up.

I nodded. "That's right. PTS something or other now," I said and took a cookie from the plate.

"These here are real good," Otis said, holding up a cookie. "You bake 'em yourself?"

"I bought them. They're called Verona."

Otis nodded. "The town of Romeo and Juliet, the star-crossed lovers," he said, once again surprising me. We settled into watching another grainy scene from WWI playing out silently. Whatever had been holding my throat had thankfully loosened. After another round of cookies, it was time to leave.

As I climbed into the Explorer, I looked back. Otis was standing on the porch in his overalls, with his long white beard and white hair like a halo around his head looking like a benevolent Santa at the North Pole. He waved and called out, "Keep on baking those good cookies, you hear." I couldn't stop smiling all the way home.

Later, while I was brushing my teeth, I remembered a time, in our freshman year at CU, when Joanie and I decided to switch boots for the day. Hers were black knee-highs with heels, exuding confidence. Mine were the dirt-brown, lace-up combat boots that made me feel like I was dodging bullets in the trenches. All that day, as I walked around campus staring down at my feet in the black leather boots, I felt all powerful. My back was straighter, my head held higher, I was supremely confident. Who knew I could be whoever I wanted to be, just by changing my boots. I spit out a mouthful of toothpaste, rinsed, and peered at myself in the small bathroom mirror. *Right on. You can be whoever you want to be. Whatever you feed, grows.*

The Twentieth Century Ends

As winter settled in, I began to worry about how to bring in more income to keep myself and the ranch afloat. I needed money for bills, for food, for boarding Rain. Looking for clues, I read through all the ways Angelica tried to keep the place going, but I couldn't see working in a chicken hatchery or starting up the sawmill.

A few days later, I stopped by Singing Acres Ranch. "Hi there, stranger," Margaret called out from the porch as I parked in front. A blast of warm air hit me as she opened the door to the cabin. Clara was reading by the woodstove, a cup of coffee by her side.

"Coffee?" she asked.

"Or something stronger?" Margaret chimed in. I chose a shot of whiskey, Margaret and I sat down in two overstuffed chairs, and I got right to my question. "How did you guys manage to keep Singing Acres going before the Appaloosa business took off?"

"We started up a ski slope across the road," Margaret answered.

"For beginners," Clara added.

"We called it Silver Hills ski area," Margaret went on. "Kind of a fancy name for a hill kids could slide down. There were a lot of naysayers."

"How did you deal with that?" I asked.

Clara chuckled. "I always said we had strong backs and weak minds."

Margaret struggled to her feet to throw a log in the stove. "Can't say the same about my back these days," she said.

I loved being in that dim room with the old leather couch the color of the whiskey in my glass, surrounded by antlers hanging from the walls, the woodstove holding us all in a cocoon of warmth. "I've never skied," I said. "I don't think that will work."

"How about Christmas trees?" Clara piped up. "We did that for a while. Pine and fir. We had to dig them and bag them and haul them to Denver. Trees, and boughs for wreaths." Christmas was right around the corner and it was sounding like a lot of work when Margaret broke in.

"You wouldn't have to do all that," she said. "We can give you the number of an outfit out of Pueblo. They'll just come up and cut 'em down and haul 'em away."

A week later, the tree cutters arrived in a flatbed truck. They drove across the valley and parked up at the saddle below the tree line. I walked slowly up after them, feeling uneasy. I heard the chainsaw start up and my heart beat faster. By the time I arrived at the scene, ten small and medium-sized fir trees were lying on the flatbed. I began to feel queasy at the thought that it was my choice which trees didn't deserve to grow up on the land. Meanwhile, more trees were piling up on the truck. Suddenly, I couldn't take anymore. "That's good," I blurted out. "That's enough." I was waving my arms, my voice straining to be heard over the chainsaw. Finally one of the men saw me waving and stopped. "It ain't a full load," he said after he understood what I was saying. "That's okay, you can just give me whatever you want . . . or nothing, that's fine." I was babbling like a madwoman. The foreman thrust a fistful of $5 bills at me and jumped into the cab. They couldn't get out of there fast enough.

If I didn't even have the stomach for cutting down a few trees, what would I have done if I had had to butcher a hog or brand and castrate yearlings? My vision of ranch living was galloping across the valley, my tawny hair flowing behind me, wearing a perfectly aged pair of cowboy boots. Real ranch living was another reality altogether.

That night I lay on the couch wrapped in a quilt in front of the antique gas heater and watched old episodes of *Upstairs Downstairs*. Each episode called to mind a world of endless cups of tea, handkerchiefs tucked into cardigan sleeves, treacle tarts smothered in Bird's Eye custard, and hot-water bottles— a world soothing and familiar.

There are no pictures of Christmas 1999, no "Howdy from Lookout Valley Ranch" cards, no stories to tell. I have tried to dredge up a memory, any memory, from that Christmas and haven't found a single one. I did find a journal whose first entry from December 26, 1999, begins:

This is my journal of winter 1999–2000, here alone with Bronco and Abby and Kitty Boy and snow. Everything is colored by the anxiety I feel at being alone, at not knowing what is happening, at meeting myself.

Reading on, the journal tells me that I spent the time taking baths, watching football, meditating, staying warm between my flannel sheets reading English mysteries, and trying not to think about all the years of family Christmases at the Piedra Blanca in La Cruz. Trying to keep the loneliness at bay.

The week before New Year's, I went into the prison for one last visit before Y2K. It was Matt's turn to give a book report on a chapter in *Cutting Through Spiritual Materialism*. He had chosen the chapter on the six realms. "I don't know, reading this I kept thinking there has to be someplace where everything works out. You know what I'm saying? Like the god realm. I mean, that has to be okay, right? Better than the hell realm."

He was starting to get frantic as he tried to nail down a linear path through the realms—from hell realm to animal realm to human realm to god realm and then, just when he figured he had it made, plunging into the realm of jealous gods and then back to hell. "Fucking hell, how come we have to start all the way back at the beginning? How do we get off this train?"

His anxiety began to permeate the room. We were all getting tense, sitting on the edge of our cushions. "Any ideas?" I asked, looking around the room. No one jumped in. "Okay, let's all sit back and take a couple deep breaths," I said, settling back onto my cushion. "How about if we look at this differently, not like train stops we get stuck in. How about we look at these realms as states of mind. What comes up then?"

"I sure know the hell realm," Matt volunteered. "And I guess I've been in the god realm a few times too, thought my shit didn't stink."

"Jealousy fucked me up," Luis shared, "more than once. It squeezes the life out of you."

"I hear you, man," said Steve. He rarely spoke more than one sentence, but kept on talking now. "I never believed any woman I was with would want to be with me."

"Man, any woman would want you," Luis said, looking over at Steve. "But, I know what you're saying."

As they each weighed in and talked about their struggles with jealousy and rage, stubbornness and stupidity, a feeling of warmth was rising and expanding out into the room.

After a long pause, Steve said, "It's all about opening our minds, man." I knew he meant it, not in a sound bite kind of way, but with genuine understanding, an understanding all of us in the room were experiencing together in a space that, in that moment, was almost luminous.

"It's pretty amazing how we can drop our shit and the world looks completely different," Matt added, and we all nodded in agreement, bringing the afternoon to a close.

"Thank you, guys. What a great way to end the century," I said as Steve and Luis stacked the cushions against the wall.

"What do you think?" Matt added as the men lined up to leave the room. "You think the computers will go haywire at midnight, and the prison gates will open, and we'll all walk out of here with open minds?"

Kenny ended the meeting with a loud, "Hallelujah!"

Driving toward the mountains as the last rays of the sun stretched across the cholla and sagebrush along the road, I let the warmth in my heart carry me. I couldn't remember the last time I had been with people communicating in a way that was so genuine, so vulnerable and open. I could see how the walls I had created around my heart were a big part of what had gone wrong in my marriage. And Joe's walls were just as thick. With both of us hiding behind our walls, genuine intimacy didn't stand a chance.

I stopped at the top of the driveway and grabbed my mail from the box. Abby and Bronco bounded up the driveway to greet me. It took awhile to get settled—put away the groceries, feed the dogs and Kitty Boy, get a fire going in the cookstove—before I could sit down in the armchair in the kitchen. I had two letters. I opened the one from Berna first. It was one of her handmade cards tied with a maroon ribbon with the inscription: "Wishing You the Blessings of a New Millennium" and a handwritten note inside. "I think of you often and hope you find joy and peace this holiday season and the coming year."

Reading her words, I felt like my whole being was bursting with what I can only describe as a sorrowful joy. Joy and peace and sadness all in one, a heady draught.

I sat for a while letting myself experience the unfamiliar sensation of letting go. Just then I heard the sound of tires on the gravel. It was late. I couldn't imagine who it could be. I turned on the porch light and went outside, wrapping my sweater around me. It was a truck, barely visible, but when the driver opened the door, I could see it was Leon. "I guess you made it in the nick of time," I said as he came up on the porch and we hugged.

"I didn't want the world to end before seeing you again," he said.

"Have you eaten?" I asked, knowing he hadn't.

I rustled something up and we settled at the kitchen table, catching up on this and that—how Augie was doing, the horses, Carol and Dave at Stillpoint. "I'm only here for a night," Leon finally said. "I'm traveling to a town far south in Mexico tomorrow."

"Driving?" I asked. He nodded. It wasn't like him to be so quiet. Something was up. "What are you doing there?" I finally asked. He started telling me about an indigenous group that was coming together to try to mediate the conflict that was still raging down there. He had been asked to join. There was a subdued quality to his telling of the story; he wasn't boasting. I realized he was scared and vulnerable, and in my heart, still tender from the time with the prison group, I felt a wave of compassion and a deep desire for him to be safe and happy. "Are you worried?" I asked. I took his hand, and he knew there was no challenge in my voice or my question. He held my hand and nodded.

"Worried and a little scared," he said.

That night we slept together in my bed, curled up close. In the morning, after a cup of strong black coffee, Leon took off, heading south, and I stood on the porch and watched until his old truck disappeared behind Lover's Leap, where the two lovers had leapt to their death. I had never shared the legend with Leon. Somehow it never felt right.

Back in the house, I noticed the other letter I hadn't opened. It was from Joe. So much for my newfound tenderness. Just the sight of his handwriting immediately shut down all systems. Before even opening the envelope, I was hit by a tidal wave of panic. I steeled myself, tore the seal, and took out one folded sheet of lined notebook paper covered in his familiar writing.

"Dear Vicki," it began, "we need to talk about selling the ranch. I want to buy a place out here, so I need the money."

I dropped the letter on the table and sat down. I couldn't read anymore. Every nerve in my body was on high alert. My throat was dry. My chest closed down. My body felt lifeless. Under normal circumstances, I never smoked in the house, but this wasn't normal. I lit up and breathed the smoke deep into my lungs. I had no idea what I was going to do.

Learning to Love Lincoln

I was pedal to the metal, Lauryn Hill blasting out of the speakers as I hurried up to Boulder in time for a friend's New Year's party. I hadn't planned on going, but after reading Joe's letter, I knew I didn't want to spend the last New Year's Eve of the century swigging a bottle of wine and watching the ball drop by myself.

I wasn't ready to sell the ranch. I wasn't ready to face the thought of selling the ranch. Even the idea of selling the ranch freaked me out. After a three-year journey that began with being overwhelmed by panic at the thought of moving to the ranch, then working with my anxiety and fear living at the ranch, beginning to feel my anger and sadness as our marriage fell apart, and now finally being open and strong enough to look deeply at the mountain of old wounds I had been carrying for so many years, I wasn't ready to leave the ranch. It was no longer a place in the mountains where I had inexplicably found myself living; the ranch was my home. It was the place where I had found a way to crack open my heart.

I was deep in my thoughts when, passing through Florence, in one of those cascading moments that happen in life, I caught sight of the sign in front of Carl's Jr. that usually said something like "Milkshakes $1.95," but that day proclaimed, "Catherine, come back, I love you." At that moment, the light changed to red, and I sailed right through it. I was still wondering whether what I had seen was real, and if so, what the story was when the sound of a police siren woke me up. There was no denying I had run the light. I tried to appeal to the young policeman's sympathy. "I'm so sorry, Officer, my husband left me, and I was trying to figure out that message. Do you know who Catherine is?" I blithered on, but he wasn't having any of it.

"I am sorry for your loss, ma'am," he said as he handed me the ticket. "You have a good day now."

I nodded politely at the young cop, rolled up the window, and burst into laughter at the insanity of it all—the earnest policeman doing his job, my broken marriage, the heartbreak of whoever wrote the sign, and the mysterious heartbreaker, Catherine. The full catastrophe.

I was happy to be with my Boulder friends toasting the end of the twentieth century together, but as soon as it was over and the world hadn't ended, I couldn't get out of town and back to the mountains fast enough. The weather channel was predicting a big storm, and I needed to get home.

Before leaving Boulder, I loaded up on supplies: real pasta, parmesan that didn't come in a green cardboard box, granola, bottles of cabernet. My last stop was a visit to Radio Shack to outfit my Explorer with a Motorola car phone the size of a briefcase with a handset attached. My idea was that in a snowstorm I could call Dee or Laura as I was turning onto Highway

165, where the snow got as high as an RV on either side of the single-lane road, and then call them from home to let them know I was safe. I had no idea if there was any real safety in the system, but having it made me feel a little less anxious.

Two days after I got home, the first storm of 2000 hit with a vengeance. It snowed for three days. The power held strong, but the phone went down. Blowing snow covered everything, swirling, flying sideways, popping upward like popcorn, filling every corner of space. We were cut off. It was truly winter in the Wet Mountains.

As soon as the phone line came back, I emailed Berna:

It felt good for the first few days. Quiet enveloped the house, the dogs were sighing in their sleep, the fire in the woodstove sputtered and crackled. No cars passed by. I know you remember what it was like. But then it did get kind of eerie after a while. I have been on edge the last couple days.

It took a few days for her to respond. When her email finally arrived, references to her cancer were there, but they were oblique.

Dear Vicki,
    I do understand the fears of living so many wintry, black, lightless miles from ranch to town. And then the memories of days when the snow fell so softly and quietly, everything was enveloped in a fragile shroud of white emptiness. In times of insomnia or physical pain, when I close my eyes and imagine the place I would like to be, I see snow-covered mountains and

meadows, and a peaceful feeling folds over me like my favorite childhood quilt. Those times I want to be there with you.

I hope you are staying warm and keeping your spirits up.

Luv, Berna

Keeping my spirits up was a tall order during those long, dark, snowy days. My mind kept circling back to Joe's letter. I finally decided to buckle down and do something. I began searching the internet for information on legal separations. The definition I found told me: "A legal separation is a popular alternative to a divorce when the parties are unsure of the state of their marriage but want to establish financial boundaries and responsibilities."

I had been unsure about the state of our marriage for years, but now I could see how setting a financial boundary was a good idea. I didn't want to be paying his gym fees in LA. And I was sure he didn't want to be responsible for Rain's hay bills. We needed separate accounts and credit cards. From templates online, I put together a document for us both to sign and file with the courts to make it legal. I read it over quickly and then pressed Send and sat back in my office chair, my heart pounding, suddenly scared shitless. I felt like I had just jumped out of the proverbial plane into thin air.

The snow had stopped falling. From my office window, I could see a thick blanket of hard-crusted snow covering the hillside and trees, the whole valley glistening in brilliant sunlight. I needed to get out of the house. I needed fresh air. I didn't care if it was ten degrees outside. I decided to plow the driveway. It would be my maiden voyage.

The truck with the plow was parked next to the house, facing outward. I trudged out, snow up to my knees, and after what seemed like hours scraping and brushing the snow off the windshield, I climbed aboard. It took an anxious few moments before the ignition caught and a few more freezing minutes to warm up the engine. I was ready to roll. I was feeling good, the air sparkling with a mist of swirling snow, the trusty engine chugging under me. I took off. Slowly. I turned on the windshield wipers and peered up the driveway. It seemed longer and steeper than I remembered. I felt a moment of panic, but I took a deep breath and powered forward.

As I headed up, the snow flying off to the sides, I was feeling almost cocky. And then, just as we hit the steepest part of the driveway, the truck crapped out. Right away I was hot and swearing. "Shit, fuck, no, no, no!" I yelled while I flipped it into neutral and slid back down the hill. At the bottom, I threw on the emergency brake, cranked the key, pumping furiously on the gas. Off we went again, and once again it died, at the very same spot. I started swearing again, pounding the wheel. "What the fuck? You can't do this to me."

Suddenly I felt my mind zoom back, and I saw the whole picture from a distance. Me, stranded in the middle of a very long driveway, in three feet of snow, yelling at a truck that wasn't doing what I wanted.

I needed to "change my attitude and relax as it is." I took a deep breath. *Relax.* I sat back and watched a load of snow cascade off a spruce tree across the road. *As it is.*

Out of the blue, I was visited by an image of finding myself in the same situation a week before with Rain. We were in the arena at Rancho Loco, and I was struggling to get him to lope. He didn't want to. Each time I asked, he would half-heartedly lope a couple of paces and then sputter back into a ragged trot. Right away, I lost my seat, my legs stiffened, my back constricted, my breath became shallow. Frustrated, I kicked him and he broke into a faster, jerkier, trot. Then it suddenly occurred to me that I was the one at fault. Whatever it was I was doing was making it impossible for Rain to keep cantering. I didn't trust that he would do what I asked him to do, and I was trying to force him. Sure enough, when I relaxed and let him do his part, everything went smoothly.

"Okay, I know you're not a horse," I said to my truck, "but I trust that you can do this. I've seen you do it. So, I'm just going to relax and let you do your job." I took a deep breath and turned the key in the ignition. The engine turned over on the first try, we were off and running, and we plowed all the way to the top.

"Yes!" I shouted, pumping my fist in the air, and then I effortlessly shifted into reverse, backed up just enough to turn, and drove back down the driveway. Mission accomplished. It was all good.

The next morning, I drove the Explorer up the plowed driveway and down to Florence to the prison for our weekly meditation group.

"Are you kidding, Kenny? You didn't really give them that number?" I asked, trying to elevate my voice over the hoots of laughter and cries of "you're fucking crazy" and "you dodged a bullet, man" bouncing off the walls of the meditation room. We had begun the meeting with Kenny telling us the story of his parole hearing for his release, still a year away. Ahmed had recently made parole, calm and cool as a cucumber, but Kenny's hearing hadn't gone so well. He told us he had given the parole board the phone number of an old friend in San Francisco who could vouch for his post-release living arrangement in his hometown. Unfortunately, the number he had was for a head shop in the Haight. Fortunately, the person answering the phone had never heard of Kenny or his friend. Nonetheless, it was a red flag, and now the authorities were planning on sending him to St. Louis. Kenny couldn't even find St. Louis on a map.

After the laughter subsided, Luis weighed in. "When I was young," he said in his low, hoarse voice, "I hated English. I didn't want nothing to do with English." He was a twelve-year-old boy when he arrived in the United States, alone, one of the 125,000 Marielitos who left Cuba's Mariel harbor on a fleet of boats headed for Miami in the summer of 1980. After months in a Catholic boys' home, refusing to learn English, he was called into the office by a priest who told him he was to be sent out of state to another home. He had a choice. "New York or Lincoln, Nebraska." Not believing his luck, Luis picked Lincoln. "The L word and N word," Luis told us, "got me confused. I thought he was saying Las Vegas, Nevada. Nebraska, Nevada. Sounded the same to me." After a moment of disbelief, we all cracked up for the second time that morning. Luis shook his head. "Imagine, if I'd just learned a little English, how different my life would have been. I was the only Cuban in all of Lincoln my whole fucked-up life." The room had quieted down when Steve started singing, softly at first.

"If you can't be in the place you love . . . "

Right away, Kenny joined in, "Love the place you're in."

The rest joined in, making up their own verses, louder and louder.

I looked at Luis. He was staring at them, as though he could strangle them all.

But then he started to chuckle, and a second later he called out over the singing, "Crazy motherfuckers, all of you."

"Yep," Kenny said. "You got to be crazy to love the shit-hole we're in."

"Crazy or enlightened," Matt added.

Our time was almost up. "We only have a few minutes left," I said, "so let's just take a deep breath, relax onto our cushions, drop into our bodies, and let our mind settle." As I rang the gong, the space expanded in a long sigh and we sat still and silent. Once again, I was amazed at how any situation can be transformed from a problem to an opportunity just by changing the way we look at it.

Some years before, my friend Howard Bad Hand had told me it was possible to rewrite our past, to create a different personal history. At the time, I couldn't fathom what he meant. How could our past not be our past—the past we knew it was, the past we had the pictures to prove it was? Of course, I knew my mind created my reality—any self-respecting Buddhist could tell you that. But could I take it that far?

That evening, as I sat in my recliner after dinner, I began to wonder what it would look like to rewrite my childhood. Could I rewrite those years I remembered as fearful and lonely, filled with constant upheavals, carted from one country to another, dragged away from pets and friends and familiar foods and cozy beds? Could I rewrite that childhood? Could I love all of it?

My mind was spinning, when suddenly it stopped, and in a flash, I clearly saw that inside every story of the past or present, another story was unfolding. The proverbial silver lining was always available. After all those moves from country to country as a child, I could now walk into any world undaunted and make a connection there. It didn't matter whether it was a prison, a rodeo, a meditation center, a hogan, or a ranch. I could embrace it and make a home for myself. Now I was being asked to do it again. I wasn't happy about it, but I knew I could do it.

The Lunar Eclipse

The sun was streaming through the window when I dragged myself out of bed and threw cold water on my face. I had to get moving; I had houseguests coming, and there was nothing in the refrigerator.

My friend Pie and her partner Lester were driving over from her ranch in Ridgway, a six-hour journey. He was an older man in his seventies, a rancher and builder, a man who spoke little, nursed his glass of bourbon in the evening, and could take care of anything—a fence in need of fixing, a house construction project, a lost calf in a snowstorm. I had known Pie since my first year in college when she lived in a farm next to Haystack Mountain outside of Boulder where many of my early LSD journeys had taken place. I was also with her on the fateful Halloween night I met Joe. We shared a lot of history. She and Lester were coming for a couple of nights. The first night there was to be a rare total lunar eclipse.

After loading up on beer, eggs, bacon, and other essentials, I began the journey home. I dumped the mail on the kitchen table, unloaded the groceries, made sure there were sheets on the guest bed and towels in the bathroom, fed the dogs, and finally sat down with the pile of envelopes. Bills, more bills, and one letter postmarked Los Angeles. I stared at the envelope, my mind racing through all the possible contents, coming to rest on the one most obvious: Joe had received the separation agreement, and this was his response.

It was short, written in pencil on a piece of lined paper torn from a notebook.

Dear Vicki,
    Is this struggle really worth it? Maybe getting divorced is too hard. Why don't we just figure something out.
    Love, Joe

I read it again and then one more time. I threw it down on the table. *Really? After everything that's happened, he wants to get back together?*

Of course, I had had the fantasy that Joe would come to his senses and crawl home, begging for forgiveness, pleading for me to take him back, professing his undying love. The fantasy always ended there. I had never come up with what my answer would be. For five months, I had tracked his journey along with mine, feeling resentment rise in my throat each time he waxed eloquent about all the fantastic things he was doing to improve himself. Gag me with a spoon. I was sick of hearing about his perfect new life as I increasingly felt doomed to become another of the solitary women of the Wet Mountains, withering away alone and annoyingly self-sufficient. *And now the son of a bitch thinks we should just stay together because it's too hard to separate? How fucking romantic is that?*

I was building up a toxic head of steam when I was interrupted by the sound of Pie's Tahoe in the driveway. I stuffed the mail into the empty grocery bag and went out to greet them.

They had brought steaks cut from one of her butchered cows, a pecan pie, and a bottle of whiskey. Pie had been to the ranch before; it was Lester's first time. "Nice place you got here," he said, standing at the picture window in the kitchen.

"How about a quick tour before it gets dark?" I asked, and we grabbed our coats and headed out, circling the property from the frozen pond to the gazebo, taking in the bare willows of the sweat lodge. Lester ran his hands along the corners of the old cabin, commenting on the perfection of its tongue-and-groove construction. The sun was disappearing in a silver sky, the air was cold and crystal clear, the pine trees brushed with shards of glistening ice. There was something painful about sharing the place with someone who could appreciate its pristine beauty. "Joe wants to sell the ranch," I blurted out as we walked back to the house, "so he can buy a place in LA."

Pie stopped and stared at me. "Jesus, you're kidding?"

"Nope," I said.

"I never did trust the son of a bitch," she said with her customary, sometimes intimidating directness.

"And you've known him longer than I have," I said, trying to keep my bitterness at bay.

After a dinner of steaks and mashed potatoes dripping in butter and something resembling a salad, we settled on the porch, bundled up, mugs of whiskey in our hands, waiting for the eclipse. The moon was full overhead, taking its time slowly completing the journey across Earth. I took a drink of whiskey and told them about Joe's last letter, his feeble change of heart. "It makes me so angry," I said. "But I don't know, maybe he's right."

"Don't even think about it," Pie barked.

Lester nodded his head in agreement and muttered, "Can't trust a man who can't make up his mind."

"And he didn't say anything about staying on here," I went on.

"Of course not; it's all about money. He always was a stingy son of a bitch. Selfish, too." With that, Pie ended the discussion.

"Looks like it's almost time," Lester said, standing up for a better view. We joined him at the edge of the porch. All of a sudden, the last sliver disappeared and the moon turned completely red. The color of dried blood. It was eerie and magical, completely otherworldly, standing under a pitch-black sky with a shimmering blood-red circle hanging over our heads. It may have been seconds or it could have been minutes. It was bone-chillingly cold; I had lost contact with my body awhile back.

And then it was over, and we all fell back to earth, shivering, our teeth chattering. "Let's get the hell inside," Pie said, "before we freeze our asses off."

Earlier that day, I had read an article online about the astrological interpretation of a total lunar eclipse. I wrote some of it down. After we warmed up in front of the woodstove, I grabbed my journal and read it out loud: "Lunar eclipses are more likely to bring about sudden endings, culminations, or powerful changes of heart. Either way, the fast-paced events of an eclipse—however rocky and disorienting—help us to let go of what's no longer serving us and embrace the truth, which allows us to move forward in a more spiritually aligned way."

Lester poked at the fire and said, "Can't argue with that." Pie was at the sink rinsing off the mugs. She turned around, drying her hands on a dish towel. "True enough," she added.

I grinned at them both. "Celestial confirmation for sure," I said and staggered off to my room.

The dogs had already turned in. I dropped my jeans and sweatshirt on the floor and crawled into bed with them. The room was spinning. I was woozy with whiskey and celestial encounters. After letting the bed settle into an uneasy sensation of swaying in a hammock, a clear thought penetrated the alphabet soup swirling in my head: *I need to make sense of all this*, the message read. *I need help.* I fell instantly asleep, clutching at what felt like a very flimsy lifeline.

A week later, I was in Canon City, meeting someone who might be able to help.

"I'm Kay," she said, extending her hand. She was small and slender with short, mousy blonde hair. Her voice had a hint of Midwestern twang, not quite grating, but her outfit set me on edge: a plain white blouse with a round Peter Pan collar tucked into the elastic waistband of her gray slacks, topped off by a blue jacket and brown pumps. Slacks, blouse, pumps, jacket. This was never going to work.

I shook her hand. "I'm Vicki."

"Come in," she said, welcoming but not smiling. I followed her and sat down in the chair she indicated. She sat down opposite me.

The pickings were slim for therapists in Canon City. Kay had come recommended by Dee, who had seen her when her marriage was falling apart. I decided not to arrive at a conclusion yet, to see what she had to say. The first thing she asked was, "What brings you here?" I launched into my story—the dissolution of my marriage, the ranch, the panic attacks. I came to a stop at the possibility of selling the place.

She didn't say anything for what seemed like forever, and then she asked, "What do you want?"

Instantly, my mind stopped. My story was suddenly irrel-
evant. The question hung in the air. I knew this question. I had
been asked this question before. It would be a few more weeks
before I remembered when that was. At that moment in Kay's
office overlooking the Arkansas River, surrounded by her
diplomas and bad paintings of longhorn sheep and bears, my
mind began to spin like a merry-go-round, stopping at one
answer after another. There were so many possible responses,
and I couldn't come up with a single one that made any sense.

"I don't know," I finally blurted out. "I thought I wanted
intimacy, but I don't know. Maybe I just want to be alone." I
sputtered to a stop.

Kay sat very still, listening. "You know that there is no formula for intimacy—we can't go out looking for it."

I had been looking at my hands knotted together in my lap.
My toes were twitching—a habit, I was beginning to recognize, that accompanied a rise in anxiety. I looked up. Kay was
watching me, her expression inscrutable and at the same time
unfathomably kind. I felt my body soften, my mind loosen,
just a fraction. Tears welled up. I could see the clock on the
courthouse. We were halfway through our session. I wanted
to stay there forever, and I wanted to get the hell out the room
immediately. "Here is the thing," Kay said. "Our inner state
creates our outer circumstances, not the other way around."
How many times had I heard those same words, how many
times had I said them? And yet I seemed to be hearing them
for the very first time.

When the session ended, Kay gave me some homework:
take note of my dreams, write them down, and make a list of
any patterns I noticed in my relationships with men. I fum-
bled in my purse for something to write on, and she handed

me a piece of paper and a pen. We made another appointment for the following week. I gathered my coat and hat and left.

A light snow was falling, not yet sticking to the ground. I brushed off the windows and got in the car. I felt drained. I sat for a while, the car running, the heat slowly warming my hands, my mind mulling over what had just happened. *Wow, not what I expected*, I thought. *What were the chances that a woman wearing gray slacks and a Peter Pan collar was the perfect person to help me at just the right time? And I stumbled on her in Canon City, Colorado's correctional capital, home to twelve fast-food restaurants and not a vegetarian option in sight.*

On the way home, I stopped at the grocery store in Florence and wandered the aisles, grabbing things off the shelves. The Eagles were piped into the sound system, and I tuned in as they were singing "Don't let the sound of your own wheels drive you crazy." Perfect. "Take it easy, take it easy . . . " kept on playing in my head as I drove up the mountain. The snow was still falling lightly in the soft light of early evening. Suddenly my mind burst open, as in that moment when a plane rises above the clouds and you can see from horizon to horizon, and I knew the truth of suffering deep in my bones. In that moment, cruising down Highway 165, I understood that birth is just a doorway to a journey of loss, that death is real, that no one gets out alive, and that the sadness I felt at the thought of the loss of the ranch was only a taste of what was to come.

It wasn't a new revelation, but I could see that before, I had veered away each time I was at the moment of fully embracing it. This time I sunk into it like a hot bath. Everything became clear and calm.

I wasn't ready to write Joe. That could wait. I didn't have to do what he wanted. I could do what I wanted, when I was ready.

The snow had stopped, and the sun was sliding down behind the mountain. The vast, steely sky slowly darkened in a long sigh, and I followed my breath all the way home.

Buddhism 101

"Does Buddhism really help anything?" Kenny asked, squirming on his cushion. "Like our lives—does it really help in our lives?" He was struggling to express what was bugging him. "I guess I want to know, has it helped you, in your life?" He finally blurted it out. It caught me off guard. I wasn't quite sure how to answer. I knew that whatever I said had to be real.

By then, I had been coming once a week to the Camp for a year. Every week, the same four men would show up, sometimes joined by one or two others. In those many hours of sitting and talking and learning together, things had gotten pretty real. Each week, the edifice of denial and posturing we had all been hiding behind when we began had weakened, and our bullshit detectors had become finely tuned. I couldn't wiggle out of Kenny's question with a superficial answer.

"Not pulling any punches with that one, are you, Kenny?" I grinned at him.

"Nope." He grinned back.

"The short answer is yes, it has helped me." The group looked at me expectantly. "But I can see that probably won't do it." I went on. "Okay, how has it helped me, let me count the ways."

I had to go slow, feeling my way through what I wanted to say. "I was a very unhappy teenager," I started out. "I tried all the usual things to dull the pain—alcohol, drugs, slashing my wrists—none of them helpful. It felt as though everything I was

being told about how life should be, how I should be happy—
go to college, have a husband, kids, a nice house—was a lie. I
always had a nagging feeling that there was something else,
something more, some kind of freedom from my unhappiness,
and it was that longing for freedom that got me to Buddhism."

I looked around the group. Maybe *freedom* wasn't the
best word to have chosen, but there was no turning back.
"I wanted to cut through the bullshit. And that's what I
found in Buddhism. A way to cut through the bullshit of
always wanting things to be different, of doing the same
things over and over that never made me happy. It gave
me another way to look at things." I sputtered to a close. "I
guess that's my answer."

We all sat still. No one spoke.

Finally Kenny nodded and said, "It looks like you found it."

"Thanks, Kenny," I said.

"I know the feeling," Matt added, "of wanting something
different, not the same old anger, jealousy, over and over. My
own bullshit always getting me in trouble."

"Your mind, man, it's your mind." Kenny commented. I felt
a certain pride welling up in me. We had talked so much about
how our state of mind determined our reality. I could see how
it was beginning to penetrate—all of us.

"So, how do you become a Buddhist?" Luis piped up.

"Is that something you all want to know?" I asked, not sure
how far to go with the answer.

"I do," Steve answered. The others nodded. Matt's and Kenny's comments gave me an idea. "Okay, so being a Buddhist
means following a path of letting go of anger and jealousy and
everything that keeps us hurting ourselves and others. It's a
gradual path." Pretty feeble answer, I could tell.

"But is there something you do that seals the deal, where you sign on the dotted line?" Matt asked.

"There is a ceremony, called a Refuge Ceremony," I said. I was relieved to have something tangible to talk about. "Not refuge like finding a place to hide out. It's more like taking refuge in our own sanity, our own basic goodness, and developing trust in that." I looked around the room. Everyone seemed lost in their own thoughts.

Luis finally broke the silence. "Is that something we could do? Take Refuge?"

Things were moving fast. I needed time to gather my thoughts. "Let's talk about that next week," I said. "We are almost out of time."

Walking across the parking lot to my car, I could see that a winter storm was brewing. Gray clouds hung low over the mountains, the temperature had dipped down toward freezing, but I figured I had just enough time before the snow started for a visit to Rancho Loco.

Rain was happy to see me as I approached his stall with some carrots. I gave him a hug, let him out into the arena, and spent some time urging him to circle around me at a trot, then a canter first one direction and then the other. Then I stopped and waited for him to come toward me. I rubbed his forelock and then we backed up, side by side, and sprinted forward. Do-si-do your partner, sashaying around and around; it was a dance we both enjoyed. After an hour, I was winded, my face red and raw from the bitter cold. But my mind was clearer.

Dee was just pulling up as I walked to my car. I waved. "I can't stop. Gotta get back before the snow gets bad."

"Call me," she answered, sliding out of her truck. "I'll be in the office."

As I drove, I could see the snow falling harder on the mountains. Reaching under my seat, I checked to make sure I had my car phone. Driving up the canyon, flakes were swirling around the Explorer, the spruce trees were blanketed in white, the black rock icy and glistening alongside the winding road. There was nowhere to pull over and turn around. I had to keep going. A couple of cars passed me going down to the plains. My heart started beating fast. After what seemed like forever, I made it to the intersection. By then it was dumping hard. I pulled over at the top of my road and called Dee. "I'm heading down 165."

"Okay," she said. "Call me when you get home. I'll stay here. Go slow."

It was eleven miles from the junction to the ranch, a trip that usually took twenty minutes, give or take. I peered through the swirling snow; the road was now snow-packed, one lane, a narrow tunnel between the verges piled high with snow on either side. "Shit, shit, shit, shit," I yelled, trying to shake off the fear that threatened to paralyze me. I knew I had to just dive in; the only alternative was to stay there and freeze to death. "Okay, let's do this." I sat up straight, put the Explorer into four-wheel drive, and let up on the brake. Clutching the steering wheel, praying that I wouldn't run into any other lunatics coming up the hill, I entered a world now completely white. No evergreens. No rocks. No road. Nothing. Only snow, whirling, shooting straight at the windshield, falling and falling. It was mesmerizing and very frightening.

The car was moving at a snail's pace, maybe eight miles an hour, but moving, the tires gripping the road. Gradually, my hands relaxed. There was nowhere to go but down through the tunnel. A calm descended on me. I realized that, even without seeing the road, I could still feel all the curves I had come to know so intimately.

After what seemed like hours, I could sense a dip in the snow on the right. I looked at the odometer. Eleven miles since the turnoff. It had to be the driveway. Holding my breath, I slowly turned the wheel to the right, slid down the hill, and stopped in front of what I imagined was the porch.

I had done it. I had driven home in a blizzard all on my own. I was euphoric and completely exhausted. Bronco and Abby had taken refuge on the blankets I had piled up for them in the lean-to next to the barn. They bounded over, crashing through the snow, whining and barking, and together we made our way up the stairs of the porch and fell in a heap inside. Lying on the kitchen floor, I surrendered to the wriggling mass of joy, wagging tails, tongues aimed at any exposed part of my body.

I could barely move. As I lay there on my back next to the old cookstove with my two dogs beside me, a Tibetan proverb I had once heard popped into my mind. "Wherever you receive love, that is your home."

I struggled to my feet and called Dee. She picked up on the first ring. "I made it," I said, smiling widely.

"You go, girl," she answered, and I could feel her smile back at me across the snowy miles.

"Wherever you receive love, that is your home." So simple and so true. This was my home, and I could feel the fear and sorrow at losing it percolating in my belly, ready to burst.

Class Dismissed

"March comes in like a . . . what is that word?" I was pacing around the kitchen, trying to remember the rest of the phrase. "March comes in like a menace, like a monster, like a tiger, like . . . a lion! Yes! *Fierce not friendly* was the idea I was circling around.

We were well into March, the days limping along under gray cloudy skies. Grim. It was a struggle to get out of bed in the morning. A blizzard always seemed to be looming over the mountains, just waiting to obliterate everything. Contemplating the word *March* set me off into images of prisoners in Siberia marching through knee-deep snow, shackled, their knuckles red and raw. Marching and marching, trying to get to the other side, of what was unclear. To get to the end of the phrase where we arrive at "out like a lamb." *April:* such a soft and gentle word.

That morning, everything, even the air on my skin, was irritating. Since my appointment with Kay, I had been working on my homework, trying to make sense of my relationships with men, tracking the back-and-forth between promiscuity and periods of frigidity when I became disembodied, my body and emotions locked in a deep freeze. I was queasy just thinking about the men whose names had disappeared, leaving only bare threads of memory. Married men, men I barely knew, and in one case, a complete stranger in London in 1970, who left while I was sleeping, taking my precious coral and turquoise Tibetan necklace with him.

So many nameless and faceless men reaching out like drowning sailors bobbing in a dark, stormy sea on a moonless night. I shook my head trying to clear the images. I needed to get ahold of myself. I splashed cold water from the kitchen tap on my face. Maybe therapy wasn't my best idea. Maybe it would be better to let sleeping dogs lie, or drowning sailors drown, as the case may be.

It was time to tackle the day. I pulled on my jeans, noting how big they had become. I needed a belt to keep them up. I was skinnier than I had been since 1975, the year before Nick was born. My hair was long, my bangs covering my eyebrows. Staring at myself, I realized my hairstyle was the one I had wanted my entire childhood, the one I had tried valiantly and unsuccessfully to talk my mother into letting me have: long with bangs. I finally had my way.

By the time I got to Kay's, I felt ready to share my findings. I was no longer raw. I had pulled myself together, cleaned up, and bandaged my wounds. The tales of my sexual encounters and relationships with men were now palatable for any audience.

I started telling my story: my first lost love, Nicky, dying in London; my search for sexual experience; and, by the way, I was raped when I was eighteen, but it was the sixties so, no, I didn't go to the police. I had a few affairs, but so did most people I knew back then; my marriage fell apart. That was about it.

I had reached the part where I was now living alone at the ranch. "Have you written to your husband?" Kay asked. I stared blankly at her. "Have you responded to his letter about giving up on the separation?" Kay clarified.

"No," I said, realizing I had swept the whole thing under the rug. "I don't know, maybe I should say yes. I don't know what to say. I don't want to be with him, but maybe he is right. Maybe I should just say yes."

I looked at Kay, hoping for some kind of homespun advice. She sat still, her hands resting in her lap, and said, "It is often the case with women who have been raped that they find it very difficult to say no to men."

It was a hole-in-one, a gut punch, a home run. There was no denying that my whole life, I had been unable to say no to men. For years, if a man wanted me, I said yes.

I felt like throwing up.

"That therapist you sent me to doesn't pull any punches," I said to Dee as we sat drinking beer at the Alibi Lounge. The rippled glass windows and dark wood interior created a perfect place for daytime drinking. The TV was muted, a soap opera unfolding silently above us.

"I know," Dee said and took a swig of her beer. "I figured you were going to need someone who knew how to use a sledgehammer just to get through the wall." She smiled at me. I started to laugh, and soon she was laughing too, and we sat back in our armchairs and let it roll.

"It takes one to know one," I said as the laughter died down.

"Relationship fuck-ups unite!" Dee countered, and we clinked bottles, downed our first beer, and ordered another. It felt good to sit there with no agenda, no plan to fix anything. I was beginning to learn that there were times when I needed to go deep and times it was good to take a break from the difficult and meaningful and just enjoy an afternoon hanging out with a girlfriend in a dark bar.

The first few days after my meeting with Kay and the Alibi Lounge debrief with Dee, I was energized. I was ready to tackle Joe, my past, my mind whirling at warp speed from one task to another, getting things done, ticking them off my to-do list:

- I wrote Joe and told him I wasn't getting back together with him and that he needed to hold his horses about listing the house.
- I contacted the Shambhala Prison Group and started the wheels turning to get permission to officiate at a traditional Refuge Ceremony.
- I scrubbed the kitchen floor and stripped all the beds and stuffed the sheets and pillowcases into the old washing machine in the basement.
- I drove to Florence on a clear, sunny day and took Rain out alone on a ride through the sparse landscape around Rancho Loco.
- I called Kay and canceled our next appointment, blaming the unpredictable weather. The truth was, I wasn't ready for any new land mines or sledgehammers. I made another appointment for two weeks later.

I was feeling virtuous. Taking care of business. Competent and in charge.

After a few days of this routine, I started to feel little twinges of unease. I was worried I hadn't heard back from Joe. Every hour or so, between compulsively cleaning the house and working on a script for the gang videos, I would check my AOL account. Finally, an email from Joe landed in my inbox. No pleasantries, no "dear" or "how are you?" He got right to the point. *Why don't you send me a list of everything you want from the house and cabin, and I'll get back to you with what I want.* That was it. My breath got shallow. I opened a FreeCell game.

It was midafternoon when I started my first game, and then I lost count. Hours went by. The house was dark, the sun had set, and the dogs were shivering on the porch when I finally came to. Feeling disgusted with myself, I poured a glass of wine and lit a cigarette to seal the deal. By eight o'clock, I had consumed two more glasses and had settled in front of the television, snacking on goldfish crackers, watching one CNN horror story after the next. Talks breaking down between Syria and Israel, a mass suicide of a doomsday cult in Uganda, Pope John Paul II apologizing for two thousand years of church errors. Two thousand years? That's a lot of errors to apologize for. It made my transgressions look like nothing.

I staggered into bed and lay there in the dark, my mind churning, unable to sleep. After a couple hours, I gave up, turned on the light, and shuffled back into the kitchen. Armed with a glass of milk and a plate of saltines, I tried to calm my nerves with a P. D. James mystery. Two hours later, I dipped into my dwindling stash of Ativan and fell into a deep, unsettled sleep. I dreamed I was outside the house, stark naked. *I began to walk up the driveway and suddenly found myself on the highway. Cars and bicyclists were streaming by. I tried to pretend I was invisible, but soon I realized everyone could see me. I scurried back to the house, locked all the doors, and closed the curtains.*

I woke up late the next morning to more snow. I couldn't get out of bed. I couldn't move. Slowly, I felt myself sink into a deep, almost comforting abyss, awake but unable to feel anything. The world was drained of all color and movement, my body scooped out, emptied of matter and flesh and bones, leaving a gaping emptiness that was slowly filling with dark clouds.

I knew that place well. I had been visiting it for periods of hours and days, sometimes weeks or even months, for as long as I could remember. Every fiber, every cell in my body was resisting. My whole being was shut down. No breath allowed in. I was four years old. My feet were dug in. I was not taking another step. The whole world was stacked against me. I knew it was hopeless, but there was no way I was surrendering. *I don't want this to be happening. I can't stop it. All I can do is not feel it.*

The hours passed. I made a cup of tea and brought it back to my bed, letting it grow cold on the bedside table, fascinated by the process of something going from hot to cold. My mind floated, latching onto random questions: *Where does snow really come from? Are my toes cold or warm?* My mind never stayed around long enough for the answer. As the sky darkened, I sunk deeper into my nest of quilts and drifted back to sleep. It was still snowing. My last thought was. *"Wow, it's April first, April Fool's Day. I guess someone forgot to tell the weather gods in the Wet Mountains about the lambs."*

The next morning I woke with a phrase flashing like neon in my head: *"class dismissed."* The bedroom was washed clean in bright sunlight. My mind and body felt rested and ready for anything. "Class dismissed." The end of a twenty-five-year relationship came down to an email divvying up the goods. We were done. Everything was clear, and I was ready to move on. That was what my head was saying. But that's not how it felt. I had been hurled back to summer camp in 1962, holding the letter I had written home the week before that my father had sent back, all the grammatical errors slashed through with lines of red ink. Failed.

As I was about to succumb to feeling sorry for myself, the words popped up once again: "class dismissed." To hell with them all. I can dismiss too. I didn't need to keep trying to teach Joe or my father how to be the person I wanted them to be. And I didn't need to be who they wanted me to be. No more trying to toe their line. Class dismissed!

I sat down in front of my computer and wrote my list. Taking my time, I let my mind travel from room to room, picking this and that, paintings, furniture, kitchenware. When I was finally done, the list was long; I had asked for everything I wanted, and a little more. I clicked send and shut down the computer. I slammed my hand down on the desk and stood up, startling the dogs. "It's all right, girls. You are good girls. We are all the best girls." I reached down and scratched them behind their ears. I felt stronger than I had in a long time. There was a lot more to face, to feel, to understand, and to grieve, but a small and powerful step had been taken in the journey ahead.

Everything Really Is Impermanent

Spring in the Wet Mountains was our reward for making it through the winter. Suddenly, one day, everything softened. The trunks of the aspen trees, silver all winter, turned a pale gold. The snow started melting, leaving patches of white dotted here and there. One morning, I dragged a rocking chair over from the barn and placed it just right to catch the first rays of sun as they slid around the side of the house. I sat down and let my body settle into the slow rocking, a warm breeze touching my face. I felt like a convalescent recovering from a long illness. With my eyes closed, I imagined the hillside beginning to flutter with new life, shoots of grass and dandelions popping up and filling the pasture. It was almost time to bring Rain up for the summer.

There was a heightened sense of living that I had experienced with friends who were dying, held in the co-emergent awareness of the amazing beauty of being alive and the pure, piercing heartbreak of knowing that, at any moment, it would end. Sitting on the porch that morning, I felt a tender sense of teetering on that edge. It was almost unbearable. Fortunately, I couldn't sit there for long. It was a prison day. I had to get moving. It was also a double-header. After the meditation class, I was to meet with Kay.

The bare branches of cottonwood and aspen along the drive down the canyon to Florence showed hints of light green; at each bend of the road, the green of the leaves darkened, became truer. As luck would have it, the song on the radio as I emerged from the canyon was an Eagles favorite, "Desperado." I turned up the volume and let it carry me all the way to the prison.

The men were waiting in the chapel foyer when I arrived. All four of the regulars were there, along with a fifth, a man I had never seen before. He was a mousy, middle-aged man from Boise named Frank who, we later learned, had embezzled a large sum of money from the bank where he worked in order to pay for his wife's cancer treatment. "Welcome," I said and introduced myself.

We sat down on our meditation cushions, Frank perching on his, ready to take flight any moment. "This is Frank," I started off, "in case you are not acquainted. He is joining us today. Let's all welcome him and introduce ourselves." I watched as the men each said their names and where they were from. I could sense a mixture of bravado, a kind of old-timers showing off, and resentment at having our little circle broken. Frank was having a hard time looking at them, his eyes darting up and then back down.

When everyone was done, I turned to Frank and asked, "Have you ever meditated or had any connection with Buddhism before?"

"No, ma'am," he said, "not really, I mean I have done some reading." I didn't want to push him, so I decided to just start our meditation.

"Don't worry," I told Frank. "I'll be guiding us through our meditation. It's very simple; we're just following our breath, letting go of our thinking mind, and trying to relax."

"Don't let her fool you," Steve told him. "It's not that simple." Frank looked up at Steve, a faint look of relief on his face.

I launched into the meditation, settling onto our cushions, back straight, heart open, jaw and shoulders relaxed, gaze down. Then we began following our breath, letting go of our thoughts, and returning to our breath over and over. After ten minutes, I rang the gong and looked over at Frank. "How was that?" I asked.

He nodded and said very quietly, "It was okay."

"It'll get easier, man," Luis told him. "First few times, ten minutes felt like a fucking year." It was just what the doctor ordered. I realized I had been treating Frank as if he were an invalid. Luis had launched us back into our groove.

At our last meeting, I had promised to talk about how to become a Buddhist. I had been thinking a lot about it, trying to get to what I really wanted to say.

"I want to talk about Luis' question about what it means to become a Buddhist. First, I want to talk about what it doesn't mean. It's not about signing on a dotted line, joining a cult with a lot of strange rules. It's not about living up to a set of commandments. For starters, Buddhism is not a religion; it's nontheistic. Does everyone know what *nontheism* means?"

"Not believing in God," Matt jumped in first. I nodded and looked around to see if anyone else had something to say.

Kenny was looking worried. "Does that mean if you're a Buddhist, you'll go to hell when you die?"

Keep it real, I said to myself and turned to him. "I never believed in a place down below called hell that we are sent to if we have sinned. I do believe that we all can experience what I would call hell, in this life, on this earth."

Kenny was slowly nodding his head. "Can't argue with that," he said. The others grunted and nodded.

No one seemed to want to add anything, so I continued, "Last time I talked about my path as a Buddhist. Each of us has our own unique troubles and pain in our lives, but the process of seeing how our lives aren't working and recognizing how we make things difficult for ourselves by trying to fix things, by grabbing something new or blaming someone else and instead seeing how we can connect with a goodness inside ourselves and find happiness there . . . that is the first step on the Buddhist path that is true for most of us."

Whew, that was a mouthful. The group was uncharacteristically quiet. I couldn't tell if I had loaded too much onto them.

"So, if I get what you're saying, this is just about us deciding to live our lives better?" Steve asked.

"You could say that," I answered.

He went on, "So why would we have to become a Buddhist to do that? Couldn't we just do it?"

Before I could answer, Matt jumped in. "Maybe it's like why we get married when we could just live together. For some reason, we feel we have to do the whole wedding thing. I did anyway." Matt finished with a shrug.

"Good point. So why did you do the wedding thing?" I asked.

"Commitment, I guess. Seemed like it was taking it more seriously."

I nodded. "Exactly. It's about committing. To ourselves. To waking up. To coming back to our path again and again when we screw up and fall into our old patterns, knowing that there is a path to come back to." I paused and then went on, "In my experience, the first step is really getting that this life isn't going to last forever, that one day it will all disappear, so we need to pay attention to how we are living it now, in this moment, because when its gone, it's not coming back."

I was about to move on and talk about the actual ceremony of becoming a Buddhist, when Frank raised his hand.

"Last month, my wife died," he began, his voice shaky but stronger than when he had introduced himself. He had everyone's attention. "I couldn't be with her. We'd been together twenty-five years, and I wasn't there when she was dying. I was here. And then one day, she was gone." He shook his head, as though he was trying to clear it, and kept speaking as he looked at each of the men. "I realized, you know, that death is the real deal. It can happen any minute. I could be the next to go. Or any of us." He had rested his gaze on me. "Everything is impermanent, and we need to stop messing around."

There was nothing I could add to that. Frank had said it all. "Thank you, Frank. I can't imagine how hard that was for you," I said.

Then Steve, who had been fixated on his hands, folding and unfolding them, looked over at Frank, and Frank looked at him, and they held each other's gaze. "That is some hurt, man. I am so sorry." It felt like the room was holding all of our pain.

Our time was almost up. "Let's sit for these last few minutes," I said. I settled onto my cushion and rang the gong, looking around the group as the sound reverberated in the space and slowly disappeared.

Nothing remains the same, nothing holds still. Every thought, every instant of joy, every moment of sadness, every connection we make, every regret we feel vanishes like a kite let loose into the sky. Here and then gone, and we never know the exact moment of its disappearance. Sitting there, I could feel the truth of that deep in my being. There was no point in talking about the Refuge Ceremony or any other Buddhist ideas. At that moment, reality was way more relevant.

Driving out of the prison gate, I turned right toward Canon City. My mind was raw and open, no concepts about this or that. As I neared the outskirts of town, the thought popped up: *Wow, there are land mines everywhere; anyone can wield a sledgehammer.* I could feel I was getting nervous about what might come up in my therapy session.

The Idea of Leaving

"Why don't you tell me a little about what it was like growing up," Kay began the session. I wasn't expecting the question, but it wasn't hard for me to crank up my story; I had years of practice telling it to myself and anyone else who would listen. An only child, clueless parents, a lot of moves, scary people, different houses, different countries, torn away from the one place I felt at home. "I never had a choice about leaving places, but the worst was leaving Madrid. For a year, I barely spoke." I was chugging along. I looked over at Kay. She was looking at me with the kind, enigmatic expression I found unsettling.

"I can see it must have been very difficult to leave a place you loved. Can you tell me more about that?"

Leave a place I loved. The words got lodged in my brain and were on repeat. I tried to oblige, to tell Kay more, about leaving my canary, Guapo; our maid, Aurora; and cook, Herminia; my school; my Spanish friends; but it felt like I was speaking from a vast distance. I finally ground to a halt.

"Have you ever seen a beaver dam?" Kay asked. The question was so out of left field it flipped me back into the room. I nodded. "So you know how solid the structure seems—solid enough to hold up the flow of a creek." I nodded again. "Yet, precarious, a balance of logs. I see childhood wounds and the traumas in our lives like a beaver dam. Over the years, they build up into a solid-yet-precarious structure, stopping the natural flow of energy. Our job, when we are ready, is to dismantle that structure, log by log." I was with her all the way, visualizing the dam, the creek, the water, and then we got to the dismantling. The words *log by log* attached themselves to *leave a place I love* and became the beginning of a strange song playing in my head.

My homework was to write about the logs, or the structure, or something. I wasn't quite listening. I just wanted to get home. I had been thinking of my life, my memories, as a puzzle to put back together, but I could feel in my bones that the idea of dismantling a beaver dam, log by log, was what I had to do. Just the thought was unnerving. All during the long trip home, I thought of Berna as a child and Angelica both having to leave the place they loved. I needed to know how they felt. When I got home, I curled up on the couch, the gas heater going, and opened up *My Life as a Mountain Pioneer.*

I found what I was looking for right away:

I did not want to face another winter alone. That fall, after the hay was in the barns, I prepared to leave. The girls were not happy, and neither was I. I rented a two-room apartment on Main Street. It was a heartbreaking adjustment. No running in the halls. We shared the bathroom down the hall and bore up under the strong smell of disinfectants. We were missing far more than our home. We were missing our friends, the animals, the sleigh rides, and the neighborhood gatherings.

I left the furniture and farm equipment and prepared to put the place up for sale. There was no other choice. One day, I received a call that I had a buyer for the ranch, and I sold it to a man named Apple. I sold 260 acres, including a team of horses, all implements, and a furnished house for $7,500. That ended my life in the land I loved for twenty-five years as a mountain pioneer.

I put the book down and stared out the little window in the alcove. The sun had slid down behind the ridge to the west, and the sky was streaked with pink and gold. The sorrow that enveloped me seemed never ending. Even with her customary matter-of-fact description, the grief Angelica felt at leaving her beloved mountain home was palpable in every line.

I knew exactly what she was feeling, teetering between "I didn't want to spend another winter alone" and "It was a heartbreaking adjustment." Between "There was no other choice" and "That ended my life on the land I loved." I felt queasy just reading those last, stark words. The reality of them was impossible to even contemplate. "A place I loved." "A land I loved." A double whammy in one day.

I had been very conscious in those last few months of not asking too much of Berna, to give her the space she needed to deal with her own very real challenge. That evening I wrote her a long email, opening up to her about the need for us to sell the ranch and sharing how hard it was to read Angelica's chapter on leaving.

> I know you have a lot on your plate right now, but would you be able to write a bit about how it felt for you to have to leave, about the move to town after living your whole life on the ranch?

The house was getting cold. It was too late to go for a walk. I felt at loose ends. Nothing appealed to me—calling a friend, cooking dinner, getting in the hot tub. It all seemed like too much effort. Every thought that arose in my mind hurt: The thought of leaving hurt. The thought of staying hurt. My whole being ached, and there was nowhere to turn. No relief. The current of emotions was running hard and fast, pushing against the dam; the logs were teetering, ready to come crashing down.

I sat on the couch in the darkening room and watched through the window as the light slowly faded. Nothing lasts. Everything ends. There is no escaping that truth. Holding that in my aching heart, all I wanted was for the day to be over.

Remembering (Leaving the Nest)

Dark shapes seemed to float in the indeterminate space of what, in real life, was my bedroom. The light was dim. I had no idea what time it was. As if in a trance, I slipped out of bed, pulled my quilt over me like a shawl, and left the room. I didn't turn on any lights. In my small office alcove, I sat down and started the computer. I opened a Word document and began to write. I had no idea what I was going to write, or even what words were coming next as I wrote. I just kept writing.

This is what I wrote, word for word, that morning:

Leaving the Nest
On the last day of my freshman year of college, I found myself curled up in a fetal position on the floor of one of the bathroom stalls on my floor in Sewall Hall. Actually, it was the cleaning lady who found me. I was babbling and gulping for air, beyond tears. She spoke Spanish, the language of my heart, of my home, the language of tears. I was removed to Wardenburg Clinic, to a second-floor room, where they bandaged my wrists with clean cloths. I didn't speak. The night before, I had taken a razor and slashed across the pale grooves just below my palms. I wasn't really interested in dying, just in penetrating the excruciating thickness of my tortured mind. The slashing was something clear and precise, like fresh air; the red drops on my white sheets brightened the vast gray hopelessness. I had wrapped my arms in strips torn from my sheets and gone to an end of semester party on Goss Street. I was light-headed, and my ears were ringing from the bottle of aspirin I'd swallowed before cutting myself. The rooms were small and dark and smoke filled, and I lay down on the grass in front of the house with a cigarette dangling from my weak hand until Benji, one

of the Dykes of Duck Lake, found me and took me up to the bathroom and gently washed my wrists and asked me "What do you want?" I didn't know what I wanted. I wanted someone else to decide, someone to take care of me, I wanted someone to move me from my room at Sewall Hall with the burnt-orange Indian bedspread and the record player you could close and snap shut and carry like a suitcase. It was a small single room where, as the year progressed, I ate less and less and drank more and more and slept with stranger and stranger men, just so I would have sexual experience to take back to London and offer to Nicky. He hadn't known what to do with my virginal infatuation the year before, and now it was too late. In May, he had died of leukemia, and all of that growing up and becoming experienced had been for nothing, useless. Now, I didn't know where to go, one used, confused, pale and oh-so-skinny eighteen-year-old. At Wardenburg, the sheets were clean and white and so were the walls. Weicker Moving and Storage packed up my Beatles albums and philosophy textbooks in boxes and placed them in a warehouse in East Boulder, and every morning my mother would come to my doctor's office in the northwest corner of the building, and I would come downstairs from my white room, shuffling in slippers and a bathrobe and sit silently in a chair between the two of them. They talked about me. Two travel agents chatting over a silent package resting on the chair between them. They discussed where I could go for the summer: India, where my parents lived, my godparents' house just across the campus, my grandmother's home in Phoenix. There were so many people

*who cared about me and would love to have a delight-
ful young woman such as myself spend a few months in
their home. I listened, disdainful, and picked at my cuti-
cles and smoked. When the hour was up, I drifted out
the door and went back to my room and let my breath
out in a long sigh of relief; another day gone by without
having to make a decision. One morning after about a
week of this, the doctor wised up and told my mother
she should just go home to Calcutta and let me make up
my own mind; it was my decision anyway. He turned to
me and asked me pointblank where I wanted to go, and
without any thought whatsoever I said Boston. He said,
fine, that's settled then and signed my discharge papers.
The next week, my mother and I flew to Boston.*

*There was some logic to it. My best college friend,
Joanie, who had been put on probation with me after getting caught signing out from the dorm to Timothy Leary
and Richard Alpert's house, had rented a house in Cambridge, in a dicey part of town. When I got there, the
living room was empty except for a record player in the
corner that played James Brown continuously. I moved
into the dining room, stringing the Indian bedspread up
to make a hallway to the kitchen. Just down the block
from the house on Franklin Street there was a jazz club.
Most everyone in the neighborhood was Black. A small
man with a German accent and a bust of Beethoven, or
was it Jung, in his office off Harvard Square diagnosed me
as manic depressive, and I smoked a lot of cigarettes and
stayed up late and once a week took the trolley to the psychiatrist's office in Belmont, and everything drifted along
just fine until one night Joanie brought home a musician*

from the jazz club who decided, when she locked him out of her upstairs bedroom, that I was fair game behind my flimsy curtain. My bed was under the window filled with huge black branches that moaned and scraped the side of the house. I didn't cry out. I stayed very still. After he left, my legs shook so badly I couldn't make it up the stairs to Joanie's room. I crawled to the kitchen and sat at the table and drank a cup of tea. It took days for my thighs to stop aching. I never told the psychiatrist in Belmont. Unknowing, my mother got on a plane and went home to Calcutta.

One day about a week later, a man I had met before leaving Boulder arrived on our doorstep. I could barely remember who he was; his name was Scott. He moved easily into my bed, and I cried as I told him, and he held me. The next morning, he found us a second-floor apartment on Green Street, across from where one of the Lovin' Spoonful lived, we were told, and the bed-spread came down and I moved in with him and his friend Brian and a large stash of weed they had driven across the country. I looked for work while they set up shop. I lasted less than a day at my first job as a waitress with my hair in a net. I could see the customers' mouths move but I couldn't hear the orders. The manager was very nice about it and told me I wasn't cut out for this kind of work as he gave me a day's wages. The heat enveloped me as I walked back to the apartment to soak in an ice-cold bath. Just up the street from our place, a sign in the window of the St. Vincent de Paul Thrift Store advertised a sales position. I went in. It was dark and cool with bins full of hats and racks of black shoes *and aluminum dinette sets with red tops and musty paperbacks. The staff were all seated on one of the living room sets, eating sweet rolls and drinking coffee. I was the first person who had walked in the door about the job. The manager, Lily, was a small, white-haired lady, and then there was Dennis, who stocked the shelves and worked in the back and lived in a group home. His head bobbed just a little, and he smiled sweetly at everything you said. Lily offered me a chair and a sweet roll, and I didn't pay much attention to the questions on the form because I knew they would never read it. I told them my name was Marion, and Lily asked me when I could start. I said why not now.*

For the rest of that steaming summer of 1966 I arrived on time each morning to do my job and eat sweet rolls and drink coffee. On Thursdays, I put out the new hats, and all the widows in the neighborhood came and watched me as I filled the bin and then they would pounce on it and paw through all that brightly-colored felt. I loved to walk to work in the morning and home again in the heat of the early evening and know that every day, from 9:00 to 5:00, I was safe in my nest of used furniture and clothes. Sometimes at night when the rage came over me, I would silently tear my white cotton nightgowns into shreds. But in the morning, I knew I had a place to go. And for those brief few months, I was strangely grateful to be alive.

I have no idea how long I sat at my computer and wrote. When I finished, the sun had risen. It was a cloudless day. I had to pee. I was thirsty. I felt like I had just come out of surgery, still held by the anesthetic, uncertain about who and where I was. I stood up, took a step toward the bathroom, and my legs buckled under me. I sank to the floor and curled up into a fetal position. I lay there for a while, and then I unfolded my body and rolled onto my back and said these words, out loud, for the first time from a place of fully being, not as a narrative, but as the truth:

"I was raped when I was eighteen years old. It changed everything. I have carried the wound in my body, and mind, and heart my whole life."

I stepped out into a world that was saturated with light, the trees a vivid green, the sky an intense blue, everything vibrant with life arising and dissolving. I had no idea how long I had been lying on the floor, no idea what time it was. It was the first truly warm day of spring. I stopped and stared, entranced, at a handful of brilliant yellow daffodils that had pushed their way through the snow by the front steps.

Bronco and Abby could barely contain their excitement as we started walking. I had no plan. I just walked at a slow, easy pace. Many years before at Rocky Mountain Dharma Center, Trungpa Rinpoche had introduced a practice he called "aimless wandering": moving slowly through space with no agenda, no destination, no purpose, just wandering with all our senses wide open. I spent the rest of that day aimlessly wandering around the valley.

I traveled up the spine of the small ridge, climbing over rocks, weaving my way through patches of snow, sure footed. The sun was hot on my face and hands. I was still wearing my pajamas, with my boots on and a sweatshirt on top. At the top, I squatted and peed on the ground. It felt good in a primordial earth mother kind of way. I felt no fear, no irritation, no concern for anything. My mind was still and open. I sat down on a rock, flanked by the dogs, and surveyed the valley below. I could see ribbons of pristine snow along Hardscrabble Creek zigzagging through the valley, the water shimmering. I took off my sweatshirt and pajama top and let my bare breasts warm in the sun, tickled by the cool breeze. My heart was so full it felt like it could overflow.

A song was bubbling up inside me, a wordless tune. I waited to see what it was. I knew it would tell me everything I needed to know about what was going on inside me, a message from a cosmic jukebox. I took another drag and exhaled. A phrase floated through the airwaves:

"Come down from your fences . . . open the gate . . . "

I heard honking above and looked up to see a straggling line of geese headed north. The words kept rolling on, "It may be raining, but there's a rainbow above you . . . "

I began to sing. "Desperado, why don't you come to your senses. You've been out riding fences for so long now." I took a deep breath and started belting out the chorus. "You better let somebody love you . . . let somebody love you." I kept singing, louder, with all my heart. "You better let somebody love you . . . before it's too late."

In a flash, I knew that was it, that was the answer to the question Benji had asked all those years ago as she bandaged my bloody wrists and Kay had asked at my first therapy visit: "What do you want?" The answer was right there; it was what I had blurted out to Pema Chödrön: "I just want to be loved." That's all I wanted. To be loved. To let somebody love me. It was all there in the song.

I was ready to go back to the house. I could see it was a long way down to the valley floor. One slip could leave me pinned to a rock forever. I climbed carefully from scrub oak to scrub oak and then followed the dragon's sloping back down to the road and kept on singing all the way home.

I hadn't eaten all day, and I was suddenly starving. I padded barefoot into the kitchen and started loading logs into the cookstove. I could feel something was shifting inside me, a crack was opening, letting in a sliver of light. *Log by log*, I said to myself, *that's how the crack will grow.*

Loving this Place

It seemed like a lifetime since I had emailed Berna my question about leaving the ranch. The next morning, I heard back from her.

> It was wrenching to finally leave for good. I cried myself to sleep at night. I felt as if my heart had been ripped out and buried on the farm. I had to leave Lindy, the love of my life, who immediately ran off and was never seen again. Strangers slept in my bed, swam in my swimming hole, ate off my kitchen table, and trampled my woods. I was stunned and bewildered. I bottled up all my misery and stayed busy, trying to keep from feeling the bitterness and bewilderment lurking inside me. All I wanted was to go home.
>
> It has been almost sixty years since I left the ranch, and I have not yet figured out how to say goodbye. If I close my eyes, I can see my parents walking from the barn carrying pails of warm milk and hear Mother's voice calling to me in my upstairs bedroom. I can see a

zillion stars unblemished by city lights and step in the footprints my father left for me in the snow.

Writing this today brings it all back. That pain. But somehow sharing it with you, Vicki, and hearing your stories and feelings from living in the place we both love has created an invisible net binding us together with the mountains and with our home there. I know intimately the sadness you must be feeling at the thought of leaving. It helps me to share that pain with you. I hope you can feel the same way.

Luv, Berna

I sent her a short reply right away:

I do feel the same way. Our friendship has been and continues to be a lifesaver. I don't know how I could have managed this last couple of years without knowing you were there, and that you were holding my hand every step of the way. I just want you to know that I am holding yours as well.

I love you, Vicki

I shut down the computer and went to the porch. A half-moon was hanging over the mountain. I sat on my rocking chair and looked up at the sky, studded with the same zillions of stars from Berna's recollections. The old corral was bathed in silver light. Soon dandelions would be scattered across the meadow.

"Living in the place we both love." The word *love* lingered in my mind. I felt raw and tender, thoughts and emotions softly bubbling up inside me. *What does it mean to be loved?*

Is it possible to be loved by a place? By a tree? By the sharp smell of peppermint? A field of brilliant yellow dandelions? Could love be the nuzzling of a horse or the unwavering attention of a dog? Could that be all the love I need? Why do I think love needs to be about the perfect romantic relationship? Could love simply be a moment of kindness from a friend, a common space of pure awareness with another suffering being, strands of light that flow through us, joining us with every living being and overflowing out into the world? Is it possible that I could start by loving myself? Could that be all I need to feel loved? Is it possible that being loved and loving are one and the same?

The days were getting longer and warmer, the meadow turning pale green with new grass, and the creek was rushing by the house, overflowing with melted snow. Art had already brought up Red and Chaz and Peanuts. I was outside, admiring the row of lilac bushes just knee-high, covered in new buds, that lined the fence around the yard, when Otis and Casey pulled up in their truck. It had been a while since I had seen them, all of us hunkered down, hibernating in our winter bunkers, now ready to emerge, pale and blinking, into the light.

Otis lumbered over to the fence. "Thought we'd stop and check on you. See if you made it through that last doozy of a storm."

I smiled at him. "Yep, still here," I said.

"I remember when you got those little suckers," he said, looking down at the baby lilacs.

"It's been a couple years. We got them from the extension office up there at CSU. They shipped them down here, free," I said.

Otis shook his head. "In little burlap baggies, no bigger than cantaloupes."

I laughed. "You thought we were crazy."

"I did indeed." Otis chuckled. "Now look at 'em, growing like weeds. They'll be real bushes before you know it."

I didn't want to think about what they would look like the next year and the year after. I changed the subject. "I'm thinking of having a Memorial Day barbecue."

"Sounds good. I'll tell Jo to make her famous tater salad."

We meandered over to the truck. "Are you up for riding Peanuts this summer?" I asked Casey, who was leaning against the corral, rubbing the little horse's forehead. He gave me one of his almost imperceptible smiles.

"Yes, ma'am," he said.

"Next weekend, then. I'm bringing Rain up this week."

Otis was easing his bum leg up into the cab when he stopped. "Almost forgot—you know the couple living up the road with all them kids, down in that gulley? The man went and had a heart attack. Forty-two years old. Left the wife and the kids." He shook his head. "I don't know what the hell they're going to do now. They been pretty close to the edge all along." He settled his leg under the steering wheel and started the engine. I couldn't think of anything to say. He didn't seem to expect a response. I waved my hand slowly as he backed the truck up.

Death seemed to hover over that stretch of road along the ridge of the Wet Mountains. Death and loss. In the years I had been living there, five people had died from accidents, heart attacks, and suicide. When I had had the brilliant idea to use my panic at moving so far out of my comfort zone as a practice for dying, it hadn't occurred to me that you can't practice for dying without coming up against impermanence, loss, and grief, my three biggest fears.

I had just heard that an old friend was dying in Nova Scotia—young too, not even fifty. A real wild woman, tamed by dharma but never boring, she suddenly and irrevocably found herself invaded by cancer in her brain, lungs, kidneys—just about everywhere.

Later that day I told Jenny, the postmistress in Wetmore, about my friend as I handed her the Hallmark card I was sending her. Jenny clucked and shook her head and then launched into a story of a friend diagnosed with some kind of fast-moving cancer, given six weeks to live. "He come by the house white as a sheet, carrying a bouquet of roses, wanting to tell me how he'd always loved me and how it was the biggest regret of his life that we weren't together. He even went on about how much he liked my kids. He was a mess." She laughed raucously. I waited for the punch line. She milked it a little longer. "He sold his horse and had a for-sale sign on his truck parked out on the road. He went around town giving shit away. A couple of weeks into it, the doctor called him. Seems they got his tests mixed up with someone else's." She chuckled as she weighed and put postage on the card for its journey to Canada.

"So I guess he had to propose after all that," I teased her.

She let out another hoot. "Never saw him again. Couldn't show his face after that. It was a damn good thing nobody'd bought that truck. He needed a fast way out of town, the little chicken shit."

We leaned against opposite sides of the counter and laughed together, and I felt a lot better about life and its uncertainties. "I've always wanted to be diagnosed with a fatal disease, just for the attention," I said to her as I gathered up my mail.

Jenny grinned and nodded. "There sure is something to be said for that."

I waved and pushed the old wooden screen door of the post office open. "Stay safe," she called out as the door slammed shut behind me.

Stay safe. What a strange thing we tell each other, as if we had any choice in the matter. And yet, hearing those words, it felt like someone cared, and I was beginning to understand that caring, like loving, was a bigger deal than I had ever thought.

Driving home, as I neared the gulley where the now fatherless family was still living, I pulled over and parked at the top of their icy driveway. I opened the back of the Explorer and pulled out a large Styrofoam cooler I had bought at the grocery store and filled with a random collection of cans of beans and bags of M&Ms and spaghetti and cheese, eggs and bread and peanut butter. A woman in a hooded coat opened the door and came out on the porch. I could feel her watching as I placed the cooler by the mailbox and raised my hand in a silent greeting. After a moment, she raised her hand in response. *Stay safe*, I wanted to say, but she was too far away to hear me.

An Old Friend Visits

"Hey, Fig." There was no confusing who it was; there was only one person in the world who called me Fig.

"Hey, Prune," I answered. "Where are you? It sounds like you're underwater."

"I'm on my car phone," my college friend, Joanie, answered. "I'm close to Pueblo. Are you near here? I want to stop by."

"Not that far, as the crow flies," I said. I gave her directions and hung up the phone. *Wow, has she somehow tuned in on some astral plane to my recent journey back to Cambridge, that hot summer of 1966?*

Joanie's life as a nun hadn't lasted much longer after I visited her at Tail of the Tiger. She kept her name, Tsultrim, after she took off her robes and married her first husband and had two daughters and moved to Boulder. I moved to Boulder, married, and had my two kids. We had stayed connected ever since, Fig and Prune. The origin story for those names had disappeared somewhere along the way.

It was just getting dark when she pulled up in front of the house. I met her on the porch as she came up the stairs wearing a long skirt clinched at the waist by a turquoise studded Navajo belt, her brown hair, streaked with gray, held loosely in a ragged bun on top of her head by a chopstick. She was carrying a shoulder bag, identical to the ones we had carried around India thirty years before. We hugged, and I ushered her into the kitchen, where, straightaway, she dropped her bag on the floor and said, "I need a bath." She had always had a way of getting straight to the point, no matter what was happening. In India, I had taken to referring to her as a sacred cow. It didn't matter if a mile-long line of cars was parked for hours, if a cow wanted to lie down in the dirt in the middle of the road, everyone waited until they were ready to stand up. Tsultrim shared that same quality of single-minded self-preservation.

I showed her to the bathroom with the deep claw-foot tub. "Perfect," she said, turning on the water and pouring in half a bag of bath salts. I went back to the kitchen and tried to figure out what I could pull together for dinner.

After a long soak, Tsultrim shuffled into the kitchen in a pair of my pajamas and slippers, her wet hair hanging down her back. We sat down to a plate of spaghetti and a bottle of red wine. It didn't take long for her to tell me what was on her mind. It had been over a year since we shared a fancy dinner in Boulder to celebrate our fiftieth birthdays, but we were always able to pick up where we left off, no matter how long it had been. "We're in a rough patch," she said, referring to her relationship with her current husband. She elaborated while I listened; I could feel her worry and fear that another relationship might be on the brink and her confusion as to what to do. She needed someone to talk to.

When she had finished, I told her about Joe's breakdown and his escape to Los Angeles. "He couldn't take the isolation, and I couldn't keep trying to make him feel better." I was keeping to the facts, hesitant to open anything deeper. We sat in silence and drank our wine.

"I wonder if things would have turned out differently if you had bought one of those pieces of land near me when you were first looking," she said. The statement took me by surprise. It had been awhile since that idea had come up. In 1993, Tsultrim had bought a large piece of land near Pagosa Springs in southern Colorado and moved there with her soon-to-be third husband to build a Buddhist Retreat Center, which they named Tara Mandala. At the time, there were other, smaller plots available surrounding it. I had forgotten that, when Joe and I started looking into moving out of Denver, she had suggested we buy one of them and build a place near her.

I shook my head. "I don't know. I don't think it was Joe's cup of tea. Probably too close an encounter with something Buddhist." Just saying those few words threw me back into the pain of the collapse of our marriage. Too much wine, too long a day, things had suddenly become raw. "I don't really know what Joe was looking for. I don't think anything would have worked for him. It was just a disaster waiting to happen. And now we have to sell and I have to leave. And it makes me sick to think about it." My voice was shaky. I was trying hard not to fall apart. For some reason, I didn't want to be seen as fragile as I felt. Tsultrim sat quietly watching me, then she reached over and put her hand on mine.

"It's a loss, Fig, another loss, a death. You know you don't do well with loss. Too many losses in your life." That did it. The tears began falling, a light rain, down my face.

"I love this place," I whispered. I felt as if my heart were bursting, as if it couldn't hold all the sorrow anymore. I was consumed with fear and regret, love and anger, and the desperate wish that none of this was happening. Tsultrim didn't flinch; she kept her hand on mine while I cried. It didn't last long. I took a deep breath. "Whew, I wasn't expecting that," I said, smiling weakly.

"It's okay," she said. "Let it hurt."

It was late. We left the dishes, sticky with tomato sauce, in the sink and retreated to our rooms. I lay in the dark, my mind swirling with unfinished thoughts and splintered images of a screaming child's hand clutching her favorite toy, her blanket, her mother's skirt, trying to hold on to something as her fingers were being pried open, one by one. Finally, I sank into a strange kaleidoscopic world of colors and sensations and fell asleep.

The house was quiet when I woke up. It was still early. I slipped out of bed, splashed cold water on my face, and went up to my attic meditation room. I needed to settle, to watch the sun rise, and ease my mind before the day began.

The sun was peeking over the mountain when I heard footsteps on the stairs. Tsultrim came into the room, holding two mugs of tea, and sat down on the old single bed next to my cushion. "Thanks," I said. "I didn't want to wake you." I took a sip. She sat cross-legged on the bed and we watched the sun rise. "I've been writing about what happened that night in Cambridge when you brought the man from the jazz bar home. Do you remember?" I said. I had been thinking about it, but when it came out of my mouth, it was unexpected. She looked at me, quizzically. "You left him downstairs and locked him out of your bedroom. And he came into where I was sleeping. In the dining room." I watched her.

Finally she said, "I don't remember much about that night. I don't think I locked my door. I don't think there was a lock on my door. I told him to leave. Maybe he left the house and came back?"

I could feel irritation rising in my chest. *The lock . . . was that all she wanted to talk about?*

"You may not have needed to lock your door. I was right there. There was just that bedspread for a door . . . and a wall." I stared out the window as I spoke, my voice bitter. I felt a wave of exhaustion wash over me. "Maybe he did leave and come back. Or maybe he stayed when you went to your room. Does it really matter?"

My breathing was shallow. Tsultrim was looking out at the mountain. I was beginning to feel that maybe she thought I had made it all up. Then she said, "Tell me what you remember." I told her what little I remembered: how a man came in through the opening in the Indian bedspread curtain and how I froze, and all I could remember was the sound of the branch scraping the window. "I knew he was the man you had brought home. I had seen the two of you making out in the living room when I woke up after you came home. He saw me too. Maybe he scared you, went too far."

I took a sip of tea and tried to breathe. Holding her mug, Tsultrim fixed her clear blue eyes on me. It was the first time we had talked about that night. After what seemed like forever, she said, "I do remember something you said the next morning. You were in the kitchen at the table when I got up. You were holding a cup of tea. I remember you looked up and kind of whispered, 'The strangest thing happened last night.'" She continued watching me.

"Was that all?" I asked.

"You said you woke up to find a man in your room. You didn't seem to want to say more, and I didn't want to push you. You weren't really yourself, so I left you alone."

Something grabbed me hard in the middle of my chest, stopping my breath. I looked up, searching for something to hold on to. The sun was shining straight into the room, blinding me. *The strangest thing happened last night.* I knew she was telling the truth. I knew that was exactly what I would have said. The queen of minimizing.

"Isn't it strange," I said as I blew out the candles on the shrine, "that you introduced me to my rapist and to my teacher?" We both stood up, facing each other.

"And you took me to India," she said. "Complicated karma, isn't it?"

We went downstairs and made some toast and then bundled up and went out to the Adirondack chairs by the creek. The day was warming. We sat listening to the song of water splashing and gurgling as it flowed by. The air was filled with a pungent mixture of peppermint and willows and wet earth. After a period of sitting side by side in silence, Tsultrim turned to me and said, "I'm sorry, Fig. I don't remember much about that night. It must have been really scary. I am sorry for being so careless."

She reached out and took my hand, and we sat together not moving, not talking, for a long time. I felt an ancient knot, held in the depths of my chest, loosen.

After a while she said, "I'm going to need to get going."

And I said, "I'm sorry about you and David. I really hope you can work it out."

"Me too," she answered.

As I walked her to her car, I had a flash of an old memory. "Do you remember," I asked, "going to see your uncle in San Francisco before we went to India?"

She smiled, "The palm reader. Very flamboyant. I don't remember what he told us. Do you?"

"I remember he told you that you would be married a few times, each time to a man from a different country," I said.

"Okay," she nodded, her eyes widening. "Dutch, Italian, American. I guess that qualifies. What did he tell you?"

"He showed me how my lifeline is split in the middle. For a while there are two side-by-side lines, and then it becomes one again. He told me I would have two very different, distinct halves to my life, with a long transition period in the middle."

"I guess you're in the transition," she said as we stood leaning against the car.

I nodded. "I guess so." I gave her a hug. "I'm glad you came, Prune."

"Me too, Fig," she said and climbed in behind the wheel.

After she drove off, I sat on the porch for a while. It felt like it should be late in the day, but when I looked at my watch it was only noon. The whole afternoon stretched out in front of me. The dishes were still soaking in the sink, the beds unmade. I was still in my pajamas. The garden needed weeding. I let it all go and stayed where I was in the glider, rocking slowly back and forth.

Dandelion Wine

The next week, I hauled Rain home from Rancho Loco. When we got to the ranch, I pulled up next to the corral, opened the back of the trailer, and led him into the corral.

The gate to the meadow was open, the other horses grazing nearby. As I released Rain, he whinnied loudly and his old friend Chaz whinnied back. A primal call and response. In a heartbeat, Rain was out the gate, cantering across the meadow, his body rippling as he shook off his winter confinement. He was home, with his herd, the ruler of his domain. I leaned against the corral, watching. Everything felt complete. It had been a long and exhausting day, and I was dusty and sweaty. It was time for a shower.

The message machine was blinking, so I hit the button. There were two. The first was from Berna. Her voice was weak but still full of that "nothing to worry about even when the worst possible situation is unfolding" spirit I had come to rely on. The message was short: "Hi Vicki. It's Berna. I just wanted to see how the dandelions are doing. I wish I could be there. Are you still planning on trying to make my grandmother's dandelion wine? I can send you the recipe. Love you."

How did she know? Just that morning I realized that the pasture had suddenly become a field of brilliant gold flowers. Even the yard around the house was sparkling with bright yellow stars. I picked up the phone and called her back, leaving a message. "Please send the recipe. I do so wish you could be here to make it with me. Sending all my love back to you." I didn't want to think about our plan for Berna to come spend a few days at the ranch, basking in the glory of dandelion season and making her grandmother's dandelion wine with me.

I pressed the button a second time. "I'm coming Memorial Day weekend." Joe launched straight in. I steeled myself and kept listening. "We need to talk. And I want to make a video of the place for Watson Realty—for potential buyers." I could feel a surge of electricity shoot through my body. How about: "Would it work for you if I came out Memorial Day weekend?" I stood in the hall by the answering machine, pulsing with a wild energy that was blowing out all my circuits. Furious and helpless. And something else I couldn't quite name. I went outside and marched up the driveway and back down, feeling the charge start to dissipate. And then I knew—it was his voice. From the night we first met, Joe's voice had drawn me to him. Hearing his voice, disembodied and unexpected, had stirred an old longing to connect with him that had never completely disappeared in all our years together. Complicated karma, as Tsultrim had said.

Just then, a last ray of sun lit up the dandelions on the hillside. *What the hell*, I thought. *I'm going to make dandelion wine and we are going to drink it at the barbecue and Joe can go fuck himself. I am not canceling my party for him.*

First thing the next morning I called Dee. "I really need your help for this party. Do you have time to come up?" I blurted out. It was Sunday. I knew she wouldn't be working.

"Sure, I'll be there soon," she answered.

As I waited for her, I wrote a guest list. Otis and Johanna and Casey; the Rancho Loco crew—Laura and Ron, who were back together, and Lee, who was back in the stables full time after his emu business failed. Dee, of course, and maybe her on-again, off-again husband, John, who had moved back in to try to stop the divorce proceedings. And Joe. A motley crew, for sure.

"Dandelion wine? Are you kidding?" Dee said as I printed out the instructions from Berna's email. "Have you ever made it?"

"I have the recipe here," I told her and launched into reading the printout:

> I helped Grandma carry bags of spiky, golden flowers from the pasture to the root cellar. There she mixed them with cold, clear spring water and squeezed their essence into a crock. Tingling, fruity smells wafted through the house as the wine fermented behind the kitchen range. By the time the planting season got under way, field hands would have a bottle of Grandma's nectar to swig at suppertime.

I looked over at Dee, who was trying valiantly to hold it together. "What?" I said, still grasping onto a vestige of hope.

"There are so many ways this is bat-shit crazy," she started. "First, picking the damn flowers, second where the hell is the wine press and the crock, and last but not least, the wine has to ferment for weeks, and the barbecue is just days away." She gave me a satisfied I-rest-my-case look.

I folded. "Okay, okay, you're right," I said.

And then she graciously ended the discussion with, "I'll bring a case of Coors and we'll pretend it's dandelion wine."

We settled down at the kitchen table and started to write down a list of supplies: chicken breasts and ribs, hamburger meat, buns and all the fixings, a pie or two. I told her Johanna was bringing potato salad. "I'll bring a watermelon," Dee said. "And Laura is a good pie maker. So who else is coming?" I read her the list.

"Joe will be here that weekend," I added. "How about John?"

"Looks like he'll be here too," she said. We looked at each other and shook our heads. "The soon-to-be-ex-wives club." Dee giggled. "Wasn't there a movie with some kind of title like that? With Dolly Parton."

"That was *The First Wives Club* with Goldie Hawn," I laughed. "And I was Joe's third wife."

After Dee left, I picked up the phone and dialed Berna's number. Usually those days, she didn't answer, but this time she picked up after one ring. "You must have had your hand on the receiver," I said after we said our hellos.

"I was just waiting to hear about a doctor's appointment," she said, sounding tired. "It's a full-time job, keeping track. But it's all right—they can leave a message. How's the wine making going?"

"I failed miserably," I said. "In fact, I didn't even get started. I gave up."

To my surprise, Berna began to laugh. "Don't feel bad," she said. "I've never managed to do it either."

"Thank God. I felt terrible letting down the team," I said, laughing.

"No, no, I have given up more times than I can count," she said. It felt good to have something to laugh about together. I told her about the barbecue, describing the guests and the food.

"Laura from the stables is bringing up her horse so we can all ride," I added.

"It sounds just like the parties we had up there when I was little. All the neighbors came with food, and there was horse-back riding and all-night square dancing in the barn. It was a good time." Her voice was wistful, and I could feel a wave of sadness wash over us.

"I do wish you could be here, even though there won't be all-night square dancing or dandelion wine," I said as we ended the conversation. "I will be thinking of you."

"I'll be thinking of you too," Berna said. "Have fun. I know you will."

Two days later, Joe drove up in his Jeep. I watched from the porch as he took his suitcase from the trunk and walked toward me. We exchanged a few terse words. "Hi, I'm having a barbecue tomorrow. You can come, or not," I told him.

"Okay, I have a lot to do. I'll be okay." He went inside, leaving me on the porch, bobbing in an uneasy sea. The combination of hosting a get-together after my long winter hibernation and Joe there to put our home on the market had created a perfect petri dish for brewing anxiety. But I was determined not to let it get to me. That evening we made small talk over dinner and then went to our rooms.

The next morning, Joe was already filming in the kitchen when I got up.

After I told him I needed the kitchen to get ready for the barbecue, he retreated outside, taking shots of the cabin, the corral, and the creek up toward Eustace's land. I began making hamburger patties, marinating the chicken breasts and setting up the picnic table by the gazebo, all the while keeping track of Joe's movements until he finally retreated to his office.

It was just past noon when Rain started making a racket in the corral, pacing back and forth and neighing loudly. How he knew his buddy was in the trailer that was just turning into the driveway was one of those mysteries of animal minds that never ceased to amaze me. I went out to greet Laura and Ron as they parked in front of the corral. "Welcome to Lookout Valley," I greeted them.

"Hi there," they called out as they got out of the truck. Laura opened the back and led her horse, Winnie, out of the trailer. Ron grabbed a box holding two fresh-baked pies from the back seat and started limping toward me, his gimpy leg from an old horse injury acting up.

"Fine day for a shindig," he said.

"What can we do?" Laura asked as she came into the kitchen. Laura had that iconic look of a ranch woman capable of shoeing five horses and making a beef stew for ten hungry men all in one day. Just seeing her in the kitchen was enough to reassure me that it was going to be okay.

I set her up at the table, slicing tomatoes and onions and cutting hamburger buns in half. Ron and I were hauling a cooler of beer out to the gazebo when Lee pulled up in his old Chevy truck, followed by Dee and John, who unloaded fishing gear and a huge watermelon and carried them out to the picnic area. Last to arrive were Otis and Johanna and Casey with the famous potato salad.

All my worries about weather and Joe being there and how it was all going to work dissolved as I watched everyone settle in with no hesitations or awkwardness. The day was perfect, sunny and warm. The beer was cold. Right away, everyone found their place. Otis grabbed a beer and set up a seat by the grill. Johanna settled her substantial

body into a lawn chair next to him. John, who was trying hard to cozy up to Dee, offered to get her a beer while
she was standing next to the cooler. Lee, a few weeks into
chemo for lung cancer, had that wired, dried-out look of
someone whose body was in trouble. But he kept his hat
on, covering his sparse hair, and lit a cigarette as though
nothing was wrong.

"Okay, ladies, are we riding or what?" Laura called out as
she walked over from the corral where Winnie was already
saddled and ready.

"We're there," Dee and I answered. "You sure you're okay
here?" I asked Johanna. "We could saddle up Peanuts for you."

"Don't you worry, just enjoy yourselves." She laughed her
deep laugh. "I'll have these fools whipped into shape by the
time you get back."

"Hell no, we're going fishing." Lee grabbed one of the rods.

John picked up the bait and held a rod out to Casey. "You
can come with us, leave the old folks here."

Within minutes, everything was set into motion. The
three guys carrying fishing rods were tromping single file
up the creek. Otis and Johanna were comfortably seated in
lawn chairs manning the fort. Laura, Dee, and I were riding alongside each other across the meadow, looking like the
Magnificent Three.

"I've got a big lifestyle change coming up," Dee said, opening a can of Coors as we ambled along. "My son is coming to
live with me this summer. Eleven years old. I'm going to have
to start looking like Snow Fucking White."

"Oops," I said, laughing.

"Whatever happened to that crazy German girl?" Laura
asked as we neared the base of the hill.

"Colorado wasn't Wild West enough for her," I told her. "She took her daughter and went up to Montana to become a real cowgirl."

"Oh, Lordy." Laura laughed. "One of those things you just can't explain."

There was something about hanging out with the friends I had made in that short time at the ranch—a quality of life just happening, without needing to torture ourselves figuring out how to make it better or what the lessons were that we needed to learn from the stuff that kept happening. Good fortune, misfortune, life was like a continuous rolling out of *As the World Turns* episodes in the Rockies.

"Come on, ladies, enough chitchat. Let's pick up the pace," Laura called out as she took off at a canter up the long slope to the upper pasture. Rain was ready to go. I felt him gather up under me, wanting to surge forward. Dee stuffed the empty can into her bag and looked over. Her smile told me everything I needed to know, everything she had been telling me for a year. *Don't let him take off on his own say-so. You tell him when it's time.* I took a breath, settled deeper into the saddle, leaned slightly forward, and barely touched Rain's sides with my heels. In a second, we took off, and Dee and I, side by side, were racing after Laura.

A mile or more of wide-open sunlit grass stretched out ahead of us. I could feel myself shedding fear, holding nothing back. A feeling of freedom, of pure harmony, of my body and Rain's moving together through space arose as we cantered fast across the meadow.

We were all smiling as we slowed down at the edge of the woods, wordlessly forming a single line moving slowly up a dappled trail. The ground was a deep bed of pine needles, still moist from the melted snow. The light was shimmering between the tall trees, catching the pale green shoots on the pine boughs. Sparrows flitted here and there. The air was fragrant with the smell of evergreens. Up ahead, I saw speckles of purple in an open space in the trees. As we got closer, I saw it was a bed of wild irises, tall and delicate, deep blue and pale lilac, in full bloom. We slowed down.

"Oh my God," Dee said. "Have you ever seen those before?"

I shook my head. "I never came this far into the forest," I said in a hushed voice. Laura looked at us both, smiling. It was breathtaking. The magic of the three of us coming upon that spot at that moment was so poignant, nothing needed to be said. After a moment, we turned around and rode back out into the open meadow. The sun was shining bright. We could smell smoke from the barbecue wafting up the valley. We were back in the real world.

The men were back from their fishing expedition and were seated around the open fire pit that Otis had loaded up with ribs and chicken. As we unsaddled the horses in the corral, I could see that Joe had come out of the office and joined them. I couldn't hear the conversation, but I could see he was the one talking, probably about the joys of his new life basking in the sun and surf of southern California. I felt a familiar gripping in my belly at the thought of him holding forth about himself as everyone around him wilted. In the next instance, I realized he was no longer my responsibility. In fact, he had never been my responsibility, but there was no point in opening that old barn door. On that day, Memorial Day 2000, I knew that whatever Joe did or said was not a reflection on me. He could do what he wanted, and I could go ahead and have my own good time.

As the sun dropped behind the ridge, we all sat in a circle on logs and lawn chairs next to the fire, balancing paper plates loaded with burgers stuffed into buns dripping with ketchup and ribs and chicken breasts sticky with barbecue sauce and German potato salad, washed down with bottles of beer. We complimented the cooks and swapped stories of fishing exploits, horse tales, and the crazy things emus did. We threw the Frisbee over and over for Abby and laughed until it hurt at Bronco and Dee's Pomeranian eating watermelon off the rinds we threw on the ground.

After a while, Joe drifted off into the house; the rest of us kept on chatting for a while until it was just about dark, and Ron got up and stretched his aching body and pronounced it a great day. Dee grabbed a trash bag, and she and I circled around, tossing in bottles and watermelon rinds and paper plates, while Otis and Johanna damped down the fire, and John and Lee gathered up the fishing gear.

Then everyone said their goodbyes, and the line of pickup trucks pulled slowly out onto the road. I watched from the porch as their red taillights disappeared into the darkness, letting the fullness of the day settle on me like a warm blanket. Even the thought of Joe being there, in the house that I had come to feel was mine, could not ruin this perfect day.

Be Grateful to Everyone

I woke up with my belly grumbling from the excesses of beer and barbecue sauce and cherry pie, but my spirits were still flying high. They stayed high up until Joe's last words as I left for the prison meeting. "I'm going to Watson's to get the listing going," he said, and I came crashing down. He had just finished reviewing the Memorial Day get-together with what sounded to me like the condescending comment, "Nice people."

"They are my friends, good friends. And tell John Watson I won't allow him to put a for-sale sign anywhere on the property," I barked as I headed out the door.

I drove down the canyon still buzzing from that exchange. I was in the perfect state of mind to talk about the day's slogan "Be grateful to everyone," or how to practice patience when dealing with difficult people. People who push every button you have. People you can't stand. I planned on starting with the Bengali tea seller story I had heard Pema Chödrön tell.

We were all seated in a circle on our cushions when I began. "There is a story that when Atisha, the Indian teacher who came up with these slogans, was invited to teach in Tibet, he was under the impression that Tibetans were all laid back and easygoing, so he decided to bring someone really irritating along with him to help his practice of patience. Bengali tea sellers had a reputation for being the most annoying people in the world, so he decided to bring one with him on the journey." The men were all looking at me, bewildered. I wasn't sure whether it was the word *Bengali*, or *tea seller*, or just the whole idea of practicing patience by creating an annoying situation that had them flummoxed. I had to come up with a translation.

"Okay, think of someone you really can't stand. Someone from your life outside or someone here in the Camp." I looked around the group.

"How many assholes can we pick?" Matt asked. He was ready to start rolling out his list, so I decided it was best to keep going.

"Now zero in on what they do that gets under your skin. And then, what you do when that happens. Can you identify how it feels? Or are you caught up in telling yourself the story of what most annoys you about them?" By now the men were sitting quietly, each lost, it seemed, in their contemplations. As I worked my way through the questions, all I could think of was Joe and all the ways he drove me crazy: all the irritating things he did, his intolerance, his judgmental mind, his lack of compassion, his inability to be present. Blah, blah, blah. "Does anyone want to report on their findings?" I asked.

After a moment, Luis nodded, and I turned the floor over to him. "I'm not naming names," he said, "but you all know the asshole I'm talking about." He went on to describe a man in the Camp who felt he was entitled to get the best of everything—the best food at lunch, the best seat in the yard, a man who had been a big-time coke dealer in Baton Rouge and thought he deserved the same kind of respect inside that he had earned through terrorizing people on the outside.

I took a deep breath, nervous that I was about to ask Luis to take a bigger leap than he was ready for. "So," I began, "is there anything about this man, these qualities you are describing, that seems familiar to you? Anything about what pisses you off that you could identify in yourself?"

Luis sat still, his impressive head of black hair gleaming with pomade, his back erect, the image of someone who demanded respect. I couldn't tell what he was thinking. I was caught up in my own realization that all the qualities I hated in Joe were ones I could easily recognize in myself. I was intolerant and judgmental, I lacked compassion, and I had a hard time staying in the present. I had to drag myself back to the room. Luis was nodding slowly, reluctant to verbalize what he was seeing, but definitely seeing something. "Ass-holes as teachers. This is some strange shit, but I get what you're saying," he finally said.

"Can anybody talk about how seeing some of those irritating qualities in ourselves might lead us to be grateful to the source of our irritation?" I looked around the room. I could tell it was hard for these men, faced with so many annoying, difficult, painful situations every day, to shift perspectives that radically. I wasn't sure I was able to make that big a leap right then either. "We aren't talking about loving everyone. If someone hurts us, we don't need to hug them and say 'thank you,'" I said. "We're just taking a step back and seeing that all situations can teach us something about ourselves, and often the tough ones teach us the most."

As I finished, Matt started to speak, his voice a little softer than usual. "I can see it with my wife. We're getting divorced, and everything she says pisses me off. Her resentments and judgments. I just want to be like, 'Bitch, who do you think has been paying for your gym membership and nail jobs all these years?' She acts like I owe it to her, the world owes it to her. And then, I look at my own anger and sure enough, I can see it all there. The same fucking thing."

I could feel my heart pounding. I was relieved we were almost at the end of our time. There was one last thing I needed to ask. "So, where are we with the Refuge Ceremony? Are there any of you who would like to take the Refuge vow? I need to reserve the larger room for next month if we are going ahead with it."

Matt raised his hand right away and said, "Count me in."

A moment later, Luia said, "Me too." The other three, Kenny, Steve, and Frank, sat quietly.

"This is not something you need to do just because it's being offered. Only if and when you really feel like it. You won't be excommunicated from the group." I smiled at them, hopefully reassuringly.

"That's good," Kenny said. "It's just not for me right now."

Steve nodded. "Me either," he said, looking relieved.

Frank piped up, "Hell, this is just my third time here."

"It's all good," I said. "Everyone can be there, whether you're taking Refuge or not. You can be cheerleaders."

We all bowed to end the meeting. As we stood up, I said, "One thing I know for sure is that I am grateful to you guys every day for your honesty and courage." I was not expecting that to come out of my mouth. Luckily, none of the men felt they needed to comment. I was already feeling shaky.

Before I left, I stopped by the chaplain's office. "So, is this some kind of graduation?" she asked as she handed me the request form to fill out for the room.

"Not quite," I said, "more like a"—I definitely didn't want to say "initiation" and finally arrived at—"a confirmation ceremony." She was fine with that.

I wasn't ready to go straight home. I was feeling a little too raw and tender, so I headed over to Rancho Loco to return Laura's pie tins instead. Laura was standing by the arena next to a skinny sorrel quarter horse. "This is Bucky," she said as I walked over. I reached out my hand to stroke his forehead, and his head jerked up and then bobbed up and down a couple of times. "He's not going to work out," she said and told me how they had bought him at an auction in Limon. "He came from Kansas. It was us or the slaughterhouse. He seemed gentle enough for kids, for summer camp. But he's got that nervous twitch." I had been watching him as she spoke. His eyes were deep and very gentle.

"He seems sweet," I said.

"He's a good boy," Laura answered. "He just needs some TLC from someone who isn't worried about his head bobbing. Someone who can be patient with him." I reached out again, slowly, and that time he stood still, letting me stroke him down his neck. "Hey," Laura turned toward me, "could we bring him up to your place? Just until we figure out what to do with him?"

"Sure," I said. At that moment, I had a strong sensation of my heart opening to this small, wounded being.

We arranged for Laura to bring Bucky up the next day. I got back in the Explorer and headed up the mountain. Only one more night of Joe being at the ranch; I ought to be able to manage that.

Joe was just getting out of the hot tub, holding an empty beer bottle, when I pulled up. I changed into sweatpants, opened a beer, and perused the contents of the refrigerator, pulling out odds and ends of leftovers from the party. Neither of us spoke until we sat down with our plates of cold chicken and potato salad. Finally, Joe broke the silence. "John has a lot of good ideas. They're hooked up now with Christie's, so they'll pull out all the stops on a brochure and market it all over the world." As he started talking about the meeting, he was getting almost giddy. My stomach was in knots. I reached over and poured a glass of wine from the bottle he had opened. I could feel the sad, tender heart I had been carrying, since leaving the prison, rise up and spill over.

"I don't understand how you can be so cheerful," I said.

"I feel good," Joe answered. "I feel optimistic for the first time in a very long time."

"Is it that much of a relief to be out of all this? Don't you feel just a little bit of regret?"

Joe shook his head. "Not a bit. It's a huge relief. Now I paint. I talk to dogs. I garden. I feel good. I felt bad for all those years of useless marriage counseling and everything you wanted us to try. I hate this power struggle between us. I hate that you make me feel so bad about myself. I am glad it's finally over."

It felt like I had just been run over by a semi. So many words. I hadn't heard so many words coming out of his mouth for a very long time. I tried to breathe. To stay open. "I just don't understand how you can let it all go so easily—the family, our life. Everything."

"I hated being on the receiving end of so much anger," Joe said, taking a long drink of wine.

I tried one last time to get through to him. "It's not anger. It's sadness I feel. I am sad about us, about the kids, what they are going through, about our family. I know it's best. I'm not trying to resurrect anything. I'm just sad, is all." I stood up. Joe looked up and shrugged. Just a little shrug, but it was enough. I left the room and went into my bathroom.

I was shaking all over. I stared at myself for a long time in the small mirror over the sink. I remembered the exchange the year before when I tried to talk with Joe about being sad. That time, when he didn't respond, I shut down. That time I stood under the shower until the water went cold, and I still couldn't feel anything.

This time, my heart stayed open. Bruised and throbbing, but not dead. Not frozen.

"Do you remember," I said into the mirror, which had become a stand-in for Joe, "when you told me you didn't see any change in me from all the years of meditation? Well, I have changed. I am a little kinder. I'm not numb. I can feel things. I can thank you for that. For bringing me to this scary place and leaving me here alone to face my demons. For that, I am very grateful."

I got into my nightgown and turned off the bathroom light. The moon had risen and the bedroom was filled with a soft, silver light. I slipped into bed and lay still, not thinking of anything, just letting myself feel sad. No storyline, just pure sorrow.

Becoming Intimate with Myself

Joe was already in the driveway packing the Jeep when I sat up in bed. I could hear the sound of him dragging boxes across the gravel. I didn't want to get up. I didn't want to talk to him. I didn't want to disturb the spacious, open mind I was in as I awoke that morning from a vivid dream of Trungpa Rinpoche.

Over the years, I had had a handful of dreams in which Rinpoche spoke directly to me, giving me a thumbs-up or down on the state of my mind and practice. *In this dream, Rinpoche was seated on a large bed, surrounded by deep blue silk pillows. He was wearing a black and white kimono. I was sitting, relaxed, in an armchair next to him, when he looked over and said, "You are doing well. You are becoming intimate with yourself."* Thumbs-up! My teacher had just confirmed that the long and torturous path I had been on all those years was working.

My path, like that of so many spiritual seekers, was born from a deep unhappiness, a longing to find something real, something true, something to ease my pain. The longing led me to meditation, which I tried valiantly to do, first in the Gurdjieff tradition, then following Carlos Castaneda's instructions, and then, during my second year at the London Film School, at the Friends of the Western Buddhist Order weekly meditations. None of it quite made sense. Then I met Trungpa Rinpoche.

In those early days, being a student of Chögyam Trungpa Rinpoche was like being given a ticket on one of those Japanese bullet trains. He was downloading the entire Buddhist path at lightning speed. It was breathtaking. There was so much to learn and, given that my default when faced with challenging feelings was to excel in the realm of intellect, I took on too much information with too little meditation. I spent years trying to be a good student, doing what I was told, reading what was assigned, chalking up hours not exactly meditating on the cushion. Then I ran into a wall; none of it was making any sense, it all seemed like so much bullshit. Just as I was ready to throw in the towel, the true meaning of being a Buddhist practitioner finally dawned on me. I saw that it wasn't about learning the right way to do it. It was about living my life, it was about looking at my mind, it was about meeting whatever came my way each day with whatever amount of generosity, discipline, patience, exertion, meditation, and understanding I could muster. At that moment I felt my life as a practitioner finally began. Trungpa Rinpoche had died a few years before, and I was on my own. I needed to figure it out for myself. I needed to stop looking elsewhere and start working with my own mind.

Ten years later, that morning at the ranch, the message from Rinpoche—*you are becoming intimate with yourself*—was the best confirmation I could have had that my path was no longer theoretical. Along the way, it had become real.

I heard the back of Joe's Jeep slam shut. It was time to leave my room and relate to what was happening outside.

Joe was just getting into the driver's seat when I came out on the porch. He paused and looked over at me. There was nothing I wanted to say. He looked away and then said, "You should start figuring out where you want to go. The listing is going public next week." I nodded just slightly, turned, and went back into the house. I heard the sound of his tires on the gravel as he took off up the driveway.

As I came in the door, I could see at the far end of the dining room how the sun, still low in the sky, was bathing the bedroom in golden light. It was so beautiful. I looked around the kitchen—at the sugar pine cabinets and the old turquoise cookstove, the round scratched dark wood table and the orange recliner. I loved it all so much. Every inch of the house was tugging at my heart.

Out of the blue the thoughts came to me: *Could I be the one to buy it? Could I somehow come up with a way to buy Joe out? Why do I have to lose the place I love, just because Joe, a man, is telling me I have to? Could I figure out a way to stay?*

There was still coffee left in the pot Joe had made. I poured a cup and took it into my office and turned on the computer. For the next two hours, I followed a handful of financing paths, each one leading to another dead end. Two hours later, all I was left with was a bitter dose of reality: As a woman on my own I couldn't qualify for a loan big enough to buy the ranch. I couldn't get help from my mother, who had her heart set on my moving back to Boulder, a plan she had already said she would help finance. My father had never had any faith in my ability to manage money or take care of myself; it would be useless to talk to him. There wasn't enough time to find a sugar daddy. My only possible way of staying was if nobody bought it. A long shot at best. The reality was that there was no way I could buy the ranch.

I turned off the computer and stared out the window. My mind was still going a mile a minute, wearing itself out, banging up against walls. As it started to settle, I could sense another reality was hiding in the wings. *Who was I kidding? Me, a fifty-three-year-old woman, a lifelong city dweller. I couldn't do another year, another winter, on my own, taking care of a 130-year-old homestead on 160 acres in a remote mountain valley. One year, yes. But a second year? Or the rest of my life here alone?*

Joining fantasy and reality is our life's work, the Dalai Lama had said. Staying at the ranch was a fantasy. Selling and moving to a smaller place, near a world that was familiar, where I knew people and could start over, that was the reality. Boulder was the obvious choice. That said, I still had a horse, two ranch dogs, and a cat I needed to bring with me.

I picked up the phone and called a friend for some realtor recommendations.

On my third call, as I worked my way down the realtor list, I reached Harvey. Harvey listened and then proceeded to ask the right questions. There was no selling job, no fancy websites to check out. Just: "Is there an area around here you like best? How many acres? How much can you put down? When can you come up here to look?" We arranged to meet and look at some places when I went up to Boulder in two weeks to bring my mother down to the ranch. I had picked the two weeks of Wimbledon for her visit and made sure I could get every game on my TV to keep her occupied.

The real estate train now in motion, I needed to eat, walk, touch the earth. It was already the middle of the afternoon, and it felt like I had spent the hours since I woke up in an alternate reality.

Before I knew it, I would be moving back to Boulder, where I could shop at Whole Foods and pay $110 for one bag of groceries and still not have anything for dinner. The idea that I would soon be living in a place where the city council was debating whether to change the term *pet owners* to *animal guardians* made me queasy.

I was slathering mayonnaise on a slice of bread when I heard a truck coming down the driveway. I slapped a piece of ham on the other slice, stuffed a big bite of sandwich in my mouth, and went to see who it was.

Laura was climbing out of her truck. She had pulled up alongside the corral with enough room behind her for the trailer she was hauling. I could see Bucky's head through the window. "Hey, there," I called out.

"Let's keep him in the corral at first," Laura said as I shut the gate to the pasture and stood holding the other gate open, waiting for her to bring out the little sorrel horse. Bucky was skittish, unsure of where he was and what was happening. His head began to bob as he stood in the center of the corral. Rain and the other horses were grazing nearby, keeping an eye on the action.

Leaning against the fence, Laura and I watched the dance unfold, every bit as intricate as a performance of *Swan Lake*. One by one, each horse approached and, pretending indifference, began to graze just outside the corral until, finally, Peanuts came right up and stuck his head through the fence. After a moment, Bucky took two steps over, and the two horses greeted each other, muzzle to muzzle. "Time to open the gate," Laura said. Rain and Red and Chaz took off across the creek, but Peanuts stood waiting as Bucky tentatively made his way out. The two lowest horses on the pecking order circled around each other and then, Peanuts in the lead, they crossed the creek and began grazing.

"Gotta get home," Laura said, giving me a hug. "Thanks for taking him."

"No problem," I answered. "He'll be fine here." I looked over at him grazing next to Peanuts and once again felt an inexplicable kinship with this wounded being who had found a refuge with me, both of us in a tenuous, uncertain world.

Wimbledon Days

"Tsultrim dropped by not long ago," I announced. I had just loaded my mother into the Explorer, and we were headed south to the ranch for her Wimbledon in the Wet Mountains visit.

"Dropped by?" my mother asked. She was sitting upright in the passenger seat, holding her cane in front of her. I was amazed at how small and fragile she seemed as an older woman, after so many years of appearing so large and formidable. "How on earth could somebody just drop by your place?" Her voice was still strong.

"I know," I said. "But you know Tsultrim; she's capable of anything."

My mother snorted just slightly. "She certainly put your father and me through the wringer. Back when she was Joanie." My parents had become *in loco parentis* to Joanie on our trip to India in 1966, having assured her parents that she would be safe with them. From both sets of parents' points of view, Joanie taking off across India with a gimpy Japanese night club singer turned monk in training was way more than they bargained for. *Loco* became the operative word.

It was time to change the subject. "I met with a realtor while I was in Boulder. He's starting to look for a place for me. A mini ranch."

"Good," my mother said, and settled back into her seat. For the rest of the trip we listened contentedly to a Dick Francis mystery on CD.

In the years since my parents retired, moved to Boulder, and got divorced, I had been revising my view of both of them. Growing up, I saw my mother as an irrational hysteric, a sloppy drunk who threw her emotions around like candy from a piñata. My father was an impeccable dresser, elegant and restrained, a man who could hold his liquor. That image began to erode in 1970 when they were living in Saigon, their last overseas post. I watched as my father shut down and swallowed the position of the government he had pledged to represent, while my mother began to rebel. She couldn't support the war. It was the death blow to the partnership that had been their marriage.

But nothing, of course, is simple. Even as I felt more sympathy for the bind my mother had been in as a diplomat's wife, I still felt the burden of taking care of her, the mother who was never able to take care of me. All that winter I had been living alone, she never once called to ask how I was doing.

"It's still all about her," I had complained to Bob, an old friend from Boulder, at dinner during his visit to the ranch some months before. "It's all about her needs. She's getting old, recovering from having a brain tumor removed, can't walk well, half blind, living alone, and I am all she has. I'm sick of it. I just want to be able to focus on myself for a change. I go crazy when she calls multiple times, needing something from me." I was a little bit drunk. I needed to vent. Bob knew my mother, he knew how difficult she could be. I thought he would sympathize.

Instead, he said, "What if you stopped thinking of her as a burden and thought of her as a warrior?" He paused to give me a chance to take it in.

"What would that look like?" was all I could think to say.

"You could call her before she calls you, offer to do something for her, take her somewhere, ask her what she needs, not wait for her to have to ask. Turn toward her instead of holding back and getting pissed off."

I took a gulp of water. "Whew, Bob, I never knew you were so wise." I had just received a heavy dose of the truth. He was right, and I had a choice: to hang onto my story or let it go and try something radically different. Did I want to keep on believing I was right, or did I want to be free? It was time to bring the slogans into action. "Okay," I nodded, "I am going to give your plan a go. Or die trying."

It was that conversation that had led to my inviting mother to come to the ranch for two weeks. Just to be on the safe side, I had scheduled an appointment with Kay for a week into the visit.

Once at the ranch, we settled into a routine, beginning with breakfast together. Mother would clean up afterward and then begin her tennis viewing. During breaks, she sat on the porch in the sun with the dogs. She trained Abby to bring a tennis ball close enough for her to pick it up by tapping her cane next to her foot. We had a sandwich for lunch, sometimes sitting outside. Dinner was more elaborate, involving one or the other of us cooking something, but still keeping it simple—hamburgers, chicken breasts, salad, sometimes a glass of wine. As she grew older, mother drank less and less. We kept our conversations easy and straightforward, talking about my move, about the weather, about tennis. Every now and then, I would join her in front of the TV and drift off, watching the back-and-forth of the tennis ball across the net, with the soothing British voice intoning, "Set. Match. Game point."

I wasn't ready to get real about what I was feeling about the move. I could talk about selling the ranch but not about my grief at having once again to leave a place I loved or my anger at Joe for forcing me to sell.

Now, when I think of all the similarities my mother and I shared in our lives, particularly our marriages that fell apart later in life after years of disappointment, I don't understand why I could never be open with her. Early conditioning is the only possible reason. Growing up, on the few occasions I had reached out, when I couldn't bear being so depressed, my mother's response was always, "But Vicki, there is no reason to be depressed. There are so many people who love you." It was an incomprehensible statement that only served to shut me up for good.

That spring at the ranch, there was an unusual sweetness to the time we spent together. The weather was perfect, warm during the day with the occasional afternoon thunderstorm. We saw rainbows almost every day.

While Mother watched tennis, I spent my days keeping busy—riding, mucking out the corral, herding cows, opening and shutting gates, watering the garden, packing a box every now and then, running to Westcliffe for eggs, sneaking off for a cigarette when the anxiety took hold. Each evening, I fell into bed and read my book on how to work with depression as a spiritual practice. Every night, I would dream of houses, cabins, tenements, motels. Houses where there was no way in or out.

I lived in fear of Watson Realty calling with a request for another house viewing. There had been two already. Both times, I had left the ranch and wandered around Westcliffe, praying they wouldn't like it.

"Why, when I know how painful it is to leave places, do I attach to them anyway?" I asked Kay at my midvisit therapy session. "I attach, and then I get hurt, and then I shut down. It's classic. I keep dreaming about houses with no doors. And of course my mother is visiting, which probably isn't helping with the moving anxiety."

It was good to be able to talk with someone about what I was feeling about the move and how even thinking of the move made me want to disappear forever. "Do you know that in the four years we lived in London, we lived in four different houses? That can screw anyone up." As I spoke, I felt myself trapped in the same old vice grip of frustration and anger and fear I had felt as a child.

"You carry a lot of suffering from those moves," Kay told me. "The houses in your dreams are all parts of you, many different parts."

Our hour was almost up. "What I want you to pay attention to before our next meeting is what you do, or want to do, to dissociate when it gets to be too much. Smoking, drinking, organizing things—whatever it is, jot it down in your notebook. Write about what brings up the urge to numb. It's not about stopping yourself from doing it. Just notice."

I nodded and gathered up my stuff. "Computer solitaire is my go-to right now," I told her.

"Good, write it down," Kay said, walking me to the door. "See you in two weeks."

I spent the journey home adding to the list: smoking, drinking, keeping busy, mystery reading, watching the weather channel.

Mother had made chicken breasts and a salad for dinner. I knew she wouldn't ask me how my therapy session went. And she didn't. The one time, at my urging, she had tried therapy, she came out of the session with a satisfied smile on her face and said, "She was nice. We both agreed I don't need therapy." Case closed! Classic.

We sat down, and I opened a bottle of wine and poured us each a glass. There was something brewing inside me that I needed to tamp down. "Who won today?" I asked. We talked tennis as we ate. Then, as I poured my second glass of wine, I changed the subject. "Do you remember a conversation with a therapist you told me about after we moved back to DC from Madrid?"

Mother looked at me, confused. "I'm not sure I do."

"It came up in therapy today. How hard all those moves were for me. Leaving Madrid was the worst. That first year I didn't speak to you or anyone for months." I looked over and could see she was listening, so I went on. "I remember you told me you met a therapist at a cocktail party who told you that most of her clients were children of foreign service officers. Do you remember?" I gave a strangled laugh and took a drink of wine. Mother was sitting very still, watching me. "Why would you just tell me about that conversation? Why didn't you sign me up for therapy?" My voice was rising; the words felt like bullets coming out of my mouth. "I mean, for Christ's sake, I had not spoken more than monosyllables in months." I took another gulp of wine. I was shaking.

Mother's face was a mask; she was holding herself together very carefully. Finally she said, "I have no explanation. All I can say is I'm very sorry I didn't help you."

My body, so filled with righteous anger, deflated like a punctured balloon. My throat was barely holding back the tears. After a moment, I reached out and took her hand. "Thank you," I said. There was nothing more that needed to be said. It was all I had ever wanted to hear. Mother squeezed my hand, let go, and pushed her chair away from the table. We both stood up and together cleared the plates and glasses. I filled the sink with warm water, and we stood side by side while I washed and she dried.

The last few days of the visit, I spent more time in the TV alcove, lying on the couch while my mother sat close to the screen in a rocking chair, watching the matches together. Sitting there in companionable silence, it felt like some deep, old wound was no longer throbbing inside me.

The evening before we were to leave, John Watson called. "Is there a time in the next few days I could bring that young couple over that saw the ranch a couple weeks ago? They want a second look." I could tell by the sound of his voice he was feeling optimistic, but he was smart enough not to get too excited when talking to me.

"It's your lucky day," I told him. "I'm driving my mother back to Boulder tomorrow. I'll be gone a couple days."

"Great," he said, and we signed off. I stood still for moment, not ready to move. I felt sick. I still had a queasy feeling deep in my belly that night when I crawled into bed.

Bucky

A light rain began as I veered off I-25 south of Colorado Springs. It was a warm day. I pulled over and got out to stretch my back, and a bittersweet feeling grabbed me as I was hit by the familiar smell of hot, wet tarmac and sagebrush I loved from years of summers in Colorado. There was a roll of thunder, the sky opened up, and I hurried back to the car. I didn't turn the engine on. I just sat there listening to the rain pounding on the roof and watching the rivulets of water coursing down the windshield. I didn't want to drive. It wasn't just the rain. A feeling of dread had moved in, a premonition of something I didn't want to know.

I wasn't wrong. The voice message light was blinking when I got home. The message was from Joe. "That couple made an offer. A good one. I think we should take it. Call me."

Of course, Watson Realty had called Joe with the offer. Not me, the person living in the house, the woman who had made the beds and swept the floor before the viewings. The anger felt clean and real. It helped keep me from collapsing in a blubbering heap on my bed. I took off my shoes and began putting away my groceries. I sure as hell wasn't going to call Joe back right away. Let him stew. Anyway, I had no idea what to say. I fed the dogs and made myself a peanut butter and jelly sandwich and sat in the armchair in the kitchen eating it slowly as the misty gray in the window faded into darkness.

The next day I woke up to fog, a Scottish kind of day. I sat in the TV alcove with the old gas heater cranking, eating oatcakes and drinking hot tea and watching a VHS of *The*

Secret of Roan Inish. I was glad the sun wasn't shining. It felt good to be cut off in a world of mist and rain and haunting Irish tunes.

The movie ended, and I began to get antsy.

"Okay," I said when Joe answered the phone. And then, "I don't want to talk about it right now," when he began enthusiastically listing everything that needed to happen next.

He stopped for a moment and then said, "Okay, I'll just get started." Cut off at the pass, but not deterred. I hung up.

The rain was letting up and streaks of light were shooting through the clouds. I could see the hint of a rainbow forming in the sky over the corral. Grabbing my poncho, I went out onto the porch and scanned the pasture for the horses. The herd was grazing nearby, their coats wet, shiny in the glow of the late afternoon sun.

Suddenly, I realized Bucky was not with them. My first thought was he was lost somewhere in the woods, but I decided to check nearer to home first. I climbed over the fence and, following some kind of blind instinct, walked to the loafing shed. Inside was dark. As I stepped in, I heard ragged breathing and saw a flicker of movement. Bucky was standing up against the back wall, shivering. My heart was pounding hard. I reached up to stroke his neck, and it was then that I saw a large, jagged slash across his chest. A flap of skin was hanging, leaving a gaping hole of raw meat, dripping blood. "Oh no, no, no," I whispered. "Hold on, Bucky. It'll be okay. I'm getting help." He stared at me with those deep, soulful eyes as I backed out of the shed and ran to the house.

The vet's office was in Florence. It would take forever for him to get there. My only hope was that Margaret was home. I dialed and she answered on the second ring. "I'll be right there," she said. "You have a hose nearby?" I did. "Get it as close as you can to him, I'm on my way," she said and hung up.

I was standing by the corral with the hose and a halter when Margaret drove up. "So what have we got?" she asked as she climbed out of her truck. Just the sight of her stocky, no-nonsense presence in her moth-eaten cowboy hat went a long way toward calming me down.

"He's over here," I told her as we walked to the shed. Bucky hadn't moved.

"We're going to have to bring him closer to the hose," she said, gently slipping the halter over his ears, talking to him the whole time. "That's good, old fella, that's okay." We slowly made our way to the gate. I held it open, then ran over and turned on the hose.

"What do think did this?" I asked as she squatted down and examined the horrifying gash. "Barbed wire?"

"Could be," Margaret answered. "Or it could be a mountain lion. Hard to tell." She picked up the hose. "I'm going to show you how to do hydrotherapy, and you're going to do it twice or even three times every day for twenty minutes. For a week or two. It works better than any antibiotic or magic salve or any of that shit. I don't think he'll need stitches." I held the halter and watched as Margaret started to spray the icy cold water, gently, onto the gaping hole. At first, Bucky tried to pull back, frantically shaking his head, but after a while, as I stroked him and Margaret kept up a steady stream of sweet talk and cold water, he slowly calmed down. Gradually, as she increased the pressure of the flow, he began to look like he was enjoying it. He even seemed to doze off. "It's like an ice pack. Numbs the surface and brings the blood circulating to the wound. That's what heals it." Margaret handed me the hose and I kept spraying for fifteen more minutes while she leaned against the fence.

After twenty minutes, the wound was clean, the flesh was pale, and the blood had begun to clot. "He is a real little trooper, this one," Margaret said as we put Bucky back into the corral with a trough of fresh water and some hay.

"I don't know what it is about him," I said, my voice shaky with exhaustion "I feel something special about him. He is kind of magical." It had been a long day, and every bone in my body was aching.

Margaret patted my hand and, for the second time since I had known her, she said, "You're doing fine. You both will be just fine."

After she left, I pulled a chair up near the corral and sat watching Bucky nibble at the hay. He was eating in a slow, contemplative way, like a patient post-surgery eating spoonfuls of Jell-O, happy to have made it through another of life's challenges.

I felt so grateful for what I had learned about horses and life from Margaret and all the other horse people I had met along the way. Paying attention to everything around me was at the heart of that wisdom. Fifty-three years old and I was beginning to learn that everything wasn't about me.

Sitting there with Bucky, I could see the wisdom of letting go of all expectations, of giving myself over completely to my life, not trying to hold a little something back for a rainy day. When everything is falling apart, what's the point of trying to hold on to any of it? It was Buddhism 101, but sometimes the simplest truths, when we actually hear them, are the most profound.

The last rays of sun were streaming down the valley, warming Bucky for a few more minutes. It was time to call it a day. In the immediacy of all that had happened, I had forgotten completely about the offer on the ranch.

PART 4

Leaving the Ranch

The Pretense of Accident

I had no idea where to begin with all that needed doing. Beyond just a house that had been sold, there was an office in the barn full to the brim with film canisters, video cassettes, and editing equipment, a fully furnished cabin, a blacksmith shop/stained glass studio, a cat, a horse, two dogs, a truck, trailer, SUV, and me. All of it needed to be packed up and moved. And I still didn't know where I would be taking us.

Bucky's hydrotherapy was a welcome relief. Standing for twenty minutes each morning and evening washing his wound had become my new meditation. After the initial impatience, I found that when I let go all that yapping in my head about everything I should be doing, I was able to relax into the space of just being there. Together, Bucky and I would breathe in and out and enjoy the sun on our backs. I don't know about him, but for me, it had become a way to let all the jumbled plans and emotions tumbling around in my brain settle for a while. Two weeks of hydrotherapy with Bucky had done as much as forty years of meditation for my practice of patience, for being in the present, not wanting to run away or numb out.

That morning, I was having a hard time focusing. I kept thinking of Berna. It had been a while since I had heard from her, and I had been putting off calling her, not wanting to tell her about the sale, scared to hear what was happening with her cancer. In one of those serendipitous moments I had come to expect from my connection with Berna, there was an email from her when I opened my computer.

Hi Vicki,
   Wow, I am getting things done this afternoon. Thought I'd send this before I forget again.
Luv, Berna

EPILOGUE
Two years ago, in a joyful phase of life, free from job demands and basking in miraculous good health, I started writing about Heart Pond, a sanctuary near me. Now, having been diagnosed with an advanced form of lung cancer, I am prone to melancholy and self-examination. I am struggling to redefine myself as a person with a life-threatening illness—to revise my existence without giving in to cynicism, self-indulgence, or despair. And I depend on Heart Pond to help me direct my quest for who and what I am in this new phase of my life. I remember the snakeskin I found here last year, and I have visions of the water sloughing away the husk of my old skin so a new, more tranquil me can emerge, a freedom yet to be discovered.

My intention today is to enter this adventure with cancer like a pilgrim exploring a new planet. And I need the frame of mind that comes from the gentle landscape, bird song, and new life I find here.

As was so often the case with Berna, reading her writing felt like I was looking into a mirror. Every word she wrote about her journey with cancer was what I was feeling about leaving the ranch. Change and loss, however it presents itself, seems to have all the same flavors of despair and melancholy and determination and longing for freedom. I picked up the phone and called my friend.

"I just read your piece, Epilogue," I said. "I loved it."

"Thank you, my dear," Berna responded, her voice weak and a little rough.

"It's been too long. I miss you," I said.

"I've missed you too. There has been a lot going on. I don't have a lot of strength," she said.

I asked her if she could tell me more and she talked about chemotherapy, about her daily ten-mile morning run having become a mile-long slow walk around her neighborhood. Listening, I felt my heart grow heavy; she was so far away, and I could think of nothing I could do or say to help.

"Everything you wrote was so familiar, so close to what I am feeling." I took a deep breath. "The ranch has been sold. The closing date is set. I am so sad." There, it was out.

"Oh, my dear," Berna said after a long pause. "I am sorry. I wish I could be there with you. I know it must be so hard." Her voice was becoming fainter. I had to let her go.

"Thank you. You are in my heart," I said. "Imagine I am giving you a big hug."

"I will," Berna whispered. "I love you too. Stay strong."

As I hung up, I felt a pain too intense for words. A tsunami of loss, regret, fear, love, and grief was building deep inside me, ready to burst. I left the house, went to sit by the creek, and tried to calm my ragged breathing.

After a while, the murmuring creek began to soothe my aching mind. It was not fazed by what was going on in my mind. It kept flowing. It didn't even know how to hold on.

Kitty Boy padded over, lay down next to me, and began rolling over in the grass, back and forth, no pesky thoughts about impermanence bothering him.

Overhead, a row of clouds slowly spread out along the mountain range, dissolving into the pale blue sky.

Far off up the valley, I caught sight of Rain, galloping toward me along the edge of the pasture. Everywhere I looked, there was movement. Everything was in flux, familiar and unfamiliar at the same time. Maybe this was what dying was like.

Some years before, I had heard a Tibetan teacher reveal that when his mind was agitated, the thought of dying was very frightening. But when his mind was calm and open, there was no fear. "Dying," he said, "is like living. The way we face challenges in our lives is the same way we will face the challenges at our death."

I had never read *The Tibetan Book of the Dead*. I had only thumbed through it and gleaned some of the basics from books and talks. What I knew was that *bardo* was the name for the period that you enter at death and travel through for forty-nine days, the time it takes to transition from death back into the next life, into rebirth. Trungpa Rinpoche had said that what we carried with us from lifetime to lifetime was our bad habits. It all seemed to come down to working with the unhelpful tendencies of our mind in this lifetime, so the weight of bad habits wasn't overwhelming. That pretty much covered my understanding of the bardo teachings.

I could hear the phone ringing as I climbed the steps to the porch. I let it go to voicemail. Those days, the phone seemed to be nothing but the bearer of bad news. I listened as a man started talking. "Vicki, hi. It's Harvey. I just saw a house up here. It may not be perfect, but I think you need to see it. You might not want to miss this one. Can you get here by nine thirty tomorrow morning? I can send you directions."

Nine thirty? I'll have to be in the car by six. This is all happening way too fast. I picked up the phone and called Harvey back. "I'll be there," I told him and jotted down the directions. As I hung up, it felt like my body was a fuse that had just been ignited. It could blow all the circuits, or it could power a moving train.

I barely slept that night. Fueled by a large Styrofoam cup of the burnt caffeinated water that passed for coffee at Carl's Jr., I was on the outskirts of Denver by seven thirty. I had already inhaled two American Spirits and was on my third. It was decades since I had chain-smoked, but that morning I was over the panic edge, my whole body vibrating with anxiety, my stomach in knots, my mind in a whirl. I felt like throwing up. I didn't even turn on the radio. I wouldn't have heard anything over the roar of the road. Both windows were wide open so I wouldn't poison Abby and Bronco with second-hand smoke.

I made it to Harvey's office in record time. He was ready, and we headed over to the property, he in his Audi, with me following. As we drove east and then north, I realized we were headed in the direction of Pie's farm next to Haystack Mountain, where I had spent many altered hours on acid in the sixties. The place we were going to was a little farther east, on the outskirts of Hygiene, a two-street town surrounded by small acreages and horse properties. We turned into a long driveway leading to a small ranch-style house, painted a sad shade of beige, surrounded by a messy collection of shrubs and trees, and sitting in the middle of six acres of pasture land with a corral, loafing shed, and hay barn.

The first thing that hit me when we opened the lock box on the back door was the overpowering smell of stale cigarette smoke. For a second I panicked, thinking it was me. "Whew," Harvey said, leaving the door open, "I heard the owner recently died. It smells like she smoked herself to death."

"I think you may be right." I nodded.

I liked Harvey, a middle-aged gay man with a direct, no-bullshit manner. I trusted him. "She lived here with her daughter, built the place for the two of them. They named it Two Broad Spread. There's a broken sign leaning on the corral."

"What a hoot," I said, smiling as we began to check out the rooms—three small bedrooms, two bathrooms, a large living room and kitchen, and a laundry room. Basic; utilitarian. All painted a white that over the years had turned a dirty, cigarette-smoke gray. It was nothing to look at, but there was an irrigation ditch, a good amount of pasture, cottonwood trees, and a view of Long's Peak from a front porch just wide enough for my two rocking chairs. The dogs had already sniffed out the whole six acres and seemed content with the smell of the place.

"I know it's not ideal," Harvey said, watching my face as I struggled with the reality of it all. "But the price is right, and I haven't seen anything comparable in this area. It's a very desirable area."

I had never been one to comparison shop when looking at houses. Of the houses I had bought, with and without Joe,

I subscribed to the "when it's time, the right property will appear" school of real estate shopping.

"Okay." I took a deep breath and looked over at Harvey. "What should we offer?" I was already visualizing what I needed to do to make the place livable. First thing, scrape all the gray popcorn off the ceilings. Then sledgehammer the hideous tiles in the kitchen. And put in a larger window in what I imagined would be my office.

"Wow," Harvey said. "Okay. Let's go back to my office. I'll give the listing agent a call. And we'll draft an offer."

By the end of the day, it was done. We had faxed over an offer. The daughter, who had inherited the place, countered; we countered; she accepted. My mother had offered me the down payment. My credit was good. I couldn't foresee a problem with financing. It felt like we'd been on a very fast roller coaster. There hadn't been time to eat, and I was shaky with hunger. "Is it okay if I go home now?" I asked Harvey. Saying the word *home*, I suddenly felt shakier.

"Sure," Harvey told me. "Don't worry about a thing. I'll take care of the inspection and keep you posted."

We hugged, and I got into my car and drove straight through to Florence, listening to the country music station, the dogs snoring in the back seat. I stopped at Carl's Jr. for a spicy chicken burger and fries and ate them in a booth, staring blankly out the window. After all those hours of flying high on fumes, I could feel my body landing and the exhaustion settling on my shoulders. It took all my willpower to drive the last forty-five minutes home.

As I drove, I thought about my soon-to-be-new home, hanging art in my mind, arranging furniture in each room. I had reached the point of placing the rocking chairs on the front porch when a memory popped up of my first acid trip, at Pie's farm, just a few miles down the road from Two Broad Spread. Sometime during the acid trip, I found a safe haven in a pile of pillows under the stairs. I have no idea how long I lay there fast-forwarding in my mind through my entire not-yet-lived life, hitting a series of high and low points—tumultuous relationships, a marriage, three pregnancies and two births, creative work, emotional upheavals, divorce, suffering and joy, winding down to a scene of being an old woman sitting on a rocking chair on a porch looking out at a field bordered by trees. Content and at peace.

So far, most had come to pass. Now I was getting older, and I had the rocking chairs. All I needed was for my mind to be at peace.

The sun was just setting as I came down the driveway. I was blinded for a moment by the last rays of light flaring off the top of the mountain. A second later, they disappeared, leaving the sky pale with a tinge of pink. When I turned off the car, I felt the silence envelop me. It was so quiet. There was no traffic, no chatter, just the deep silence I had come to love.

The house was cold and dark inside. It felt abandoned already. I turned on the lights and started a fire in the stove. The dogs had circumambulated the house and barn and were ready for their dinner.

I made a cup of tea and sat in the recliner with my feet up. My mind was flitting around, touching on all that lay ahead. There was so little time, and so much that needed to be done. I began counting how many days there actually were. It was July 18. Closing had been set for September 4. One, two, three . . . I counted on my fingers. *Oh my God: forty-nine days! The exact number of days that a being travels in the intermediary state after death before rebirth. A bardo!*

It felt like another moment of being "guided by the pretense of accident," Trungpa Rinpoche's instructions on how to find our way in life when we have no idea what to do. I had always imagined it like headlights illuminating a windy road through a dense forest. All you can see is what is right in front of you, and you just have to trust that, eventually, you will reach the other side, arriving safe and sound in the exact spot you need to be.

I still hadn't met the buyers—a young couple, both stockbrokers in Chicago. None of it made sense, and I didn't want to know any more than I had to. I just needed to keep my focus on holding myself together and preparing to leave—letting go of a lot of stuff and keep breathing at the same time.

Playing

As the countdown began, so many simple, everyday actions carried a tinge of sadness, a poignant awareness that this was the last time I would be doing them: the last time I would pick runner beans off the vine, the last time I would gossip with Jenny at the post office, the last time I would get my hair cut at Supercuts in Canon City.

There was one last Friday-night girls-gone-wild with Dee at the Westcliffe Rodeo. The big lights were on in the arena, the sounds of bulls and broncs snorting and whinnying, mixed with the twang of "Mammas, Don't Let Your Babies Grow Up to Be Cowboys" blaring through the rickety speakers. For two hours of pure mindless fun, we sat in the bleachers, cheering and clapping as four-year-olds rode bucking sheep, teenage girls galloped around barrels, their long blonde hair flying behind them, and sandy-haired cowboys picked themselves up from the dirt and limped out of the arena. I felt like I was in a movie of someone else's life. But none of it was strange anymore; it was all taking place in a world I had come to know intimately.

"Whose crazy idea was it to repave a road only a handful of people live on?" Scott, the farrier, complained on his last visit to shoe Rain and Bucky. I was leaning against the fence as he worked, and we chatted about this and that—the price of hay, the lightning strike that took out one of Vernon's cows, and the new road repair that for the last two weeks had been holding up what little traffic there was on Highway 165.

"You know it's now a Scenic Byway, Scott. Not just any old road." I smiled as I said it, and he kept right on going.

"Why the hell can't they use the money to fill up some of the potholes on 50, a real highway instead of a road for damn tourists." He hammered the last nail into Bucky's hoof and gently laid his foot back on the ground. "This old fella is doing good. That wound healed up just fine."

"The magic of Margaret and Clara's hydrotherapy," I said.

Scott shook his head and chuckled. "Those two. They broke the mold when they created them." He began putting his tools away in the back of his truck. "Okeydokey," he said as he took off his heavy leather apron. I handed him a check. "You know where to find me. Call me when you need me."

"You got it," I said, looking away. I couldn't bring myself to tell him this was the last time I would be seeing him. Reality had definitely set in; moving was no longer a concept. I had the place, but I still hadn't a clue how I was going to get there. The next morning, Pie called.

"I've got just the thing for your move," she told me. "I'm not going to tell you what it is. Lester and I will bring it over later today."

"Wow. Okay, I'll be here, waiting with bated breath," I said and hung up.

I needed something to distract me while I waited. I decided to try out some of the games I had been reading about in a book about the Parelli method of natural horsemanship. Grabbing a halter and a lunging stick, I took off to look for Rain.

"Okay, big boy, let's have some fun." I started with the Friendly Game, rubbing his neck, his ears, his withers. Then I flicked the rope over his back and around his legs, which was supposed to get the horse comfortable with sudden movement. Rain stood there, looking at me with a condescending expression on his face. I took a deep breath and switched to the next game, the Porcupine, using my fingers to move Rain this way and that. Pretty soon he was turning to face me and backing up and walking and trotting beside me, stopping on a dime, twirling, sidestepping, and coming back to face me. It was a goofy two-step, and we were both enjoying it. I was smiling, and he was licking his lips to show me he understood. Parelli's instructions were simple: *Leave them alone when they are doing the right thing. The goal is to create a partnership through play.*

Being in a partnership where neither side was trying to control the other was not something I was familiar with. Power struggles were more my thing. It felt good to be able to enjoy playing with another being. In a flash of insight, I saw how my ability to be playful had been badly damaged as I child. I had stopping knowing how to play when the game with the young Italian man had gone so horribly wrong. Dancing around the corral with Rain, I saw how playing didn't have to lead to fear and shame—it could be a way to express love.

I opened the gate to the meadow, but before taking off, Rain came up and nuzzled me, dropping his head as I gave him a last scratch behind his ears. He nudged me one last time, then took off across the creek. The day was turning out to be a warm one. I was dusty and hot and starving and relaxed. After showering and eating, I sat down on the porch and closed my eyes.

I was jolted awake by the sound of heavy wheels on gravel, followed by a loud screeching of brakes. A big truck, with Lester at the wheel, hauling an enormous stock trailer, was rumbling to a stop in front of me. Pie rolled down the window, grinning from ear to ear, and said, "Well, what do you think? This ought to do it, right?"

"Oh my God," I said, jumping up. "You are amazing. Where should we put it?" After conferring, we decided to park it on a stretch of lawn in front of the office barn. Pie and I stood on either side, directing, and Lester navigated the enormous beast into place.

They had brought more steaks and whiskey, and we settled in for the evening. "This is definitely the first time I have ever moved my belongings from one house to another in something that just carried my dinner," I said, marveling at how little that bothered me. "Now that you've solved one of my problems, how about helping me with another one? How to fix the new place up?" We were sitting around the kitchen table after dinner, leaning back in our chairs, the plates stacked in the sink, nursing our last glass of whiskey.

I told them about the dreary colors, the smell of smoke, the popcorn ceilings. "I have an idea," Pie interrupted me. "What about Joe? Get his ass up there. Work off some of his guilt."

"Brilliant. You are a certified genius, my friend." I raised my glass. "Did I tell you the place is just down the road from Haystack Farm?"

Pie took up the banner. "To old acid memories!" she called out, and we clinked and drained the last of the whiskey.

I was too wired from all the activity of the day to go to bed. I washed the dishes and cleaned the kitchen, scrubbing the top of the cookstove, wiping down the table. I felt better than I had in a while. Things were starting to move; the logjam was shifting.

Taking Refuge

The next morning, after a last flurry of activity, Pie and Lester took off, and everything became eerily quiet. I poured some coffee and headed to my chair by the creek. Sitting with my bare feet stretched out in the cool grass, with the murmuring sound of the creek a constantly changing song in the background, my nerves, as usual, began to unscramble. I let my mind drift along, meandering here and there, my feelings arising and dissolving like jumping trout. It felt good to be there on my own, not needing to pay attention to anyone else's needs.

That year, I had found that I enjoyed people coming to visit for a night or two, or even a week, but I was perfectly happy to no longer live with other people. It was an unexpected relief to not have to engage with another human's mood swings and opinions. I had spent years of my life avoiding living alone, scared of being lonely. But strangely, I found that living alone at the ranch I didn't feel nearly as lonely as I had living with Joe.

Sitting there that morning, I had the realization that in solitude there is no one to hurt me. There is no way to misinterpret. No need to numb out or run away. No need to hide.

After a spell of sitting by the creek, I felt ready to tackle the day. First on the list was to prepare for the refuge ceremony, which had somehow crept up on me and was now happening the next day. I settled myself with my notebook and pen on the old iron bed in the shrine room and sat staring out the window. What did it mean to take refuge?

It had been twenty-five years since I had taken refuge myself, with Trungpa Rinpoche in the shrine room on Pearl Street in Boulder. Forty of us sat on cushions lined up in rows, Rinpoche on his meditation cushion facing us. At the end, each of us received a refuge name, something to remind us of our basic nature, who we really were under the layers of confusion. The name I was given was *Divine Torch of Holy Dharma*, the sound of which was so insanely unlikely it took me years to accept it as mine. I thought it must have been a mistake.

I hadn't mentioned refuge names to the prison group. As I was only a stand-in, not a real preceptor, I wasn't allowed to give them names. I didn't want them thinking they were getting the made-in-China knockoff, so I kept quiet about what they were not getting.

I took a gulp of cold coffee. I needed to focus. Refuge. Refugees. What did "taking refuge" mean to me? What had I taken refuge in?

I certainly hadn't taken refuge in comfort or safety, a warm and fuzzy blanket to protect me from my sorrows or the sorrows of this world. So what was it? The first words that popped into my mind were: *a path to freedom. A path to sanity.* By taking the refuge vow, I had committed to a path of letting go of the habits and opinions and judgments that kept me stuck in my suffering mind, the mind that drove me crazy trying to get everything to work out my way.

I picked up my notebook and began writing. As I wrote the word *sanity*, I suddenly remembered Trungpa Rinpoche's question all those years before when I asked him about getting together with Joe. "Is his allegiance to sanity?" I still couldn't answer for Joe, but were he to ask the same question of me, I would have said yes, however flawed, my allegiance was finally to sanity.

An hour later, my notebook was filled with random scribbles of ideas and phrases. I had to trust that the next day they would fall into place in the right order. I had butterflies in my stomach, but that may have been because it was late afternoon and I was very hungry. I was ready. All that was left was to figure out what to wear and to get a good night's sleep.

"We are born brand new into this life, and the challenge is to figure out how are we going to live in a way that doesn't make our own and other people's lives miserable."

It wasn't exactly what I planned as an opening for the refuge ceremony, but at that point there was no turning back. We were all seated in the larger chapel, the men in two rows on meditation cushions. Matt and Luis, the two "refugees," were in the front, the others behind them. I was on a cushion in front, next to a simple shrine I had put together on a table covered with a piece of Indian silk, two candles, a small wooden statue of the Buddha, and a vase of daisies. I was wearing my best black jeans and a turquoise blue silk shirt, my hair held back with a beaded clasp. I had added some turquoise earrings.

The men had made an effort to press out the creases in their shirts and brush their hair. There was a feeling of anticipation in the air. I took a deep breath and kept going. "We are here to support Matt and Luis, our two friends, who have decided to take refuge in the Buddhist path. They have chosen to commit to this radical path, the path of awakening to the true nature of reality, to how life is, to their true selves. This ceremony is the formal acknowledgement of that commitment."

It was warm in the room. I could see beads of sweat on Matt's forehead. His expression was serious, almost scarily so, his sharp features hawk-like. For a moment, I could see how intimidating he must have been as a coke dealer. Luis sat tall and dignified, with perfect meditation posture, his hair slicked back, his shirt and pants immaculate. It was a far cry from the arms-crossed slouch he had been when we started the group two years before. Now he looked as though he could sit cross-legged on his cushion forever.

"When I say 'taking refuge,' I don't mean hiding out. When we take refuge, we aren't searching for a new home. We are embracing the reality of being a lifelong refugee, of having no permanent home, of living our lives as they unfold, moment by moment, with open hearts and minds."

I wasn't sure how any of what I was saying was landing. I felt like I was circling slowly in a pond of words. I needed to get back to earth. Suddenly, something Matt had said in one of our classes popped into my head. "I just want something different. Not the same old anger, jealousy, revenge. It's always my own bullshit that keeps getting me in trouble." The Buddha couldn't have said it better. I just needed to paraphrase.

"What this means is that we commit to using everything, our whole life, the good, the bad and the ugly, to wake up.

We see what is working and what is keeping us trapped. We commit to taking an honest look at what gets us in trouble every time. We take the logic that we have been living by that there is a way to get everything we want by manipulating our world, and we throw it out the window. We acknowledge there is nothing out there—no relationship, no job, no political party, no drug, not even a religion—that will bring us ultimate satisfaction. We abandon our master plan of trying to secure more and better, and we commit to working with the lives we actually have, here and now, no matter how impossible it might seem. Instead of security, we embrace impermanence. We throw out our old baggage and embrace the basic goodness that is our true nature. We stop looking outside, and we look to ourselves for our happiness. That is what we are being invited to do when we take refuge."

Whew! That was a lot. I looked around the room, at the two men taking refuge and at the others there to support them. They were all listening, attentive and open. I felt such a tenderness toward them. In the two years since we began our journey together, a fellowship had grown among us that was deep and unexpected. A lot had happened in all our lives, and a lot of changes were coming up for us all.

Kenny was heading off to St. Louis. Matt's wife had divorced him, and he was looking at less than a year before he would be returning to a world very different from the one he had left thirteen years before. Luis was petitioning to be sent to Miami, not Lincoln, when he was released in two years. I looked at Frank, our latest member, newly widowed, who had told us in his very first meeting, "Now I know impermanence is about every minute of our lives." So much wisdom, so much goodness, held in that room.

"So, what is it that we are taking refuge in today?" I began again. "First, we take refuge in the Buddha—not as a savior, but as a role model of someone who actually let go of all the old baggage that was holding him back. We take refuge in the Dharma—the teachings, the truth of impermanence, the path itself. We take on the challenge that we can learn something in every moment in our lives and meet our difficulties with an open mind and heart. Finally, we take refuge in the Sangha, which is where it gets hard, because it means that we commit to working with all the suffering souls who are trying to walk the path of waking up as well. And guess what that means? It means us. No matter how much we might irritate each other, how much we might want to walk away, we don't. We are a Sangha. We are on this journey together. We never give up on each other."

I was half expecting that one of the men would be unable to resist cracking a joke at that point, but no one did. We were all holding the deep solemnity of the moment.

"So, now we've come to the formal part of the ceremony where we recite the words of the vow. For this part, I will be joining you, facing the shrine. If I were an ordained teacher, I would stay in front, but I am a refugee, like you. You are welcome at some point to take the vow again with a real teacher. But you don't have to. This is real enough."

I smiled and carried my cushion over to the front row, next to Matt and Luis, and got down in a kneeling position with my hands together in a gesture of prayer. "First, join me by kneeling in this posture, and then recite the words after me, one line at a time."

The two men struggled into a kneeling position and brought their hands together.

"I will say each line three times as we take refuge, first with our body, then our speech, and finally our mind."

As I began the recitation, the room took on a deeper quality of stillness. The space felt almost luminous.

"I take refuge in the Buddha," I began, and the two men repeated the words after me. Then, "I take refuge in the Dharma," we continued. "I take refuge in the Sangha," we finished the first round and began on the next. Each time, our voices became stronger and deeper. I let the final recitation hang in the air until it disappeared. Then I looked at each man in the room, ending with Matt and Luis. "That's it," I said. "It's very simple and very profound. Just keep putting one foot in front of the other and follow the path to sanity."

I could have kept going, trying to come up with the perfect final note of inspiration, but as I had just spent a half hour explaining, there is no perfection. "Okay," I said instead, "congratulations to our two refugees. Let's celebrate!"

Everyone clapped and cheered as we stood up, and the men formed a circle around Matt and Luis, pounding them on their backs. They were all beaming and bowing at each other.

I had enlisted Steve to help me organize a party for after the ceremony with drinks and candy bars I had bought at the vending machine. He set up the cushions in a circle, and we all sat down with our goodies.

"So," I said, "full disclosure: the other thing, other than sitting next to you guys, was that I wasn't authorized to give you each a refuge name, which is also part of the ceremony when it's given by a real preceptor. I am so sorry."

"Okay," Matt said, standing up. "I have something to say to you." He sounded like he meant business, and for a moment,

I felt a twinge of panic. "First of all, you *are* one of us—I mean, not that you are a felon, but I wouldn't be taking this step if it wasn't you giving us the vows, and I don't give a shit whether you are sitting in front. In fact, from my point of view, I would *rather* you were sitting next to me and Luis. We are a Sangha, right?" The guys all started cheering. I could barely hold it together, waving my hand feebly, trying to get them to stop.

"And," Luis continued, "I wouldn't want some stranger to give me another name. Shit, man, when I moved to Lincoln they tried to change my name to Lou. I am fine with my name. Or you could give me one yourself. Whatever."

"Thank you, to you both," I said, smiling. We settled on our cushions, eating our Mars bars. It felt like we had been through something big together, something life-changing—a birth or a death were the only things that came to mind.

I was about to wrap up the festivities when Matt turned to me and asked, "So what is your refuge name?" I had hoped to avoid having to reveal it.

"Divine Torch of Holy Dharma," I said in a low voice.

"Divine what?" Matt asked.

"Torch," I said a little louder, "of Holy Dharma." Nobody said anything; they all just looked at their hands.

Matt finally spoke. "Heavy. I don't know what the hell I would have done with that kind of responsibility. You've lived up to it, though." He looked over at Luis and finished with, "I guess we dodged a bullet on the name."

Luis smiled his enigmatic smile and said, "For sure, sangha amigo." With that final word, the ceremony was over. We all filed out of the room, the men to go back to their cells and me to my car and the long ride home.

It is hard to put in words what I was feeling as I drove up the canyon. It wasn't sad or happy. It was full of all of it, of everything. It was painful. It was pulsing. And it was truly alive.

Standing Up

I was in Boulder to check on the progress at my new place and talk with Joe about the divorce papers. We were driving down 28th Street, heading back to Hygiene after meeting with our lawyer. I was at the wheel. We were talking about the few last bits and pieces that needed to be settled. It was a low-key conversation, familiar from similar exchanges over years of living and raising our kids together.

The ease of the moment lulled me into taking a step out of our limited comfort zone. "I am worried about how hard this all is for Julia—the divorce," I said. "I wish we could make it easier." I glanced over at Joe; he was staring out his side window.

"How many years has Rayback's Plumbing been there? Seems like forever," he mused, oblivious, or just ignoring me. I looked over again, and he was staring at me as though he actually wanted me to answer the question.

"Really? Is that all you have to say?" I was seething, but I had to keep my anger reined in. I was the one driving. We both went silent for the rest of the trip. The good news was that when we got back to the construction zone that was my soon-to-be new home, I could smash some more old kitchen tiles with the sledgehammer.

Joe had been working there for two weeks. The work showed some of his signature lack of precision: the new picture window in my office was slightly askew, a perfect Bengali tea seller for years to come. But the price was right, and I was grateful for his help.

I was getting ready to leave, cleaning up the residue from the scraping and smashing, when Joe came into the kitchen from the laundry room where he'd been laying tiles. He had the strained look around his eyes of someone about to say something they had been rehearsing in their heads for a while.

"I'm thinking we should each just keep our own royalties. Not split them all fifty-fifty. Don't you think that's fair?" He was working hard to keep it light. I stood there and stared at him, trying to work out what he was actually saying.

For twenty years we had made a good living producing educational video programs for which we received royalties. Joe made science and history-based videos, core curriculum programs with names like *The Black Death* and *Understanding Cells*. They were short, he could churn out a lot of them in a year, and they had an almost infinite shelf life. Each year, I would produce one or two longer three-part series with titles like *Violence: Inside/Out* and *Hooked: The Addiction Trap*. The return on them was substantial for the first few years. Then, as hairstyles changed and different issues were on the front page, the income gradually dried up. That year, many of my programs were close to reaching their expiration date. The bottom line was that royalties from my videos were slowly sinking, while Joe's programs were staying on an even keel into the foreseeable future. The idea of each of us keeping just the royalties from our productions benefitted only him.

Standing in the wreckage of a house I had not wanted in the first place, everything in me was ready to do what

I always did—to clamp down on the screaming rage I felt in my belly and run away. For the first time ever, I didn't. Instead I said, "Are you kidding?" My voice was icy cold. "Do you really believe this has just been a business partnership? Have you forgotten that we have been married for twenty-three years, that we have children together, that we have been a family, not just a business?" I paused; it felt like steam was coming out of the top of my head. "You really think that is a fair split?" Joe had frozen, like a rabbit caught in the headlights. "And by the way," I finished my speech, "I brought a fully paid-for house into this marriage. You gave ownership of your house to your ex-wife." I stopped and waited, staring at him.

"Okay, I get it. That's okay, that's fine," Joe mumbled. "It was just an idea." I nodded and held off twisting the knife any deeper. "Good. I have to get back to the ranch tonight. I have therapy tomorrow. We'll talk later about when is a good time for you to come and get your shit." I turned and walked out the door. Abby and Bronco were lying in the shade of the big cottonwood by the car, panting in the heat. They jumped in the back seat, and we took off south.

My heart was racing. I kept coming back to that moment when I stood up for myself and said what I needed to say. On the spot; not later in front of a mirror but face-to-face. It felt good. Scary as hell, but good.

I turned on the radio. As luck would have it, the Rolling Stones were playing an old favorite, "I Can't Get No Satisfaction." "Hell, yes," I yelled. I cranked it up and sang the chorus. The windows were open, the dogs hanging out on either side in the back. It felt like the car was flying down the highway.

First thing the next morning, I drove into Canon City to see Kay. It was our last therapy session. The timing couldn't have been more perfect.

"Another log went shooting down the river," I started in, telling her about my exchange with Joe. "Every time I think the last straw has broken, there's another one," I went on. I felt energized, maybe a little giddy.

She nodded. "That's good. Good work."

"Hey, is it a common thing for women to reach a point at middle age when they've had enough of being married, of taking care of someone else?" I asked, out of the blue.

"It's not uncommon," Kay said. "Is there something about that you want to talk about?"

"I don't know," I said. "Sometimes I feel a little guilty about not being able to just give in to Joe—let him be in charge. It feels like I spent twenty-three years resisting him. And then I just got to a point where I'd had enough."

Kay bypassed my *mea culpa* moment and went straight to my question. "There is a theory that, as women get older, we find it harder to give power to a man who doesn't have any connection to his own power." She paused there. My toes were twitching like crazy.

"It does feel like I am sick of the bullshit. Like I just want things to be real," I said. "And if I can't have that in a relationship, I would rather be by myself."

"That is something to explore going forward," Kay said as we came to the end of the session. "Try writing about what it means to be real, to be true to yourself."

"Thank you," I said, shaking her hand. She didn't have the hugging gene, for which I was thankful. "I've really appreciated my time here. I wish you could come to Boulder, like a hologram or something."

She smiled. "You'll do fine," she said.

I drove out of Canon City, taking the back road to Florence. The radio wasn't on. Nothing was on my mind. All of a sudden, I remembered being in the ER with Grandma Vic when she was in her eighties. She was sitting on the hospital bed, with her straight back and long patrician nose, her legs hanging off the side. The young ER doctor was listening to her heart. "Have you ever had trouble with your heart before, Mrs. Miller?" he asked.

She sat a little straighter and then said, in her deep smoker's voice, "Not to my knowledge, unless you count the three assholes I married." I'll never forget the look on that young doctor's face. She got him good. "Little punk," Grandma Vic said in the car as she savored the moment.

There was no way around the fact that I came from a lineage of complicated, difficult women, constantly disappointed in their relationships with men. Why should I expect to be any different? In fact, why not embrace the crazy reality of the whole messy truth of who I am?

The Bardo

If this was the *bardo of dying*, I had now passed through the wrenching and shocking early moments of coming to grips with the fact of being dead and had begun the more arduous process of letting go of my ties to being alive. I had entered the *bardo of becoming*.

It was twenty-five days until closing, and the tightfisted sorrow that had been gripping me was beginning to relax. At that point, it was just about dealing with the day-to-day reality of leaving. Sometimes I longed for summer to last forever; other times I couldn't wait for it to be over. I was leaving in early fall when the valley would be preparing for winter, when aspen trees would quake and drop their leaves onto the ground, when there might be a silver frost on the grass at dawn. Each shift in the weather throughout the year was imprinted in my mind. The contours of the land were as familiar as the shape of my own hand. In just two years, I had come to know this valley better than anyplace I had ever lived.

Throughout that August, friends came to visit for a day or a night, each of them helping to box something up or load something onto the stock trailer: pots and pans, a chair, paintings wrapped in bubble wrap, boxes of old videos. "Please take anything you want," I told them, desperate to prune the piles of possessions.

Old friends from the film world, Don and Marianna, who years before had introduced me to Leon, came for a weekend. Marianna was Swedish, a woman with a deep connection to nature; Don was a New Yorker who could handle anything without hesitation. "This is so perfect. We can dismantle the sweat lodge Leon built," I said as I gave them each a big hug.

At dawn the next morning, we made our way to the island where the bare structure still stood. We lit sage and sat under the open dome and, as the smoke billowed up into the sky, we made offerings of song and prayer. "May all beings be free from suffering and the causes of suffering," I recited. "May all beings be happy." I remembered how much heart Leon had put into the construction of the lodge. Sitting there with the smoke swirling around us, permeated with the smells of peppermint and burning sage, I let the feelings of guilt and remorse and sorrow arise and fill me. I didn't grab hold of them or push them away. I just let them be there until they began to soften and dissolve and flow through me and out into the space around us. I rested my head on Marianna's shoulder and felt the weight of so much loss lighten. Then one by one we lifted each willow branch from the dome and burned them in a fire in the rock circle. When we were done, something felt complete; the space, inside and out, felt clear and open for whatever was to come next.

One night, Otis and Johanna and Casey came for a last dinner of spaghetti and Prego marinara sauce, followed by ice cream and Verona cookies, washed down with bottles of Coors. "You did good with that dinner," Otis said—as he always did—while I cleared the plates from the table. "Have you thought about how you're going to get that monster all the way up to Boulder?" he asked, staring out the window at the trailer looming large in the waning light.

Of course; every night, I thought. I sat back down and said, "Honestly, I'm not sure what I'm going to do with it when it's full. Maybe start a big bonfire."

Johanna chuckled. "That's the spirit! We could haul it a ways up the road to Useless's and then set fire to it," she said.

"And dance naked around it," I added, and Johanna and I kept egging each other on until we were breathless with laughter. Casey had drifted into the TV room to get away from the craziness. Otis was leaning back in his chair, looking on with his usual benevolent expression as we started to wind down.

Then he said, "We can haul that thing up for you, Johanna and Casey and me; you just name the day. If we leave early, we can get her done in a day—up and back down."

I looked down at my hands resting on the table. My eyes were suddenly moist. I was having a hard time saying anything, or even breathing. Finally I looked up. Johanna was watching me with her I've-seen-it-all-and-I'm-fine-with-it expression. Otis was harder to read. If the light hadn't been so dim, I might have thought he too was tearing up too. "Would you really do that for me?" I asked him.

"Hell yes. Of course we'll do that for you. You're our neighbor. Our friend." That did it. I had to get out of the room. I pushed my chair back, mumbling something about needing air, and left the house.

It was dusk, that long dusk that seemed to last forever in the mountains in late summer. The sound of crickets filled the air, the grass under my bare feet was damp and cool. I stood with my back to the house, staring out to where the trees disappeared into the darkness of night, trying to breathe deeply enough to ease the pain in my heart. After a while, I heard footsteps, and before I could turn around, Otis was there, standing behind me. Resting his hands on my shoulders, he said, "We're going to miss you too, girl."

"It's really hard to leave," I whispered. We stood there for a while longer, looking out into the dark, held in the silence of the valley and the evening and the sorrow of living and of dying, knowing that there was nothing we or anyone could do to change it.

"You will be buying the gas for this expedition, darlin'," Johanna said as they got ready to leave. You could always trust her to get us back to earth.

"Of course," I said. "And I'll take us all out for the best steak dinner ever." Casey was the last to load up in the truck. "I am sorry we couldn't squeeze another ride in," I said. "I hope you can keep it up, somehow."

He mumbled something that may have been, "Thanks." I knew he would probably never ride again.

After they left, I sat down on a rocking chair. As I slowly rocked back and forth, I thought of a teaching I once heard Pema Chödrön give. "Once you open up, you're open to the whole thing—both the sorrow and the beauty," she had said. "This does require courage—to allow yourself to feel what you feel and be with yourself. But it also connects you with humanity; you realize your interconnectedness with other people. It's a whole different experience of being alive."

The connection I felt with the people I had come to know and love those years in the Wet Mountains had shaken up so many concepts that had been holding me hostage forever. Concepts about what is important, judgments about how to live, unnamed fears I had held for years. The world I had entered was so foreign and so welcoming it let me be whoever I wanted to be, to remember who I was deep down and reinvent myself as an embodied, kick-ass, heartbroken cowgirl. It was beautiful and painful, and I was grateful for all of it: the full catastrophe.

The next day, I got a call from my neighbor Bill Donley: "I need your help," he said, straight out of the gate.

"Of course. What can I do?" He had caught me on one of the few days when I was slumped down in front of the computer, playing FreeCell.

"Some cows got loose and are headed up the road toward you," Bill said, his voice even and unfazed. "Would you be able to get out and stop 'em before they hit the highway?" It took me a moment. Was he asking me to wrangle cattle, for real?

"Sure," I answered. "I'll meet you on the road."

"We can drive 'em back down together," he said, hanging up.

Luckily, I was dressed. I shoved my feet into my boots and grabbed my hat. Rain was hanging around in the corral, waiting for the game of the day. I saddled him up in record time, and ten minutes after I got the call, I was at the top of the back road. Bronco and Abby joined us as we started down. Rounding the first bend, I saw the stragglers coming toward us. My heart was pounding hard. *What if I fail? What if I can't turn them around?* Abby, who hated cows, took off into the woods, but Bronco's herding instincts kicked in and, crouching down and flattening her body, she headed toward them. Rain perked up, thinking it was a new game. Holding the reins loose in my hands, Rain and I began weaving back and forth, facing the oncoming herd. They kept on coming, and I was beginning to get nervous when, all of a sudden, they turned around and headed back down the hill. Which was when Bill joined us.

I felt like I had just landed an airplane on my own, but the best part of the whole thing was that Bill barely thanked me. He just settled into his stride next to me and together we ambled behind the renegade cows, pushing them back down the road to his place. "Is that the same horse that fell through the old root cellar last year?" he asked at one point, and we had a laugh at the memory of Rain sauntering out of the wreckage.

"I was afraid you were going to have to shoot him," I said. He nodded and smiled. It was all good. The day, the cows, Bill Donley and me riding down the dirt road. It was a hell of a lot better than playing another game of FreeCell.

An hour later, I was on my way home. As I passed by the sign that said we were leaving San Isabel National Forest, I remembered the moment on that first day when Watson had pointed out the sign and said, "This is where the property starts."

Joe had kept asking, "So, is that hill part of the land, is that mountain part of it?" And each time John said yes, Joe got more excited, and I couldn't understand why he was so excited about the idea of owning everything as far as the eye could see. Riding up the road remembering that day, I realized how much I had come to love this land, how it had become my land, every inch of it, and nothing would ever change that love, that connection.

The week before I was to leave, I threw one last barbecue. It was a birthday party for Laura and Dee, and all the regulars came. I had never been good at baking anything, but I had a Betty Crocker chocolate cake mix and icing pistols in different colors, and I was determined to make a cake and decorate it with a horse. In my mind's eye, I had envisioned a perfect horse. "Is it a bird, is it a plane? Is it . . . ," Dee said, laughing, as I carried the finished product out to the table.

"Now, don't be mean, Dee," Laura said. "Of course, it's a horse. Or maybe an emu?" Even Lee cracked up, and I laughed along with them, and we all ate way too much cake and ice cream.

"Could you guys help me load something into my car?" I asked before they left, and Ron and Lee lifted the heavy wooden table into the back of the Explorer, and Dee and Laura helped clean up, and the party was over.

As I walked toward the house, I was suddenly hit by a wave of sorrow so intense I felt dizzy. I leaned over, trying to catch my breath, and Bronco came up and licked my face. "Oh, baby," I whispered. "What would I do without you?" I let myself fall onto the grass, and Bronco and I lay there for a long time together under the vast sky filled with countless stars.

The next day, cruising along Highway 69 from Westcliffe, I found myself making a mental list of all the things I'd done for the first time in those years at the ranch. I had not just driven a three-quarter-ton truck, I had driven it with a snowplow pushing three feet of snow up the driveway and hauling a horse trailer. I had used a drill for the first time, fixed a fence, changed a tire, found a bear in the gazebo, nursed a wounded horse, and driven a car through a blinding snowstorm, alone. I felt ready for just about anything. The mysterious world of taking things apart and putting them back together no longer scared me. I had become curious about the tangible details of my own life. I had become intimate with myself.

Lost in thought, I almost missed the driveway for Singing Acres. I hadn't thought about how I was going to get the table out of the car, but luck was with me and one of their ranch hands was just leaving. "Goodness, what do we have here," Margaret said, eyeing the strange parquet-top coffee table with large bulbous legs. I had brought along a flashlight so I could demonstrate what made it truly special. Propping it up on its side, I showed her the Christmas lights nailed underneath and, in the middle, the words etched into the wood: Made by Sid in the Nuthouse. "Now, that is something special," Margaret said, tracing the words with her finger. "I love it." I knew Singing Acres was the right place for this strange, hand-carved artifact that I had first seen in the old cabin that had been in my godmother's family for years.

Clara brought over mugs of coffee, we all sat down, and Margaret launched into a story about a horse they had sold on the internet to someone in Santa Barbara. "We get this email from them," she starts in, "saying they were having behavior problems with Rex." She looks over at Clara. "No one ever has problems with our horses, do they?" Clara shook her head, smiling just slightly. "So here's what they did. They called an animal . . . what the hell was it?"

"Communicator," Clara filled in.

"Right, communicator, who had a long conversation with Rex, and he told them he had been abused as a colt. Abused." She looked at me. "Can you believe that?"

I shook my head. Then Margaret added the *coup de grâce*. "That son of a bitchin' horse always was a liar." I burst out laughing. Her timing, the story, the punch line—it was all too perfect.

"So, have you decided what you are doing with Bucky?" Margaret asked as I was leaving.

"He's coming with me," I said. "There is no way I am leaving him."

"Good. He's a special horse."

"I know," I said. "I'm grateful to you for keeping him alive. I couldn't have managed without you."

"You did just fine," she said for the last time. There was no more to be said. It was time to leave. A light rain had begun to fall. At the curve of the road, I looked back. Margaret was on the porch in her baggy jeans and old flannel shirt, waving wildly. I put my arm out the window and waved back.

Driving home through the rain, I put in a cassette of Miles Davis's *Kind of Blue*. I remembered the first time I heard the album in London on a gray and rainy autumn day, the bare branches of the trees in the street gradually fading as night fell. It was a melancholic moment, maybe the end of a love affair.

When I pulled up in front of the house, I sat in the car with the windshield wipers going, letting the cool, melancholic sound wash over me, enveloping me once again in the same sweet sorrow. The rain was easing up and a rainbow was forming above the corral where Rain and Bucky were grazing, the last light of the day shining on their gleaming coats.

The thought arose that in years to come, I would remember sitting in my green Ford Explorer at Lookout Valley Ranch, listening to the haunting sound of Miles Davis, filled to the brim with a feeling so exquisite and excruciating it could only be love.

Leaving My Tree

It was the final Sunday. Dee was coming up for one last ride. The cattle were all gone. Art and Paula had come for their horses a few days before. "It broke my heart to see them load up Peanuts. I don't know where he'll end up," I said as we rode out up the road.

"Don't go there, girl. You saved Bucky. You couldn't take on Peanuts. He'll be fine," Dee said. We rode for a while in silence. It was a clear day, sunny but not too hot. The valley felt strangely empty with the cows and horses gone.

While I was drifting into melancholy, Dee had begun working with Bucky on the road, starting him from a standstill to a gallop, then getting him to stop on a dime by raising her arm. I finally noticed what was happening. "What are you doing?" I asked.

Dee trotted back and said, excitedly, "I think he's been a roper. Either on a ranch or maybe rodeos. Watch." She took off at a gallop and raised her arm above her head, pushing up in her stirrups. Bucky screeched to a stop.

I trotted up to them. "Wow. That's amazing. Look, he's not bobbing his head," I exclaimed. Bucky was holding his head high, looking proud to have been able to show off his skills. My heart went out to him, and in that moment, I had a glimpse of why I felt the kinship I did with this scrawny little horse. He was just like me, awkward and wounded. All he needed was someone to care, to see him, to understand and accept him just as he was. All he needed was to be loved.

We'd reached the end of the valley and were headed up the old mining road into the forest. Light was flickering on the pine and spruce branches. The gold aspen leaves were dancing in a soft breeze. A hawk was flying ahead of us, just grazing the treetops. The road petered out, and I followed Dee on a trail deeper into the woods. Everything—the smell of pine, the sound of the creek rippling, the hooves muffled by the deep bed of leaves—was magical. Even Bronco and Abby were silent, weaving in and out of the trees alongside us. Suddenly the trail opened up to a grassy area, a few fallen logs scattered around. We dismounted and let the reins fall, and the horses began to graze. We sat down, leaning back against a log. "It doesn't get any better than this," Dee said.

"It sure doesn't," I agreed.

I contemplated the few clouds moving above us. Everything felt like slow motion—the sound of the horses chomping on the grass, a leaf falling, spiraling to the ground. Dee lit a cigarette and was blowing lazy smoke rings into the air. I got up and wandered behind a bush to pee. Squatting down, I looked over at what, at first glance, seemed to be a random pile of rocks. When I stood up and pulled up my jeans, I looked more closely.

Maybe it wasn't random; maybe it was part of what had once been a building. Exploring further, I found a pile of hewn logs, barely visible, overgrown with vines and mushrooms. "Hey," I yelled. "Come see this. I think there was a cabin here." We dug around some more and found chunks of iron from a woodstove and a piece of metal with a scrap of old newspaper glued to it. A memory stirred in me, not quite rising to the surface.

It was getting late, the horses had had their fill, and the dogs were getting restless. It was time to head home. Dusk was when the bears came out to feed. But first I needed to make one last stop.

"Would you like to see the true magical spot on this land?" I asked as we rode back to the house. "It won't take long."

"Of course," Dee answered. I veered off and started down the trail through the high grass toward the aspen grove along the creek. I could tell Dee was dying for me to tell her where we were going, but I kept quiet.

The air was cooler as we entered the grove, and the last of the afternoon light was faint. The path was a blanket of gold leaves. I could feel my heart in my throat; I was never sure exactly where I would find it, but suddenly there it was—the tree with my initials—held in place by two precise periods: V. H. I stopped and waited. "Oh my God," Dee whispered. "I don't believe it." We dismounted and I traced the letters with my finger. "Magic doesn't begin to cover it," Dee said, in an unusually soft voice.

"What do you want to bet this is the only place in the world where there is a tree with my initials perfectly carved on it?" I said.

"This is your place," she answered. We held each other's gaze for a long moment.

Then I nodded slightly and said, "A piece of my heart will always be here. Forever."

Dee mounted Bucky and started slowly down the trail. I reached up one last time and touched the gnarled bark with my left hand, resting my right hand on my heart and whispered, "Thank you for being here. Thank you for finding me." I leaned over and rested my head on the old aspen one last time, then, climbing up on Rain, I rode out of the grove.

"Is this it? Will I see you again?" Dee asked as she loaded her saddle up in the back of her truck.

"Of course we'll see each other. You'll visit. Who else can get Bucky to show off his moves?"

Dee gave me a big hug. "Then we'll see each other soon," she said.

"Sooner than that," I said. "I need your help, one last time. Can you come on moving day?"

"I'll be here," Dee said as she climbed into her truck and left.

A fragment of memory had been nagging me since finding the cabin ruins. I went in the house and started searching for Angelica's book. Luckily, I hadn't packed it yet. Thumbing through, I found the page I was looking for: "We started our married life in a one-room cabin furnished with a cookstove, bed, kitchen cabinet, and $11 worth of groceries, there was wallpaper on the tin walls made from old newspaper."

That was all I needed to read. I picked up the phone and called Berna, praying it wasn't too late. "Guess what," I said when I heard her weak voice on the other end of the line. I was so excited, I had forgotten to say hello. "I think we found your parents' honeymoon cabin. I mean, the remains of it."

"Oh my," Berna said. "Where was it?" I described as best I could the route we had taken up the old road and onto the trail along the creek.

"My goodness," Berna said when I had finished, "I believe you have. How wonderful." I was smiling like a fool, and I could almost see her smiling back. I kept it brief; she knew from my email that I was only a few days away from leaving; why spoil this joyful moment? We each said, "I love you," and I said I would be in touch soon.

At the very end, she said, "I may have to go into the hospital for a bit. Just tests. I'll tell you more when we talk next." I didn't like the sound of it, but I didn't press her.

It was time for a last soak in the hot tub. I pulled off the heavy lid, slipped out of my clothes, and sank down into the bubbling hot water. As the sun disappeared behind the mountain, the sky went from silver to pewter to a deep purple black, the color of a bruise. One lone coyote howled in the distance.

I could have felt sad and forlorn, but instead I felt grateful. Grateful for a life fully lived, for everything that had brought me to that moment. My childhood, meeting Joe, bringing two amazing beings into this world. Grateful to the Buddhist teachings. Grateful for having had this year alone, to fall apart and come back together, changed.

Two days later was moving day, a major production. The cast assembled at dawn: Otis, Johanna, Casey, Dee, and me. Right off the bat, Rain took off for the far end of the pasture. It took me and Casey and a bag of apples to coax him into the trailer.

Finally, after a lot of maneuvering and hitching and loading up, our caravan was on the road. In the lead, Otis, in his massive truck, was pulling the stock trailer filled to the brim with all my worldly goods. Johanna rode shotgun and Casey was in the back seat. Next came Dee, driving my old truck, hauling Bucky and Rain in the horse trailer. I brought up the rear, driving the Explorer, carrying Bronco and Abby and Kitty Boy and assorted potted plants and garbage bags stuffed with clothes.

We were moving at a snail's pace, slowly traveling from the Wet Mountains to Boulder County. It was an epic journey that took five hours. But finally we pulled into the long, narrow driveway at Two Broad Spread. "You are kidding me," Johanna said when she heard the name. "That is too crazy. Who is the second broad?" After it was all over, the vehicles unhitched and put away, there was no time to linger. We had to get to the Outback Saloon and eat massive amounts of steak and potatoes, so they could get home by dark.

After our feast, as the truck was pulling out, Otis reached out his large arm and waved a big wave, and I waved back. I felt queasy, shaky. Too much steak and too many emotions roiling together in my belly. But there was still a lot to do; I couldn't collapse.

I needed to find something I could sleep on. I needed to feed and water the horses and dogs and cat. I needed to come to grips with the fact that I had a roommate, the other "broad," a friend who was a little further along in her journey of divorce. All of it was daunting, but the most difficult part was that I couldn't just jump in and start my new life. A few days later, I had to turn around and drive back down for the closing. During those few days, Joe would be at the ranch loading up a U-Haul with the furniture he was taking to his new place in LA. As usual, we were tag teaming.

A Final Moment

Here is where it gets tricky in the way that memory can get tricky. I have tried hard to remember the closing, where it was and if the buyers were there, but I have completely erased it all from my mind. What I do remember is every one of the last few minutes I spent at the house that day in September 2000. It was after the closing, after the papers were signed. The ranch was no longer ours. There was no reason to go back there, but something in me said I needed to do one final check.

My heart was in my throat as I drove down the driveway. The weather was exactly as it had been four years before when we first laid eyes on the ranch—clear and sparkling. I pulled up in front of the house. I was by myself. I had left Bronco and Abby at our new place.

The door was open, as though the place had been abandoned in a hurry. I walked in. The kitchen looked as though it had been ransacked. Cabinet doors were hanging open, and the counter-tops were covered in coffee grounds, an unwashed coffeemaker and scattered Tupperware lids. A banana peel was lying on the turquoise stove. A few greasy plates had been left in the sink.

In a daze, I started to walk through the rooms. A towel lay on the bathroom floor, rumpled sheets on the king-size bed we had left. Joe's frantic last few hours, the panic he was in to get out, was written all over the house. I was so angry I could barely breathe. *How could he show so little respect for this place, for my beautiful home, for me?* I stared out the window for a long time, then I began cleaning up, stripping the sheets off the bed, picking up the damp towel, washing the dishes, and wiping down the countertops.

As I worked, cleaning and setting things right again, the edges of my anger softened, leaving an unbearable sorrow. I knew there was only one person in the world who would understand exactly what I was feeling. I picked up the phone. Berna answered on the third ring. "Hello, my dear," she said when she heard my voice. "How are you? I have been thinking of you."

I took a moment, still trying to ward off the overwhelming grief I felt gathering from every corner of the valley, filling every room in the empty house. "I'm just leaving," I said. "I wanted to let you know. I am leaving the ranch, right now. I just came down for a last look."

"Oh, Vicki, I am so sorry," Berna said. "I know you must be very sad." Her voice was faint.

"I am so, *so* sad. I knew you would know what I am feeling. I have been thinking of you too. How are you?" I asked. There was a pause.

"Not so good, I am afraid," Berna said. "They can't do anything more for me."

"What does that mean?"

"They say it won't be long now. They've sent me home. I have maybe six more months."

"Oh, no . . . "

The tightness in my chest squeezed the last breath out of me. I held on long enough to tell her I loved her and for her to say she loved me and for both of us to say goodbye. I put down the phone and went outside and collapsed on the porch glider. The sky was a vivid blue. A slight chill was in the air. Nothing stirred, no horses grazing on the hillside, no dogs careening wildly off in pursuit of enemy hawks. The corral gate hung open. The barn door was padlocked.

In that moment, the edifice of denial and dissociation, and the excruciating pain I had stored through move after childhood move came crashing down, my heart no longer able to contain the weight of all the sorrow. In that moment, sitting for the last time sitting for the last time on the porch of my beloved ranch, the unbearable reality of loss engulfed me, and I wept—gasping for air, blinded by tears, no thought of stopping, of past, present, or future, no thoughts at all, just pure pain erupting in a wild wailing of grief.

Even now, all it takes is a flickering memory of that moment to bring me to my knees. Even now, I can feel the exhaustion of total surrender to sadness envelop me as I write these words. That moment washed clear all the murky, hidden corners of my heart and bathed it in the distilled essence of pure feeling. And the knowing of it will never leave me. From that moment, I couldn't con myself anymore. Impermanence is real. Suffering is real. There is no escaping any of it.

I know now that life is a journey. A quest. An open question: Who am I? How will the story end? Can I meet each moment with an open heart? We don't know the exact moment our story will end. I now know in my heart there is no point ruminating on how the story ends. We are not in charge; we are along for the ride. We are here to experience each moment along the way. With our bodies. With all of our doors of perception: eyes and ears, touch, smell, taste—open. And most importantly, with our hearts. Our heart is the navigator of this vessel. Smooth sailing or rough waters, our heart is here to guide us.

It was time to leave. I stood up and, without going back inside, I locked the front door, put the key under the mat, and walked away.

As I got in my car, I heard wings flapping above, and I looked up to see an eagle circling above me. "Goodbye, my friend," I called out and watched as it swooped one last time and took off for the mountain. Everything had come full circle; everything was complete. It was all good. I let out my breath in a long sigh, got in the Explorer, and let the road take me all the way to my new home.

The sun was just setting over Long's Peak as I drove up to the house, the last rays long across the pasture. Bronco and Abby ran to greet me. Bucky and Rain were standing in the corral, waiting for their dinner. It was going to be hard, but it was going to be okay. We would be fine.

It all comes down to one simple phrase, simple to say and the hardest thing in the world to do. The Beatles told us first: "Let It Be." All along, I thought if I could find the right answer, all the pain would go away. If I could create my perfect world, the pain would go away. But it doesn't work that way. The answer is as elusive as the pain: let it be.

The answer can be found in the aspen trees that drop their golden leaves when it's time, in the clouds that arise and disappear without a trace, the bird that leaves no imprint in the sky, in the creek that keeps flowing through twists and turns, freezing and unfreezing, year after year. Even a beaver dam will in time collapse and be carried away, log by log.

I am not a solid me, I am just fragments blown apart, attaching to this and that—a person, a feeling, a memory, a place, and, as hard as I try, I can never hold it all together. Over time, everything changes. How many seasons has my tree weathered, dying each winter and being reborn each spring? How many lifetimes does it take to transform confusion into wisdom?

I grabbed an armful of hay and dropped it into the large trough and, leaning against the fence, I watched Bucky and Rain meander over and begin eating. After a while, I reached out to stroke their necks, leaning in to breathe deeply their reassuring, earthy smell before heading inside to the place where, for the time being, I would be making my new home.

ACKNOWLEDGMENTS

I want to thank my writing team, without whom this book would never have happened: Berna Jean Finley, whose idea it was in the first place; Brad Wetzler, without whose guidance and support I would have given up long ago; Skye Kerr Levy, for her impeccable editing; and the team at Bold Story Press— Emily Barrosse, Nedah Rose, Christine O'Connor, Karen Polaski, Pam Nordberg and Jocelyn Kwiatkowski for seeing the potential in my manuscript and offering their invaluable guidance and assistance turning it into a book. And finally, thanks to my friend and publicist Gail Kearns, who brought her wisdom and experience to launching it into the world.

I wouldn't be here without my family—all those who went before me, my mother who showed me what courage is and my father who saw me in the end. And I thank my children, Nick and Julia and grandchildren, Isabella, Rasa and Adrian for showing me what love is.

Thank you to the friends who read and helped shape the story—Helen Green, Anne Raitt, Irma Velazquez, John Cunningham, my daughter, Julia Sitko, and Carol Wilson. And a deep thank you to Joe for reading this story about a time we shared, even though it was painful. I would also like to acknowledge the many friends and acquaintances, too many to name, who visited Lookout Valley Ranch, some staying awhile, who didn't end up in this book. I will never forget the time we spent there together.

Special thanks to my spiritual friends, who were there at the beginning of my journey and continue to be with me—Tsultrim Allione, Pema Chödrön, and my unsurpassable teacher, Chögyam Trungpa Rinpoche, who opened my eyes to all that life has to offer. And to Tsoknyi Rinpoche and Anam Thubten who have continued to guide me on the path.

Finally, a huge thank you to the people I met and grew to love in the Wet Mountains: Dee, the Rancho Loco gang, Otis and Johanna, Margaret and Clara, and the men of the weekly meditation group at the Federal Correctional Institution Camp in Florence, Colorado. I will never forget any of you.

RESOURCES

Help is available 24/7 if you are experiencing any form of sexual violence, whether it is a current situation or a past abuse that is still affecting you. In my case, I called a rape crisis line when I was having a full-blown rape flashback soon after I left the ranch. It changed my life.

Here are some resources that are available in the US:
The National Sexual Violence Resource Center (NSVRC) is the leading nonprofit in providing information and tools to prevent and respond to sexual violence. Visit https://www.nsvrc.org/.
RAINN: Rape, Abuse & Incest National Network is the largest anti-sexual violence organization in the US. Visit online.rainn.org to chat one-on-one with a trained RAINN support specialist, anytime 24/7. Or call 800 656-HOPE.

Here are some resources available in Canada:
The Ending Violence Association of Canada is a national organization that works to amplify the collective voice of those who believe it is possible to end gender-based violence. Visit: https://endingviolencecanada.org/
A list of helplines for people affected by sexual abuse: https://findahelpline.com/countries/ca/topics/sexual-abuse.

Here is a resource available in the UK:

Rape Crisis England & Wales: https://rapecrisis.org.uk/. Rape & Sexual Abuse Support Line open 24 hours a day, every day of the year: 0808 500 2222.

ABOUT THE AUTHOR

Victress Hitchcock grew up in London, Paris and Madrid as the daughter of a diplomat. She graduated from the London Film School and spent 45 years making award-winning documentary films and educational videos. A long-time meditator, a poet, a mother and a grandmother, she lives in Boulder, Colorado. You can learn more about her creative work at victresshitchcock.com.

ABOUT BOLD STORY PRESS

Bold Story Press is a curated, woman-owned hybrid publishing company with a mission of publishing well-written stories by women. If your book is chosen for publication, our team of expert editors and designers will work with you to publish a professionally edited and designed book. Every woman has a story to tell. If you have written yours and want to explore publishing with Bold Story Press, contact us at https://boldstorypress.com.

The Bold Story Press logo, designed by Grace Arsenault, was inspired by the nom de plume, or pen name, a sad necessity at one time for female authors who wanted to publish. The woman's face hidden in the quill is the profile of Virginia Woolf, who, in addition to being an early feminist writer, founded and ran her own publishing company, Hogarth Press.

Made in United States
Troutdale, OR
04/22/2025

30840420R00216